Sunshine and Shadows

To Ella Jo—
May your life
be full of sunshine.
Sunny C. Eppler
Marjorie M. Woodcock
2001

Love 'ya'
Lois

Sunshine and Shadows

The Sunny Marie Eppler Story

SUNNY C. EPPLER &
MARJORIE M. WOODCOCK

Writer's Showcase
San Jose New York Lincoln Shanghai

Sunshine and Shadows
The Sunny Marie Eppler Story

Writer's Showcase
an imprint of iUniverse, Inc.

For information address:
iUniverse, Inc.
5220 S. 16th St., Suite 200
Lincoln, NE 68512
www.iuniverse.com

ISBN: 0-595-20382-5

Printed in the United States of America

This book is dedicated to the nuns, clergy, and staff at St. Patrick Hospital in Lake Charles, Louisiana and also to all the other Earth Angels that were sent by God.

EPITAPH

I was born knowing. It is a useless and unfulfilling journey to go in search of one's self. There is no self to find except for the self within, one that remains a constant companion throughout the trek.

My knowledge of such metaphysics had been deeply implanted by the ones who gave it.

My frontier for exploring an untapped resource was thought. I survived on the processes of ponder and marvel, and functioned through fertility of the mind.

I was an ideologist of no particular ideology, a philosopher of forever growing philosophies, a passive iconoclast of no establishment.

By the synthesis of truth all philosophy dulled at death and was a disappointment.

All earthly contemplation remains a memory of a life well spent in reflection. Yet, one concept was confirmed to me in my passing from substance to ethereal…there is no flesh.

Thought is life as soul is self.

Being immortal I still exist, if not more so, like the breathing person on solid ground.

By Sunny Marie Eppler

PREFACE

SUNSHINE AND SHADOWS IS A TRUE STORY, WRITTEN FROM MEMORIES, LETTERS, JOURNALS, AND DIARIES. NAME AND IDENTITIES OF SOME OF THE PERSONS HAVE BEEN CHANGED IN ORDER TO PROTECT THEIR PRIVACY OR PREVENT EMBARRASSMENT TO THEM AND THEIR FAMILIES. THE REAL NAMES OF DR. SHAMIEH, DR, JIMMY JONES, SUNNY MARIE'S FAMILY, NUNS, AND ALL MINISTERS ARE USED. BECAUSE SO MANY DOCTORS WERE INVOLVED AND TO MAKE THE STORY FLOW, SEVERAL DOCTORS WERE CONDENSED INTO A FICTITIOUS, DR. MILAN.

ALL PROSES AND POEMS AT THE END OF EACH CHAPTER WERE WRITTEN BY SUNNY MARIE FROM THE TIME SHE WAS THIRTEEN-SEVENTEEN. MOST HAVE WON LITERARY AWARDS WHILE SHE WAS LIVING.

ACKNOWLEDGEMENTS

Thanks to Phil Eppler, Johnny Woodcock, Marilyn Weishaar, and Rose Simar. Without their support, this book would never have been published.

INTRODUCTION

"Hi, baby," I whispered, "It's Aunt Marjorie. Your mother and I finished your book last night." In silence, I knelt down on the grass. Very carefully, I dusted the marble headstone, letting my fingers trace the deeply carved rosebud and letters that spelled out, Sunny Marie Eppler, 1962—1980. The grassy grave held only the name and date…not the soul.

Feeling her presence, I gazed up at the crystal blue-sky expecting to see my niece's beautiful face smiling down at me. I smiled at the clouds above and began talking to her from my heart.

"Oh, Sunny Marie, after all these years, the memories of everything we shared are still so fresh in my mind. I see you in every glorious sunset, I feel you when the rain slides gently down the windowpanes (you always loved the rain), and you're like that one perfect rose in the garden that stands out from the rest (but you never approved of picking the flowers, did you? You wanted them to stay intact until they fell to the ground, untouched by human hands.) "I smile when I think of how you refused to pick the flowers but I conjure up a picture in my mind that on the day you died, God was walking in His garden and picked one of His most beautiful flowers for heaven.

"When I see my Bible, I'm reminded that you asked us all to always keep the faith. When I hear the song 'Jesus Loves Me' (your favorite song,) I can still hear your clear, sweet voice singing. In so many ways you remain here with us. "Emotionally, I've always thought of myself one of God's weakest children—frail when facing a crisis, but now I know how much God truly loved me by allowing me to experience such growing pains.

"There were so many times when your mother and I doubted our ability to put your story on paper. We wanted it to be as beautiful and powerful as it was etched in our hearts. It took us years to read through the hundreds of poems you left behind, picking just the right ones for your book.

"We combined our daily journals, diaries, and personal letters. We tapped your two brother's, Philip Troy's and Derek's memories of your final year. Your daddy, grandparents, aunts, uncles, cousins, and friends were also eager to add their memories so that your book would be realistic as possible. It was painful reliving that year over and over again-writing and rewriting. The pain is still hard to bear but we wanted your story told so that it would offer courage to others who are at a critical point in their lives and help soothe their aching hearts. Hopefully, the readers will see God's glory and know that we are never alone on our journey through life.

"The last year of your life on earth had such an impact on all the people you touched. You taught us about courage, faith, and love. I've always felt that we each have a reason for being here, but you accomplished your mission faster than most of us. Maybe after reading your story, everyone will remember to hug their children and stop long enough to say, I love you, I love you very much. Those were your words. I still hear them over and over in my heart.

"Death is still the 'big mystery,' the last grand adventure and those of us here constantly seek some assurance, some small glimpse of that other side. As a result of coming in contact with you, we went away with the conviction that God has indeed planned something better for us than this short journey we call life.

"Through your eyes, as a window we were able to look at another place, known only to God and those who are privileged to have residence there. A place of such wonder, that a beautiful unafraid eighteen-year old rushed with eagerness to embrace it.

"Maybe after reading your story some will face the fact that all we have to do is love one another and then we'll be able to face pain and suffering a little better. Growing pains will always be necessary.

"There was more laughter, more tears, and more 'I love yous' in that one year than most people will have in a lifetime.

"As the evil brain tumor set out to destroy, God used you to teach us so much. God dimmed the negatives so we were able to see and hear more positive feelings of love, courage, faith, and surrender. That was our first big lesson in learning that fear and faith are not compatible and should not live under the same roof.

"Totally in awe of your relationship with God, we all wanted a little of what you had. Your room glowed with an aura that even today can't be described.

"Sunny Marie, your faith and love made us realize the family circle had to be kept intact no matter what. Because you touched us with God's love, we're all less earthbound. Christians never say good-bye, just see you later.

"You witnessed for the Lord and left us hungry to learn more, but we kept you here longer than you wanted to stay. You didn't give up until you showed us we could turn loose.

"We watched your beautiful body become a thin almost transparent shell. Inside your little body was a soul so ready to come into God's light like an exquisite butterfly emerging from a cocoon getting ready for flight.

"God places our souls in our very own cocoon and gives you a chance to develop as slowly or as quickly as we choose. You developed faster than most of us and I feel because of the time I had with you, I am now able to see more color and strength in my own soul. I feed my soul with the nourishment it will take to prepare for my flight when my time comes. I find myself getting impatient for that flight, but now I know it will be in God's time…not mine.

"God loves the plain little gray moths, but it's His beautiful butterflies that He uses to get our attention.

So my little butterfly, you held us up. When we wanted to cry, you would smile. When we wanted to scream, you spoke softly of God's love. When we were afraid, you showed courage and we were forced to do no less.

Because of you, we're learning not to ask 'Why?' but instead learning to ask for courage and faith to face each new day…one day at a time. I realize now without earthly problems, our soul would not be able to grow. No one ever said it was going to be easy. We want our mansions and streets of gold. We want to walk through those pearly gates and see the face of Jesus. We want that perfect ending like you, Sunny Marie.

Thank you, little girl, for showing us that God is still alive in our hearts and our lives. Rie, I think you would be proud of all of us, but then again you always were."

Brushing the tears away, I stood on shaking legs. Memories of that last year I had with my niece flooded my heart.

Happy/carefree pictures of events flashed in front of my eyes. It had been a memorable time. Sunny Marie and I had enjoyed a complete summer of sunshine.

But I should have known that even on the brightest days of sunshine when light surrounds us making us feel carefree, filling us with happiness, and giving us a false security, we all must deal with the shadows waiting outside the rim of light.

Life is made up of sunshine and shadows.

CHAPTER I

"No…wait!" Rie cried out. "Aunt Margie, please don't pick the rose!"

My hand quivered just above a full blooming rose. I hurriedly jerked it back expecting a bumblebee to sting me any minute. When nothing happened, I turned glancing at my niece, Sunny Marie (known to her family by her nickname, "Rie." A name given to her when she was first born by her small cousins.)

Sunny Marie—how the name suited her! Her long red hair, softly curled, danced around her shoulders, framing a small oval face whose complexion was perfection. There was a bright, sun-kissed aura that lit up her face when she smiled.

She was blessed with the widest, most breathtaking, and expressive gray-green eyes. Her eyes were forever changing color from gray to blue to green.

Her dimpled chin, as well as the dimples in her cheeks, gave the appearance that she would erupt into laughter at any moment. Just to look at her conjured up visions of beautiful princesses in childhood fairy tales. She was a real beauty, never showing vanity whatsoever. Everywhere she went people noticed her, actually stopping her and making comments about her beauty. At their compliments, she would often duck her head and blush timidly while saying a soft, "Thank you." She showed an honest embarrassment; totally unaware of the impact she had on others.

1

I suddenly became conscious that Rie was quietly observing me. "Why can't I pick the rose?" I asked.

A soft smile played over her lips. "Mom and I planted this rose garden," Sunny Marie stated proudly.

"No one remembers better than I do when you and your mom planted these rose bushes and how excited you were that they already had leaves and blooms. You and your mom did a great job; but there's no reason you should be stingy with your roses. I only want one…just one," I pleaded.

She started laughing and said, "Aunt Margie, I'm not stingy with my roses."

I looked over the dozen roses in every shape and size. "They're so pretty?"

Sunny Marie smiled with pride. It was a sweet smile that showed all her dimples at once. She stood quietly regarding one of the tall climbing roses. Under the hot Texas sun, beads of perspiration dotted her forehead and cheeks. It was a lovely day, hot with the slightest of breeze.

For a moment, I observed the girl standing in front of me, drinking in her beauty. Suddenly I was aware of the budding woman shining through the sprinkle of freckles on her face. At five feet five inches, slim at ninety-six pounds, she stood erect with her long radiant hair blowing in the Gulf heated breeze. The June sun was already causing her alabaster skin to turn a soft pink.

Determined to have just one rose, I quietly reached over while she wasn't looking. Just as I was poised for picking, Sunny Marie took hold of my hand. I felt like a naughty child that had just been caught with their hand in the cookie jar. Sunny Marie eyes filled with merriment. "Caught you. Don't you ever give up?"

Before I could answer a small yellow butterfly fluttered by and landed, like a tiny scrap of paper, in the middle of an open rose. She released my hand. Then she held one slender finger toward the butterfly. To my astonishment the tiny insect transferred itself onto the tip of her finger.

Not to be outdone by her, I held one of my fingers close to hers, thinking I could entice the animated creature away from her, but it flew away in fright to the bright marguerite daisies and giant purple Petunias.

"That thing with the butterfly, how did you do that?" She shrugged. "Butterflies just seem to like me."

"Evidently you must look more like a flower than me." She gave a soft girlish giggle. Then turning her expressive eyes toward me, she said, "Oh, what a beautiful day this is. How can anyone not believe in God? Can't you feel Him?" She spread her arms wide. "God is here."

At that precise moment, the expression that filled her lovely face was one of happiness and wonder of the world. But it was the wisdom behind her large round eyes that amazed me. They were intelligent eyes of the "speaking" sort, eyes that were far too old for her seventeen years. So many times before, I noticed how her eyes had the ability to see things far beyond her surroundings.

Before I could comment, she turned once again to gaze at the sky. Maybe it was the silence or the expression on her upturned face, but I had the feeling Rie wasn't aware of me at all. There was an expectancy of waiting. She cocked her head to the side, almost as if she was listening to a voice…someone speaking to her beyond my hearing.

I caught my breath, holding it least I break the spell. If Sunny Marie had been in an evening grown, she couldn't have been any prettier than she was at that moment in her cutoff blue jeans and faded purple shirt.

My mother's words whispered in my mind, "Rie is just too beautiful for this earth." At the time I laughed, replying, "Oh, Mother, don't be ridiculous. Every grandparent feels the same way." But all at once, I knew what my mother was trying to say. Sunny Marie's beauty wasn't of this earth. She had an inner glow. So many times we teased her about being our butterfly because she had to try everything in life;

like a butterfly kisses each flower in the garden, she too had to embrace each new thing in life and rush onto the next.

"Sunny Marie," I whispered. Enthralled, she continued to stare at the sky. When she didn't answer, I touched her arm to gain her attention. Slowly she turned; her eyes were soft and gentle as they met mine.

Giving a slight shrug, she replied, "Sorry, Aunt Margie, I guess I lose myself in all this color of life. Life's beautiful isn't it? It…," she searched for the right words. "It kinda vibrates around me." Her words were spoken with a slight catch in her voice.

I looked up at the perfect sky, at the bright vibrant flowers, at the surrounding greenery and then back at her. "Yes, life is beautiful." I answered and then in the same breath before I became emotional, I said, "So when can I pick a rose?"

As if she was remembering a painful experience her expression became sad. "Never!" she cried. Then she touched my face lovingly. "Aunt Margie, promise me, you'll never pick the roses."

At such a strange request, I was caught off guard. I frowned. "But why…I don't understand."

Her wise eyes impaled me. "Because it hurts them when they're picked," she stated simply.

I wanted to laugh but one look at her face told me she was serious. Instead, I said, "How do you know roses have feelings?"

With her long fingers, fingers that could make a piano talk; she touched the center of her chest. "I feel it here."

"But doesn't God put them here to be picked?"

"Sometimes, but He really places them here for the butterflies and bees. Butterflies are the pollinators. That's why we need the flowers," she stated. "We can enjoy their beauty until they wilt and fall to the ground. After all, what would a garden be if there isn't any flowers to view and smell?" Lovingly, she touched the red velvet bloom. "A rose bloom reflects God's perfection…doesn't it?" Before I could voice an opinion, she laughed unexpectedly, "If you think of the world as a garden, then I guess we're all God's flowers. Some are picked early while others are left to age."

"Are you saying I'm a dried up old flower? Evidently the butterfly thought so."

Her musical laugh filled the garden, competing with the birds singing in the trees. I watched the wind feather her curls until they danced upon her shoulders.

"Oh, Aunt Margie, you're an orchid," she said good-humoredly.

I raised both my eyebrows. "An orchid?"

She nodded. "The rarest kind."

"Well, in that case, I promise," I crossed my heart, "your roses will not be touched by these human hands." I waved my fingers in front of her face.

She bubbled with laughter quickly hugging me with both arms. I hugged her back, maybe I hugged a little too tightly, but suddenly I wanted to keep her from vanishing like a mirage. That feeling never went away.

As we walked into the house chattering, Sunny, Rie's mom met us. She has long, dark blonde hair with laughing dark green eyes. Everyone tells us we favor even though I have auburn hair and gray eyes and twelve years older. She met my glance. Happy and carefree, she remarked "How do you like our rose garden?"

"It's beautiful but Rie wouldn't let me pick one little rose."

"Shame on you, Rie," Sunny playfully admonished her daughter. "Surely you could let your aunt have just one of your roses."

Rie glanced over at me to make sure my feelings weren't hurt. Giving me a big grin, she replied, "Oh, Mom, Aunt Margie understands."

"Don't feel bad." Sunny laughed. "I have to wait until Rie's not here to cut blooms for the house. When I do, Rie tells me she can hear them scream."

I was home visiting that summer with my parents. Mom and Dad lived only a few blocks from my sister's house. It gave us time to spend together, to catch up. I was the Gypsy of the family. My husband,

Johnny, works in Bontang, Indonesia. Prior to that we raised our family in Puerto Rico. He's employed with oil companies. I try to spend my summers visiting with Mother and Daddy, my two sisters (Sunny and Marilyn) and their families, and my four grown children (Woody, Marilyn Sue better known as Dedo, Benny, and Art) and their families. No matter how long I stayed, it was never long enough.

It was during this summer of 1979. Sunny Marie was able to take a few courses at the local University. It was fun to hear her talk about her future, dreaming of the day when she and Doug (her boyfriend of four years) would be married.

Handsome, brown-eyed, brown-haired Doug was in his third year of college. Doug was Rie's first love and as far as Rie was concerned her only love. On the days he was home from college, they were inseparable.

There wasn't a day I didn't go to my sister's house that it wasn't full of young people. The house would be literally rocking. Rie would be playing the piano, belting out a song, while her brothers, Philip and Derek, would be playing guitar and drums. It was amazing to hear Rie sing. For someone so dainty and ladylike, she had a deep-blues voice.

One late afternoon while Mother, Daddy and I were watching the evening news on TV, we heard a knock at the door. Mother opened the door to a beaming Sunny Marie. She ran past Mother waving at us. "Come out!" she cried. "Hurry before you miss it." Rie practically danced around the room, "Hurry, Mawmaw, Pawpaw, and Aunt Margie!" She waved us to the door, pushing us as we hurried.

I stood on the porch looking around. I had no idea why she was so excited. "Look!" she pointed toward the western sky, "Behold what the Master has painted for you," she cried.

We all gazed at the beauty that was captured, as the sun was setting, red, gold, purple, pink, and blue. Indeed, it was a beautiful sight. I glanced over at Rie, her face was glowing, and her hands were pressed together under her chin, almost as if in prayer. I wondered how many seventeen-year-old girls would get excited about a sunset.

I placed my arm around Mother's shoulder and whispered, "Does she do this often?"

Mother laughed. "This is nothing, you should see her when she sees a rainbow."

We stood there until the living blend of colors faded into twilight, Rie applauded loudly and said, "That was good God." Only then did Rie consent to go into the house.

A couple of days later, I walked into my sister's house while a loud argument was taking place. Rie, Derek (her younger brother), and Sunny was standing in the middle of the living room.

"Mom," Rie fumed, pointing over at her twelve-year-old brother, Derek. "If I find him in my room one more time, I'm going to pull his ears off."

Derek made a slight grimace but continued to wear an expression of innocence.

"Goodness gracious, Rie," Sunny replied, "Derek is just curious."

"Well, let him be curious about something else but tell him to leave my diary alone," she yelled.

"Hey," I shouted playfully, "did I come at a bad time?" Derek giggled. "You came at the right time, Aunt Margie. You just saved me from having my ears pulled off." Giving me a quick hug, he hurriedly passed me heading away from the turmoil he had caused.

"What did I miss?" I asked.

Exasperated, Sunny threw up her hands. "That boy has been told to stay out of Rie's room. When he thinks Rie isn't around…he sneaks in and reads her diary."

"And he meddles with all my things," Rie stated still visibly upset. "Just last week he had my jewelry in knots."

In seventeen years, I had never seen our soft-spoken Rie angry before. I kissed her cheek. "Maybe it's time you have a lock on your door with your own key."

Rie laughed glancing over at her mother. "Would that be all right?"

Sunny looked relieved. "Why didn't I think about that?" All seemed happy until that same afternoon when Phil (Sunny's husband), Sunny, and myself were sitting around the dining table having coffee and cake when Rie came back from Doug's house. Sunny had just explained to Phil about the problem with Derek and Rie.

Rie waved at us as she headed toward her room. From my position I could see into Rie's room. In all the years Rie had taken karate, to my knowledge she had never used it until this day.

When Rie entered her room, Derek was caught red-handed in the act of snooping. There wasn't a scream, or for that matter not even a small noise but in a blink of an eye, Rie placed her foot on Derek's chest, literally picking him up from a sitting position, propelling him out into the hallway. He was lifted about two feet into the air coming to rest on the opposite wall.

Derek wasn't hurt but thoroughly impressed that his sister could achieve such a magnificent display of strength. He came off the floor with a big dimpled smile, exclaiming in awe, "Gosh, Rie, that was really cool. Do that again and show me how it's done. I can use it at school."

"No!" Rie stated firmly, wagging her finger in his face. "I love you. I don't want to hurt you, but consider this the final warning. Don't you invade my space again." Then in a louder voice Rie yelled, "Daddy! Daddy, I need you." I always thought that Phil was a handsome man with clear blue eyes and dark blond hair. He stood around six feet tall with broad shoulders and slim hips. Phil adored his children and they adored him. When anything was broke and needed to be repaired they came running to him. As far as they were concerned, their daddy could move mountains.

So it was today that my easygoing, sweet-tempered brother-in-law, Phil, glanced over at his wife and gave her a slow dimpled grin. "I guess this means I better put a lock on Rie's door immediately before Derek gets into anymore trouble."

Phil met his distressed daughter in the hallway. Rie practically pulled her father's arm off as she explained, "Oh, please, Daddy, do something to keep the menace out of my room. That little stinker is at it again." She pointed to her now opened diary. Her eyes met his urgently. "It's not as if I write secrets that shouldn't be read, but I don't like the idea of Derek telling everyone at school what I write in my diary."

"It's all right, I understand," Phil said in swift reassurance. "I had a younger brother and a younger sister. Sometimes you just need your privacy. Your mom and I have already decided that you need a lock on your door today."

From the squeal of joy Rie emitted, one would have thought she had just won the lotto. Both down on their knees with their heads inches from each other, father and daughter worked together installing a new lock.

Rie proudly placed her new key on her key chain, giving the second key to her mother with instructions, "Mom, whatever you do, don't let the imp know you have a key to my room."

After the lock was in place, Derek never had the chance to plunder Rie's room again.

A few days later, Rie came over to Mother's to visit. "Mom and Dad are both working, so I came over to see if I could take you all to get an ice cream...I'm buying."

Daddy and Mother declined but I jumped at the chance since that was one of the things that we didn't have in the jungles of Indonesia. My mouth was watering for a big triple-dip cone of any flavor with a million calories.

Somewhere between the first dip of the melting Chocolate Swirl Delight and the third dip of Very Berry, Rie and I found ourselves in deep conversation about the writings of Kahlil Gibran and Edgar Cayce.

"I love Gibran's poems," she said passionately. "They have a gentleness that the world needs."

I agreed. Her eyes lit up, She reached over squeezing my arm, "You know what?" Before she continued, she took a huge lick of her chocolate ice cream. "I just read a book about Edgar Cayce." She waved her ice cream in my direction, "He believed in reincarnation. What do you think about it?"

"Until you asked," I laughed, "I haven't thought much about it. I feel it really isn't necessary for souls to keep coming back again and again because Jesus has made it so simple when he died on the cross. If we accept Jesus as our Savior, we live forever. Besides," I said, "even if I came back many times, I would probably keep messing up."

Rie giggled softly. Then smiling that mystic smile of hers, she said, "I know what you mean, I believe in Jesus but I also feel that this universe holds secrets that are yet untold." She studied me for a long moment and then almost reluctantly she said, "The universe is dark, but somewhere there's a light far greater than anything we can conceive." Her eyes became dreamy, then in a much softer voice, just above a whisper, she said, "Sometimes, I can almost feel the light beyond the universe surround me. It's like I know things."

"What things?"

Rie closed her eyes. "If I tell anyone what I know no one would believe me."

Rie surprised me with that statement. "Well, try me. I'm all ears." When she gave me a negative nod, I persisted, "Ah, c'mon, what things do you know?"

Weighing my question, she stared at me with those big soft eyes while taking a big bite of her ice cream. When she didn't answer, dubiously I said, "You're teasing me, right?"

She smiled and started humming the theme song from the TV show, Twilight Zone.

"Get out of here," I teased. "You little stinkaroo, you had me going for a second." She threw back her head and laughed, but for just an instant, I had this funny feeling she had been really serious. I gazed over at Rie to calm my doubts and was relieved to see the child instead of the wise sage. For all her wise ways, at that moment, she was a child, a messy one. While driving, she managed to smear ice cream on her bottom and top lips. "Look at you!" I cried. "You're a chocolate mess."

After a quick glance in the rearview mirror and a hasty wipe with the back of her hand, she apologized, "I'm so sorry, I always manage to get it on me."

By the time we arrived back at Mother's house we were discussing life after death. I said, "Okay, let's keep an open mind; if I die first, I'll send you a message from the other side. When you go, you send me proof that all is well."

As if trying to picture something in her mind, she stared at the windshield. A slow smile parted her lips, and then she giggled. "Oh, this is absolutely great," she declared. She reached over and touched my arm. "Okay, okay, get this. If I go first…"

"Oh, but you won't, you know," I said smugly, "I'm twenty-eight years older than you,"

"No really…listen," she squeezed my arm tightly, "I'm serious. If I go first, look for me in flowers, butterflies, rainbows, and…," widening her expressive eyes she thought for a moment. "Oh yeah, I almost forgot…and birds."

"You rascal," I said indignantly, "you aren't leaving me anything to come back as."

The grin she gave me was pure mischief. Then wearing an innocent expression, she asked, "What are you coming back as?"

"That's not fair. You took all the pretty things. You think you're so clever." Her chuckle was more like, "He, he, he." Her face was glowing, her eye shining. She was looking, for all the world, like a cat that swallowed the canary. "Well, Miss Smarty, since you haven't left me anything pretty to come back as, I'll just have to come back at night…" I poked her in the shoulder, "as a fat little ghost and scare the hell out of you."

Like two naughty children sealing a pack, we laughed making our promise binding by hooking our pinkys together. Rie assured me this was the correct way to seal a pack before we walked into Mother's house.

With coffee cup in hand, Sunny met us at the door announcing cheerfully, "Well the two prodigals have returned." She stopped in the hall. "What are you two laughing at?"

"Hi, Mom." Rie hugged her mother. "Oh nothing, really. I'm just trying…" she broke into peels of laughter once again. "I'm trying to picture Aunt Margie as a fat little ghost."

"A what?" Sunny asked in bewilderment.

"A ghost," Rie once again replied, this time with a wide-eyed innocence.

Sunny looked from me to her daughter with questioning raised eyebrows. "A ghost?" she replied with a frown. "The scary kind?"

Rie's eyes sparkled; she bit down on her lip while she still kept the innocent expression intact.

"You're serious?" Sunny pronounced.

Rie's face sobered but her mother failed to notice the shining lights in her eyes. Slowly Rie nodded her head.

"Let me get this straight," Sunny glanced from Rie back to me. Then she gave her daughter a longer look. "You're trying to picture your Aunt as a ghost"

A dimple appeared at the corner of Rie's lips threatening at any moment to erupt into a full-blown smile. "No," Rie managed to say, "not just a ghost but a fat little ghost." The smile blossomed. Rie covered her lips with her hand to hide it while rocking back on her heels fighting to keep from laughing. "Aunt Margie promised me, she's going to be the kind of ghost that's going to scare the hell out of me if she dies first?"

"Shame on you, Rie and Margie. I can't believe you two can make a joke about dying," Sunny cried out. "Isn't anything sacred?"

Rie and I took one look at each other and both of us broke into laughter once again. Sunny gave up and started laughing as hard as we were.

Laughter flowed like bright water over the three of us. It was a silly time but one of those times that would always be remembered.

THE CHIMERA

My hopes became butterflies and flew away to brighter flowers.
My dreams never came true so they withered and died.
My thoughts became extinct and the species struggled yet had no
protecting sanctuary.
My soul opened to release the dark secrets only I knew.
And I, blindly trusting, saw the world read the etchings on my heart.

Aunt Maraie

CHAPTER 2

"Where's a pencil?" Rie ran through the house searching under magazines and newspaper. "Where's a piece of paper?"

Doug was right behind her. He found a pencil and handed it to her while she located a clean sheet of notebook paper. Rie hurriedly sat down at the dining room table and began writing. Doug stood looking over her shoulder shaking his head.

Just as I started to say something, Doug placed his finger to his lips to quiet me. Quietly, I asked, "What is she writing?"

"A poem," he whispered back. "We were sitting in the living room and she suddenly had to write it down."

"She's always doing that," Sunny laughed.

With the last line written, Rie gave a great sigh. She looked up sheepishly. "Sorry everyone, but if I don't put my poems down immediately, I forget them." We all took turns reading her poetry. It was neatly written and titled with few scratched out words. I marveled how neat it was and very well thought out. It read:

THE QUESTION

In quiet repose I count the ticking of the clock
anticipating the movement of each hand.

The rhythm synchronizes with the tempo of my brain as it
ticks off each thought, word, and deed.
In the realm of reality my logic is strong, my judgement
unbias, so why must there be doubts.
I'm seeking the answer to yesterday's question, "I'm here
today, but will I be here tomorrow?"
Blindly I grope to stop the ticking of time, hoping to
hold my future at bay.
Comprehension tells me turning back the clock will not
stop the procession of tomorrow.
For the real clock is housed within us, slowly ticking
away each measured moment.
Reality is the simple answer, "There's really no tomorrow,
the only future we have is today."

"Rie, where do these thoughts come from?" I asked.

"Who knows?" she shrugged. "They come while I watch TV, play the
piano, and sometimes right in the middle of school tests," She giggled
softly. "Thank goodness, most of my teachers are aware of why I constantly scribble on pieces of paper."

Sunny interrupted, "Rie's won awards at school for her poetry and
was published in the area school publication 'Perspective,' four years in
a row."

"Mother likes for me to write rhyming poetry." Rie said, "Sometimes
I do just for her." Then she cut her eyes to Doug. "I write love poems for
Doug when he's away at college." Tenderly, she touched his hand. "But
most of the time, like just now, I'm forced to write the words that come
hurriedly from my head. Those are never in rhyme form." She stood up,
passing the poem over to her mother.

Placing the sheet in a large notebook, Sunny stated proudly, "I keep
all of Rie's poems. Some date back to the first grade."

Doug sat down in Rie's chair and pulled her down on his lap. Snuggling against him, she smiled and replied, "To be honest, Aunt Margie, I really don't know why the poems come the way they do. I know when I write for Doug, it's because I love him or miss him. Rhyming poems are like summer sunshine. They're fun but as soon as I put the deeper poems on paper, I feel a warm glow in the depths of my mind." She shrugged, "Sounds corny doesn't it."

"No," I assured her, "I don't think it sounds corny at all. You're just talented and talented people are filled with passion.

For those of us that aren't as talented as you are, like myself, I have to rack my brain for hours to compose a simple poem, but you can write deep ones in a matter of minutes without using up an eraser."

"Oh, I don't feel like I'm all that talented. Writing poetry only fills a need. It's like my piano playing. I love to do both. Even if it's not the best—it satisfies my soul."

I had to laugh. This was a child that oozed talent. There was nothing she couldn't do. She was forever learning new things. No sooner then she mastered one she would hurry to the next. So busy with life. Life was her adventure, a blessing to be enjoyed to the fullest, and a gift to be treasured. I always told her God made a mistake giving her everyone's talent and good looks. Everything she did—she did well. She could play the piano, organ, guitar and clarinet; sing, dance, twirl, karate, write short stories and poetry; and if that wasn't enough, she was an honor student. All of us in the family wished we had just a little of what she was blessed with.

One of the joys of Rie's summer was the fact that, Philip Troy, (her four-teen-year old brother) outgrew her. She came prancing into the room.

"Look at me everyone," she drawled. "I'm wearing my little brother's jeans and shirt." She modeled for us in ridiculous poses. "Philip's outgrowing me."

Hearing his name, Philip walked into the living room.

"Hey, big handsome dude," Rie lovingly placed her arms around her brother's neck. Half shy, half-proud, she murmured, "Please, don't ever get too big that I can't hug you." Philip was built long and lean like Rie, but had pale blond hair and wide, dark green eyes. Under Rie's tutoring on how to treat girls, he was fast becoming the heartthrob of the school. Philip's friends were forever spending the night at his house so they could visit with his sister. It never ceased to amaze Philip how his friends fell madly in love with her. To his embarrassment, they would bring Rie small tokens of their affection.

"Hey, Red, what are you doing in my clothes?" Rie struck a jaunty pose. Replying with a mock demureness, she said, "But they fit me."

"Wrong answer," he warned just before picking up his sister in his viselike arms. As if Rie weighed no more than a sack of feathers, Philip swung her over his shoulders before dumping her unceremoniously on the couch. "Take my jeans off before you split the seams," he demanded.

Not one to take defeat lightly, Rie immediately jumped up and tackled Philip to the floor. In the tangle of arms and legs and before her brother could react to her fast maneuver, Rie had Philip face down sitting on top of him. "Are you saying I'm too fat to wear your jeans?" She replied with a fiery sweetness. When he refused to answer, she tickled him.

"Okay! Okay," he cried. "I can't help it if your bottom is bigger than mine," he crumbled, his voice rising in pitch until he was literally cackling.

"Wrong answer. Take it back," she commanded, "or I'll make you eat every word."

They tumbled around the living room until Sunny ordered them outside. At a fast gallop, Rie chased Philip into the front yard. Sunny threw up her arms in mock disgust. "Kids!"

"Enjoy it," I said, "they won't be kids for long. Look how fast my four children grew up."

Sunny nodded. Her face contorted into an ugly grimace, "How well I remember! I used to be your babysitter."

"Only because you came cheap," I countered. We laughed together remembering the years like they were only yesterday.

I noticed when my sister would scold Rie, Derek and Philip would intercede, taking the blame. When Rie's heart was broken, the boys would sit for hours cheering her up. If she had a bad dream at night, they would sleep on the floor of her room so she wouldn't be afraid. They were her protectors.

One day, Sunny was upset with Philip for not taking out the trash and raised her voice at him. Philip became very quiet, withdrawn, walking from the room. Sunny started after him. "Mom, wait!" Rie commanded. "Please don't yell at him again."

Sunny stopped with a surprised expression on her face. Rie didn't give her mother time to answer before explaining, "He's a quiet, sensitive person, the minute you raise your voice he shuts you out. Just try talking to him in a normal voice."

"Remember, young lady," Sunny warned, "I'm the mother."

"Mom, I know that," Rie smiled, her tone of voice becoming sweet, "and you're the best Mom any kid could have…but just don't scream so much at Philip. Okay?"

"Do I really do that?" Sunny asked. "Do I really scream at him?" Rie rolled her eyes heavenward and hummed tunelessly. "Okay, maybe I do," Sunny conceded. "No more yelling at Philip."

"Oh thanks, Mom," Rie hugged her mother lovingly. "You'll see a difference in him. I know you will."

Later I walked outside and found Rie in the front yard busy twirling her two batons. No sooner than she had exercised her arms she then picked up her two machetes with hooks on one end. The hooks enabled her to attach the two together, swinging them over her head or under her legs. The machetes were sharp enough to sever a head of cabbage (something she did many times in twirling competitions for effect). In her routine, she threw the knives high into the air catching them one at a time as they came down, ending the act in a split with the knives under her throat. It was a spectacular routine, one she won many medals and trophies with.

Two little boys and three little girls from the neighborhood sat around the yard watching Rie while she practiced. "Are you getting ready for a contest?" I asked.

Rie nodded. "There are always contest to practice for, but school starts soon and that means football season. I need to keep in practice."

"You like twirling?" asked one little girl.

"I love twirling," Rie answered as she did a hand flip in the grass catching her batons as she landed upright.

"How many medals do you have?"

"Well over a hundred," Rie stated simply. "When I march with the band, I have the nickname of 'Metal Chest' because I wear all my medals on the front of my uniform."

"Wow! Do you have trophies, too?"

Rie laughed, "My mother thinks I have too many. She complains that she's running out of room on the bookcase. Here," she said to the little girl, "let me show you how to twirl." Rie placed the long baton in the small hand, closing the fingers over the silver shaft. She rotated the child's wrist in a figure 8. "Practice with an old stick and next week, I'll show you how to run the baton through your fingers."

Each child wanted Rie to show them. Very patiently, she showed each one how to twirl from the wrist. After an hour, she gazed at her watch, "Okay, kids, be sure and practice."

"Honey," I placed my arms around her shoulders, "that was nice that you took the time for the little ones."

"I still remember how wonderful it felt when I was small and people took time with me," she said. "Even at my age now, it still feels wonderful." She looked at her watch again and squealed, "Doug, is going to pick me up in ten minutes. We're going to a movie. Wanna go with us?"

I laughed and declined, "You two go and have fun. I need to spend more time with Mawmaw and Pawpaw."

Early July, Mother was rushed to the hospital with heart pains and a tightness in the chest. Since the hospital was only a few blocks away, Daddy and I took Mother. Sunny, Phil and Rie met us there. No sooner than we arrived at the emergency room, the staff immediately started working on Mother. The situation became a comedy rather than a tragedy.

The doctor on call rushed in with a team of nurses. They began to pull Mother's blouse off so they could hookup an electrocardiogram but they weren't prepared for Mother's modesty or her stubbornness. Mother's face became alarmingly pale, her eyes went wild and her hands became fist, swinging blindly in every direction. The sound of half squeals, half squalls filtered through the emergency room corridor. "Let me alone," Mother yelled menacingly, refusing to let anyone near enough to touch her. As if that wasn't confusion enough, my sweet little mother began screaming and pushing and even kicking the nurses and machinery away.

"Now, Mrs. McQueen," the head nurse warned breathlessly, "if you don't let us treat you, we'll have to send you home." Mother took the lady at her word. By now she had extricated her arm from the blood pressure cuff and was actually starting to get up to leave.

Sunny and I tried to intercede but Mother glared at us as if it was our fault she was in pain.

Then the cavalry arrived in the form of Marilyn and Dave. Sunny and I breathed a sigh of relief. We thought since Marilyn was the oldest of the three of us and a nurse to boot, she would be able to talk Mother into rational behavior. WRONG!

The more Marilyn tried to talk to Mother the worse the situation became. It would have been funny had the situation not been so serious. I mean here was a woman complaining of heart pains, screaming like a banshee, and caring on as if this was a torture chamber. Little did our mother care that she was causing all three of her daughters to have heart failure? Our dignified Mother had decided to act like a very bad little girl and nothing her children did was going to change the fact.

We called in the big gun, Daddy. At our cries of help, Daddy tried his hand at calming his wife. Our very angry mother insisted she wasn't about to disrobe in front of a room full of strangers. Her statement prompted the resident doctor to throw up his hand in frustration. Puzzled, and totally confused, he abruptly walked from the room mumbling under his breath that other patients needed him.

Daddy, losing his capacity of endurance, was the next one to leave. Marilyn, Sunny and I glanced at each other. We wanted to leave too, but we each waited for the other to give the word.

A wide-eyed Sunny Marie stood in the hallway taking everything in. Silently she walked into the emergency room. A nurse tried to stop her but to no avail.

Rie said softly, "Oh, Mawmaw, what are they doing to you?" After Rie cuddled her grandmother into her arms, Mother began crying.

Softly, Rie whispered, "Shhh, don't be afraid, Mawmaw. Everyone here wants to help you. The nurses need to take your top off and place little pads on your chest." She placed a kiss on her grandmother's cheek. "That way they'll know if you're having a heart attack." Gently Rie stroked her grandmother's hair. "They won't hurt you. I'll stay right here and hold your hand. Just take deep breaths." Mother's eyes closed while taking deep breaths. To our surprise she became calm. The head nurse made a quick decision.

Sunny, Marilyn, and I were ushered from the room while Rie stayed. Dr. Jimmy, (the family doctor) came into the room and finished the test. After the results of the electrocardiogram, he admitted Mother into the hospital. We marveled how Mother reverted back to the perfect lady and went in like a lamb. Dr. Jimmy diagnosed her as having angina.

The next day while Mother was sleeping, Rie came to the hospital to visit. She had just finished college classes for the day and decided to quietly sit in the corner doing her homework before going to work. The afternoon sun was coming through the window engulfing Rie in a soft, golden illumination. Dust particles danced on the air currents giving the effect of floating diamonds. Rie's face, alight with a radiant glow, had the most serene expression, almost as if she had been painted by an artist. Chills went up my spine and all at once, I had an emotion surge through my body…again I felt that this child was not of this earth. I saw an aura surround her. Standing transfixed, I watched this beautiful child. She looked up and caught me staring at her.

I said, "Forgive me, Rie, but you're so lovely. I just noticed how God has placed you in His heavenly spotlight."

She seemed embarrassed. She ducked her head for a moment, and then raising her head with tears in her eyes, she smiled sweetly. "Thank you, Aunt Margie. My greatest wish is to be in God's Light."

I motioned for Sunny to follow me. No sooner than we were out of the room, I asked softly, "Are you aware you have a special child? Sometimes when I look at Rie, I feel…" I took a deep breath, "I feel she's not of this world."

I was expecting my sister to laugh in my face but she wasn't shocked at my observation. "I know," she said, "I've known since Rie was thirteen-years old and it frightens me. I sometimes have this overwhelming feeling that we won't be allowed to keep her." I placed my hand on her shoulder and squeezed. "I think all mothers must have that same feeling sometimes in their lives."

"No," a sad smile passed over my sister's face. "Oh, if you only knew how many times Rie comes in after a date and wakes me up asking if I want to hear her theories of why the universe exists. I would laugh and say, 'Ask me if I care? At this hour, who cares about your ideas concerning the universe? Just tell me about it tomorrow.' Then she would say, 'If you don't listen, mom, while it's still fresh in my mine then you'll just have to remain dumb the rest of your life.'"

Sunny bit down on her bottom lip to keep it from quivering. She spread her hands helplessly. "I read her poems and I get frightened because Rie talks about the universe and heaven. Things I know about but her writings are so much deeper than I can comprehend. What if she does have knowledge…what would it mean?"

"Ask her?"

"Someday I will," she sighed, "but not now. I don't want her to be wise and worldly. I just want her to be my little girl." Her eyes met mine. "Is that wrong?"

"No, honey, it's not wrong. You have a very special child. Rie's the kind of child every parent would like to have."

On Mother's return to home, life began to return to normal. Hot, muggy, windless August soon arrived. I was one week away from flying back to steamy Indonesia. Sunny and Rie decided to take me shopping; assuring me there was a great summer clearance sale at the shopping center.

Rie insisted on driving her car. Sunny was sitting in front fiddling with the radio knob while I sat in back. For some reason none of us were very talkative. We traveled about ten miles when all of a sudden, Rie turned slightly toward her mother and said, "There's evil all around me."

Sunny finally found the right knob, clicking off the radio, silence. Sunny gazed over at her daughter with a blank expression and then her mind assimilated Rie's words. "What?"

Rie repeated, "There's evil shadows all around me."

I waited for the punch line. When it didn't come, I laughed and replied, "Hurry, Sunny, roll down the window and let it out. I was expecting Rie and Sunny to laugh or say something funny in return but the laughter and words didn't come. Bewildered, Sunny continued to stare at her daughter in silence.

"Really, mom, Aunt Margie, I feel as though it's trying to get into my head."

I felt a stir of uneasiness; this was so unlike Sunny Marie. She never talked about evil things. I glanced at Rie's face reflected in the mirror. She wasn't joking or trying to be funny. A quick look at my sister convinced me that Sunny was aware of this also.

"Honey," Sunny reached over touching Rie on her shoulder, "it's really bothering you...isn't it?"

"It's hard to ignore," Rie stated with a catch in her voice.

"Are you having headaches? Do you feel sick?" Sunny asked.

"No, I'm not in pain. I feel great except having this apprehension of evil surround me...about to pounce into my head."

"Maybe it's the devil playing games with you," I replied.

Rie glanced from her mother to me. "Have you ever had anything like this happen to either of you?"

"I think everyone is faced by evil or evil thoughts at sometime in their lives," I stated. "You know what I do when I have these feelings?" Rie shook her head no. "I just pray it away."

Relief washed over Rie's face, softly she said, "I can do that."

Two day later, Sunny and Rie were helping me pack when Rie made another statement. "Aunt Margie, I did what you told me. I prayed that the evil would go away." Sunny and I both stopped what we doing as we focused on Rie.

"Well?" Sunny urged. "What were the results?"

Rie hesitated for a moment before answering. "You're not going to believe this but now I'm hearing voices in my head."

"Oh great," Sunny inhaled loudly, "now your losing your mind. First evil shadows are trying to get into your head, now you're telling me that evil voices are talking to you, too."

"They aren't evil voices, Mom," Rie said indignantly. Then she smiled sweetly. "No, these are beautiful voices saying comforting things."

"What kind of things?" Sunny coaxed. Sunny and I stood in silence waiting while the seconds ticked by. At first I didn't believe Rie was going to answer her mother but then her face beamed. "The voices are saying, 'Don't be afraid' and 'Keep the faith.'"

Bewildered, Sunny tightened her arms around Rie possessively. "It's okay, baby, don't be afraid."

Rie reared back in her mother's arms fixing her mother with an intense expression. Then she smiled until all her dimples showed.

"Oh, but, Mom, I'm not afraid…really, I'm not." Her clear gray eyes sparkled. "I have this overwhelming feeling that God is taking care of everything. It's as if He's wrapped me in a security blanket, protecting me."

Maybe Rie wasn't afraid but one look at my sister's white face showed me that she was definitely frightened for her child. I was just thankful that Rie was hearing beautiful voices in answer to her prayers.

"This is beyond my scope of understanding," Sunny remarked. "This talk about evil all around you and now you tell me that beautiful voices are talking to you." Frowning she studied her daughter's face. "Honey, it scares me. You've never talked like this before. I don't understand any of it. Explain. What is God taking care of?" Sunny asked quietly.

"I feel as if something is about to happen…" Before Rie could say more, Mother came into the room announcing lunch.

Maybe had we had more time Rie could have told us more, but the subject never came up again. My vacation over, I stood in the airport saying good-bye to Mother, Daddy, Marilyn, Dave, Sunny, Phil, and their families, and my own children and their families. The entire family was sending me off. We took up most of the space in the small Airport. Rie and Doug came running in.

Before I walked to the plane, Rie presented me with a long stem red rose. "For you, Aunt Margie," she whispered softly, "because I love you so much."

"I love you, too, baby," I said. Then I gazed at the beautiful rose recognizing it as one from her garden. I gasped, "For me?"

She grinned, nodding her head. "But this is one of your roses from your garden."

"The most perfect one," she said softly. "But you don't like picking your roses."

"Just this one time."

"But you said they scream when they're picked."

"Well, maybe it screamed just a little bit but when I explained it was for your going away present, it was proud to be picked." The rich musical echo of her laughter caused heads to turn. "I wanted you to have something special from me before you left."

I entwined my arms around her shoulder. I knew what it must have cost her to pick one of her beloved roses. I would treasure this moment, this child, and our enjoyable summer together. "I feel guilty taking one of your roses," I said. My eyes began to water.

"Don't, I wouldn't pick one for just anybody." She snuggled closer. "You're special, Aunt Margie. I'm going to miss you." Then her laughter filled her eyes. "It's okay," she giggled softly before she kissed me. "I made sure there were plenty of roses left for the bees and butterflies."

"I'm glad you told me that. That makes me feel better," I teased.

Waving a teary farewell to my family, I boarded the plane. I was going to miss them and all the good times we shared. My memories of them would have to last me a year, I wouldn't be back until the following summer.

Through watery eyes I found my row, literally falling into my seat. Leaving family behind was always so heartbreaking. Clutching the perfect rose in my fingers, I silently thanked God for my beautiful summer of sunshine.

A POET

A poet is an odd sort of creature.
The species of poets range from lyricists to avant-garde.
But the poet must feel where others are left cold.
The poet must be able to cry when others are unmoved.
The poet must be able to think when others dream
    and dream when others think.
He must be totally different, non-conformist mentally.
Most of all, the poet must make others think and dream.

Rie as twirler

CHAPTER 3

January eighteenth, 1980 was like every other day in Bontang, Indonesia. The jungle was every shade of green as it spread like a living plush carpet that threatened to engulf everything in its path. The growing season here is constant for there is only one season…summer. I love the blue unblemished skies that flowed forever in an endless sea of unpolluted splendor.

A warm, gentle breeze caressed me into a false sense of security, making me think nothing ugly or bad could touch me in my green and blue world, devoid of all harsh city sounds. Oh, how easily we mortals can be deceived. This is not the real world. It's far from the hectic pace of city living. It's a small encampment with a couple of hundred people from different parts of the world.

We live only a few blocks from the Liquefied Natural Gas plant where my husband, Johnny, is employed. The only way in and out of our camp is by small planes, with over hundreds of miles of jungle and water to civilization. Because of our isolation, the people in camp are very dependent upon one another. It is easy to become addicted to the adventures and money that this way of life offers but we still miss our loved ones back home. The only lifeline we have with family members is strictly through the mail. Telephone calls are too costly.

Quickly looking through the mail, (I had no reason to suspect the letter I was holding was to be the beginning of events that would change so many lives forever.) The letter was from, Sunny. Usually we exchanged letters on a regular basis, but since coming back to the jungle her letters had been nonexistent. Not even a Christmas card, which was very unusual for Sunny. I was more than anxious to hear that all was well with her, Phil, and their family. I was especially worried about Rie. Some of the things she told me during the summer still weighed heavy on my mind.

Since the beginning of December, we'd been receiving letters from different members of our family, telling us that Rie was having health problems. The doctor had first diagnosed her illness as a virus. Then we were told that she was suffering from bronchitis and severe headaches.

On Christmas Day, I called Mother and Daddy and was told Rie was being released from the hospital that very day. Her tests were finished and she was coming home for Christmas. Mother advised me not to call Sunny and Phil since they were busy checking Rie out. I felt like a weight was lifted from my heart. On January first, we received a telex from our youngest son, Art, who lives in Houston, Texas, stating, "Sunny Marie has spinal meningitis and is now in recuperative stage. Long recovery is anticipated. Will keep you informed. Love, Art," That sounded bad, but we were happy Rie was recuperating. Evidently that's what the hospital stay and all the testing had been for. I mailed get well cards and letters, praying that by the time she received them, Rie would be totally over her illness.

I tried calling my sister numerous times but we never caught them at home. After calling my parents again, I was informed that everything was going well and that Rie was improving daily. They begged me not to worry and told me they would tell Sunny and Rie that I phoned.

When Sunny's letter arrived, I was so excited to finally get a letter from her. The envelope was thick and heavy. I noticed the postmark was dated the fifteenth of January. I couldn't believe how fast the letter had arrived. Usually, it takes more than a week for a letter to reach us. I couldn't wait to open it. I was anticipating good news of Rie's recovery, maybe Christmas photos of the family. Instead, I read a letter that was filled with pain and fear. My sister's letter began:

Dearest Marjorie and Johnny:

Jan. 15, 1980

I bet you thought you were never going to hear from me.

For a while I had my doubts. Please forgive me for not writing sooner but our days and nights have been spent in and out of hospitals. It's hard to keep up with the dates. Time means nothing anymore except the dream, that in time, Rie will be well. I know how confused you must be with what is going on here, but no more so than we are.

Find a chair and sit down. This is going to be one hell of a long letter. The only way I can bring you to the present is to start from Rie's first severe headache.

When school started, she was so happy and excited to be a senior. In late October, she volunteered me as a sponsor for her journalism class. I agreed to chauffeur and chaperon six students to a journalism convention in Dallas. The journalism teacher took the remaining six students with her.

After the convention, while we were preparing to leave Dallas, we assembled at the motel's swimming pool waiting for Rie's teacher. When her teacher, Mrs. Noshari came walking toward us, her first words were, "Oh, no!"

Startled by the distressful tone in her voice, Rie and I asked if she was all right. Margie, this lady grabbed at her chest and replied breathlessly, "I just saw something."

Rie and I turned cautiously and looked behind us expecting to see something terrible. There was nothing there. "No! No!" Mrs. Noshari replied, pressing her hands over her eyes, "It was a vision."

Rie and I stared at each other. "What did you see?" I asked.

"Water, blood, and Sunny Marie," she replied. Rie whispered in my ear, "I can see me and I can see the water but where is the blood?"

"I don't know what she's talking about," I whispered back. "Well, I don't like it," Rie mumbled under her breath. Mrs. Noshari is one of the sweetest people I know. I could tell she was truly distressed at causing us apprehension.

She quickly explained, "Don't be concerned, I often have visions." Taking a deep breath, she replied, "Maybe I better go back to our room and call home."

Moments later, after she talked with her husband, Jami, we found out that the American Embassy in Iran had been taken over by the Iranians. Mrs. Noshari's husband was Iranian and his family still lived there. She had the feeling that maybe this was what she was seeing in her mind, but she couldn't explain why seeing Rie had triggered it.

I really didn't believe Rie was all that happy about being part of her vision. I know I wasn't. All the way home I had this feeling as if icy fingers were playing along my spine.

When Rie's headaches started November fourth, I wondered if this was something caused by worry. Rie was unable to go to school. (I begrudgingly blamed Mrs. Noshari for Rie's added stress. I can't write the names that I called Mrs. Noshari. You'd have to cover your eyes and then you wouldn't be able to read my letter.)

Later, in my mind, I had to apologize to Mrs. Noshari. That same week we found out that most of the kids that went to the convention were sick with stomach virus or flu. Even Mrs. Noshari had not been spared. She and I were both sick during this time. The two of us even joked about the fact that maybe we had contacted the dreaded legionnaire disease.

But after every one was well, Rie continued to complain of headaches. Once one of her friends had to bring her home from school because Rie's headache was so severe she was unable to drive herself home. By November fifteenth, the doctor was treating Rie for migraine headaches.

Headaches, headaches, and more headaches and no relief in sight. Sometimes we would be up all night; sometimes the headaches wouldn't come for days.

At the end of November, the doctor decided it had to be a viral infection. They put Rie in the hospital for bronchitis. Because she was in a semi-private room, I couldn't stay with her. Rie and I were upset but there wasn't much we could do about it. The hospital was full and they had their rules.

Every morning at 2 a.m., Rie would call me complaining of a headache. She didn't like to ask the nurses for medication so I'd go to the hospital and ask for her. Thank goodness the hospital was close to the house.

During the wee hours one morning, the nurses had to give Rie an enema for a test. Well, little Miss Rie refused; informing them they couldn't touch her until her mother arrived. (Doesn't that remind you of Mother?) The head nurse called me, requesting I come as soon as possible. When I arrived, the head nurse sighed with relief but asked me to leave the room until the other nurses finished their job. Rie calmly stood up and put on her housecoat. The head nurse asked, "Young lady, where do you think you're going?"

My sweet, gentle child very stubbornly replied, "If Mother leaves, so will I."

The nurses and I had a hard time keeping straight faces. I stayed and without any complaints, they gave Rie her dreaded Enema. The next day we were assigned a private room. What else could they do except send us home?

Tests, tests, and more tests. I didn't know there could be so many. We came home for a week. Then we went back. Rie referred to us as YO-YOs, up one moment and down the next. By December twentieth, we were back at the hospital again. This time in a private room for yet another...you guessed it...TEST. Did you know TEST is a four-letter word? One that Rie and I decided could be just as foul as anything could in the English language.

After the last test results the doctor came to talk to us. This time I saw frustration in his eyes. At one time, I caught him with his head in his hands and tears in his eyes. While Rie was sleeping, I asked him, "What's wrong, Dr. Jimmy?" I watched the professional mask slip back over his face. He reached for my hand. His hand was cold. My heart froze. He cleared his throat and in his best bedside voice, he replied, "I've done everything possible, Rie needs experts."

"Why? What do you know?"

"The test appears to show Rie might have had meningitis," he answered, but his eyes didn't quite meet mine.

The word "meningitis" hit me in my solar plexus. Didn't children die with this disease? Then I remembered he said the word "HAD." She "HAD" meningitis'. I found myself breathing again. "HAD" was a better word than HAS. I decided I could cope with "HAD."

Doctor Jimmy sent us to a neurosurgeon on Friday, January fourth for Rie's examination in Lake Charles, Louisiana, at St, Patrick's Hospital. Dr. Milan (the expert) stated that he agreed with Doctor Jones' findings. Sunny Marie HAD a bad case of viral meningitis and she was now in recovery. Doctor Milan told us if the headaches were to get worse to come back to him instead of our family doctor. We left his office with high hopes. The next morning Rie had severe pain in her head plus vomiting. Her little body would go limp in my arms when she heaved. It was so bad, I can't begin to tell you how helpless Phil and I felt. I was petrified when Rie slipped into a semi-coma state. Lake Charles was forty-five minutes away; our city hospital was a couple of blocks away. I opted for our family doctor. Dr. Jimmy gave her an injection to relieve the pain and told us that it should last the rest of the day, but I called Dr. Milan just in case he wanted us to bring her over to Lake Charles. As luck would have it, on a weekend, the expert was out of town, but I was able to talk to a neurologist on call, Dr. Shamieh. He told us to bring her in if the medication wore off and she became worse.

The injection started wearing off just two hours later. Dear God, she was worse than before. I was paralyzed with fear. FEAR, another four-letter word, wrapped around my entire being. My precious baby girl was in such excruciating pain. We rushed around getting ready to go. Mother and Daddy came to pick up Philip and Derek. We drove off leaving a confused Mother, Daddy, Philip, and Derek standing in the middle of the street waving good-bye. I didn't even have time to kiss my little boys or thank Mother and Daddy for their help. We had no way of knowing when we would return.

All the way to the hospital, Rie kept repeating over and over, "Somebody please help me." Totally out of her head, she had no idea where she was or that her daddy and I were even there. Phil drove and I counted the bumps in the pavement. It was just something to keep my mind occupied. It took so long to go forty-five miles down a dark highway that I couldn't see, didn't care to see. My eyes were ever watchful on my sick child. Phil was breaking the speed limit and praying out loud the whole way, "Our Father, which art in heaven…" We rushed her into the emergency room and immediately they began to give her an IV. They had such a difficult time finding her veins. We had to give the doctor her entire history, since he had never seen her before. I wasn't even sure I was making sense. I felt like a person detached from my body watching myself in slow motion. Everything had an unreal look to it, as if I was watching a movie.

Dr. Shamieh immediately took a spinal tap. I stayed in the room while this was being done. I asked him why he was taking a spinal tap, and he said he needed to obtain a few drops of spinal fluid. He said it would only be a pinprick. They leaned Rie forward and the doctor inserted a needle approximately four inches long into the middle of Rie's spine. Rie didn't move or cry out. I felt every inch of her needle and when it was all over, my knees were so weak, I had to sit down. I must have changed colors. Rie looked at me with those big eyes and asked, "Mom, are you all right?" Can you believe that?

Sunny Marie asked the doctor what he thought he was going to find, and he explained to her that it would be a good sign if they found a virus in the spinal fluid. On the other hand, he said, it would be a bad sign if they did not find a virus. She reached over and squeezed my hand and together we waited for the results. It seemed like hours but in reality it was only a short time. A silent scream was going through my mind and I tasted panic in my mouth, I could only guess what my Rie was going through.

Later the doctor came back and told us that a normal spinal fluid pressure was 180, Rie's was up in the 400 range. The prognosis was bad, NO virus was found in her spinal fluid. She was immediately admitted to the hospital so they could run tests to determine the cause of her trouble. In a way, I was thankful we were in the right spot for help and in another way frustrated and angry because we still were not any closer to the cause of the illness and pain. Rie is so fragile. I do not know how she endures the pain.

Oh, Margie, you'll never know how scared and sick I was. You know me, I am not one to stay away from my home or go off by myself. Here I was sitting on the fourth floor of the hospital with my ill daughter. Phil had to go back to Orange to work. Rie and I didn't know a living soul in Lake Charles. Not having anything better to occupy my nervousness, I opened the drapes to gaze out the window, just to see which direction we were facing, hoping we could see the lake. Would you believe that all I could see below me was a cemetery? No, not just a cemetery? If it had been a modern cemetery maybe it wouldn't have been such a shocker, God as my witness, this one looked as if it belonged in one of Vincent Price's horror films. It was an old unkept graveyard. The large oak trees surrounding its borders had few leaves left on the snarled branches. The fallen limbs and decaying leaves covered the ground. Streetlights illuminated the gravestones peeking out of the debris. Shivering, I hurriedly pulled the curtains closed with the intention of never opening them again.

"Well," Rie asked. "What's outside?" I couldn't tell my Rie what I was looking at. So I lied and said, "Nothing really. It's too dark to make out anything. I'll take another look in the morning, but I don't think it's going to be one with a good view." I promised myself that I would have Rie moved by morning light.

The nurses gave Rie shots all through the night so she could rest easily. I stayed awake just to make sure she was breathing and prayed as I've never prayed before, glad when morning came. Even the view from the window wasn't as bleak as the night before, but without her knowing why, Rie's room was changed.

Dr. Shamieh informed us he wanted Rie to take an EEG (brain wave) and Monday morning Phil and I were to take Rie across town to Lake Charles Memorial Hospital for a CAT scan since St. Patrick didn't have one. Phil used his vacation time to be with us for the results of the test. We made the trip across town so Rie could get her CAT scan, also known as a computerized tomography. The nurse told us the equipment employs a narrow beam of X-rays to scan a patient's head in a series of flat sections, much like slices. To make a long story shorter, what I could gather about the whole thing was that it's a super duper computer X-ray machine that gives a three-dimensional picture on a TV screen.

Later Rie explained how she lay on what appeared to be an examining table waiting while a big machine traveled around her head. She claimed she didn't have any discomfort just stress. In no uncertain terms, she hated it. She likened it to a big opened mouth about to devour her head.

Phil and I tried our best to joke with Rie, keeping her mind off the test results. We sat there with tension building; our insides tied in knots not knowing what the outcome was going to be. We were trying so hard to be brave and normal at the same time.

Monday night Dr. Shamieh came into Rie's room and told us the results of the CAT scan and EEG. I remember I was standing at the foot of Rie's bed when the doctor came in; we all said, "Hello" but he didn't look too happy. My heart stopped and I held my breath. Rie was sitting up in bed watching, with that big-eyed stare, never blinking an eye, and Phil was somewhere behind me. The doctor nodded to Phil and me, then proceeded talking directly to Rie. She didn't look afraid but continued to stare eye to eye with the doctor as he proceeded to inform her. "Your EEG was abnormal and the CAT scan showed swelling of the brain. This is called edema of the brain. There are two more tests I would like for you to take to make sure it is not a tumor. One is another CAT scan and the other is an arteriogram."

She asked, "Will it hurt?" and he said, "No, you'll be sedated." Rie smiled sweetly, thanking him for explaining the situation directly to her. Not too much was said after that, we both kissed Phil good-bye. He had to go back to work. Then we both fell apart. We couldn't stop crying. The nurses came in, sat with us, and explained how the test would be run. They told us the doctor would cut into the main artery in the upper leg, and then they would push a tube up into her neck and inject dye in the arteries in the brain. The nurses said Rie would be able to watch on a screen if she wanted to but, needless to say, this brought little comfort. Around 2 a.m., Rie and I decided to read the Bible. I remember reading it out loud, but inside I was praying. My mind was screaming, "NO! NO! Please let this be a nightmare!"

We decided to keep the news about the arteriogram from Mother and Daddy because this test was the most dangerous of all. When I talked to Mother on the phone, I told her we had another test to run. She informed me that your son, Woody, was coming from Houston to stay with the boys so that Phil could be at the hospital with us. Mother wanted us to come home and have the test run at the city hospital in Orange. She and I got into a shouting match because I couldn't tell her the seriousness of the test and what they were looking for. She thought we were foolish to have a specialist working on Rie with just a headache. Mother claimed she wasn't feeling well enough to keep the boys all the time. Bless her heart, she wants to control every situation and right now she's not in control of this one.

Oh, Margie, you'll never know how close I came to asking you to make that long trip to be here with us. I would sit and tell Rie, "If your Aunt Margie was here, she would think of something funny to make us laugh and get us through these long nights." When Rie would fall asleep, I would take the pillow, place it over my mouth and cry into it to keep Rie from hearing. The night before the arteriogram I cried buckets of silent tears.

When morning came, they took Rie for another CAT scan. Phil wasn't supposed to come until 8 a.m. so when they came for Rie at six, I knew we had to go alone. At eight o'clock we were back in our room waiting for the arteriogram. Phil got there just in time to kiss Rie before she left. We stayed in her room but we were so afraid. We didn't talk; we just took turns reading the Bible. Time stood still and we held our breath waiting, praying, and reading the Bible.

The telephone rang beside the bed and I think I jumped two feet in the air. It was the doctor calling to let us know the arteriogram was over and they had taken a hundred pictures and found no tumor. He said she made it through just fine but her leg would be sore for two weeks or more. We were overjoyed and tears were streaming down our faces.

When they brought her back to the room I wasn't prepared for what I saw. Oh God, they had mutilated her beautiful leg. Her right thigh was solid black from her hip down to her knee. She was sleeping but I had to run into the bathroom and throw up.

Dr. Shamieh came in to tell us he was going to start her on steroids to hold down the swelling in the brain. He said he believed she had encephalitis instead of meningitis. Meningitis attacks the outside of the brain while encephalitis is an inside infection in the brain. This is what was causing pressure on her spine and head. All the arteries inside her brain were swollen. He started her on anti-edema medication and there was an immediate change for the better. The steroids caused an increase in her appetite. Would you believe she makes me go down to the cafeteria to load up on three hamburgers, pies, and cakes to get her through the night? It is so funny to see her eat so much. She stuffs those cheeks so full of food she looks like a chipmunk. I have laughed so much because she has to have her food for security. When people come into the room and see all the food stored in the corner they ask, "Whose food?" She puts on her sweetest smile and explains that it's her mother's. The terrible thing about it is, I am the one overweight and she is the one that's thin. She loves to play this joke; she says it's good for my nerves. Mrs. Noshari and her husband come to see us just about every night. As I sat in this hospital room knowing we are only a block away from the lake I wonder if Mrs. Noshari's vision is coming true. After all she did say she saw water, blood, and Sunny Marie. So far it all fits. I have often wondered what else she might have seen in her vision that she couldn't tell us.

I wish you could see the huge envelope of get well letters that came from Rie's journalism class. Rie sat up in bed while I read them to her and laughed until tears rolled down her face. An incident happened at school and the kids had over a hundred versions to tell. An English teacher was standing in front of the class reading "Macbeth" when she sneezed and her false teeth flew out of her mouth and landed on one of the student's desk. She calmly picked them up and put them back into her mouth. The students were trying to suppress their giggles when she told them if they felt the need to laugh, then do so. Well, the whole class completely fell apart. Later in the day the entire class was invited in pairs to visit the principal's office and given discipline slips. They read: "Failed to maintain composure when teacher's teeth fell out." Can you imagine the conversation in the office that day? As it turned out, it was only a joke to get back at the students. Now that Rie is showing improvement and making plans to return to school, the world is once again a happy place.

Philip Troy and Derek call daily and talk to their sister. They seem lost without her. Philip has always talked to her after school. He values her opinion. Derek hasn't found Rie's key to her room yet. He's still having withdrawals from not being able to meddle in her diary. Every time he talks to Rie he tries to talk her into letting him sleep in her room. I have a feeling he thinks that if he makes her mad enough she'll come home. The boys have been so torn up since Rie has been in the hospital. Last week both boys missed school. They don't like staying at Mother's house.

I'm so thankful Woody is staying for a week at our house keeping them. God bless your eldest son for taking his vacation. Philip and Derek love him so much and think that at twenty-nine, and being a big Houston policeman, he's super cool. Poor Woody, he has his hands full with those two. Philip has a paper route and Woody has to take him everyday to deliver them.

I wish you could see this room full of flowers and cards. We are literally running out of room. The nurses from the other floors come in to see all the gifts that Rie has received, Kids from school come and go daily. Doug misses a lot of college coming to see her. He loves getting her food and eating with her.

A few days have gone by since the last paragraph was written. We were busy bringing Rie home from the hospital. She feels fine and looks good. She will start school next week with a home bound teacher until March, then hopefully she will be able to return to school for half days. Right now she tires easily and gets depressed. The doctor seems to think time will heal the brain. They say medication will help but her brain will have to heal itself and it will take a long time. The death rate for encephalitis is 50% so we are overjoyed she lived through this. Only time will tell what damage has been done. In one month she will go back for another CAT scan to see if the swelling has gone down. Just continue to pray for us.

We have all four of your children to thank for beautiful flowers, cards, and numerous phone calls. They stay in constant touch. Art and Sherri brought Rie a beautiful pantsuit. I sure hate to see them go to South Africa but I know it's a wonderful opportunity. God bless you and Johnny and your sweet children.

I'm sorry this has turned into a book but there was so much to tell you. I wish we were having a cup of coffee together. I wish I could reach over and hold your hand; maybe I could draw on some of your strength. Right now I'm holding my family and myself together...barely. I can't say that I was prepared for all of this. I wish I was stronger but I'm not. Years ago Horatius Bonar wrote, "Sickness takes us aside and sets us alone with God." I never knew how true that was until now. I'm learning to lean on God like never before, but that doesn't lessen the fear that seems to seep into every pore of my body. I never knew this kind of fear before. It never goes away...ever.

Have you ever had the feeling that if you complain too much that things could get worse? Well, I live with that sick feeling in the pit of my stomach constantly. I hate going to sleep at night, frightened that if I close my eyes for a second something awful will happen to my child. I pray...oh, how I pray, and then I wonder if God hears me.

I wish you were here. You always know the right thing to say to put everything in perspective. Maybe we could find something to laugh about. Laughter doesn't enter our life anymore. Rie and I have had enough tears to last a lifetime. Our world is getting far too serious.

Please pray that nothing else happens so my next letter will be shorter. I love you and miss you.

Love,
Your Sis

PRESENCE

In the aromatic flavoring of surrounding greenery, I lose
myself in a living blend of the vibrating color of life.
Neither remembering, nor forgetting the present time cannot
occupy my freed thoughts, lost in a limbo of their own.
Yet there is pain in such a meditative experience.
One must come back into the physical reality.
Like one must reach inward to reach out.
So one must reach out to return to the substance found inside
oneself.

Sketched by Sunny before Rie was born

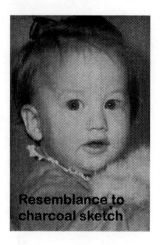

Johnny Woodcock

CHAPTER 4

The letter frightened me. Shutting my eyes I prayed, "Please, God, don't let this be as bad as it sounds." But my sixth sense said otherwise and I knew in my heart that it was.

My little sister was always the one that was so positive about life, strong with an iron will determination, and would tackle situations where even angels refused to venture. This letter wasn't positive at all. Sunny was afraid for her daughter...very afraid.

My mind drifted back to the time when Sunny and Phil were expecting Sunny Marie. It seemed like only yesterday. Sunny hadn't known she was going to have a girl, but she only had one name picked out and that was Marla Kay. An artist, Sunny drew a charcoal sketch of what her baby would look like and kept it on the wall so that she could see it every day. She was positive that her baby girl would look just like her sketch daring any of us to tell her differently. When the baby arrived February 21, 1962, Phil, Mother, my brother Arthur, my older sister Marilyn and I were the first to see Sunny's and Phil's redheaded daughter. A red cape of curls covered the little head. Even the doctor made a comment that her hair was red enough to glow in the dark. We all took our turn inspecting this beautiful child, but she only had eyes for her daddy.

Phil said, "Well, hello, Sunny Marie." That was the moment he named her. Later, he explained to us how much he loved his wife's name Sunny but he took the middle name Marie from me, Marjorie Marie.

It wasn't until the hospital showed Sunny the birth certificate that Sunny realized her baby had been named Sunny Marie. In our excitement of viewing the baby, we forgot to inform Sunny of the change in her baby's name. She eyed all of us suspiciously. Marilyn and I pointed to Phil. "He did it," I said. Phil simply shrugged with a wide grin and replied, "But I never liked the name Marla Kay."

"Never?" Sunny questioned. "Never," he calmly stated. Sunny glanced down at her new daughter (the exact copy of the charcoal sketch she had lovingly gazed at for nine months) and rolled the new name off her tongue, "Sunny Marie." She touched the tiny lips with her finger. "The two names sound pretty together...don't they? With all that red hair, it even suits you, but I want you to have your very own name. I'm Sunny too, so we'll call you, Sunny Marie." As if the child agreed, she stretched her tiny fists out making a gurgling sound.

Later, when Sunny Marie came home from the hospital her name was to be changed yet again. All her little cousins shortened her name to Rie, a name she was to be known the rest of her life by. A name only those that loved her would use. There was one other name my oldest son, Woody, called her by and that was Rosebud. He noticed that all her clothing and blankets had printed or embroidered pink rosebuds around the edges. He claimed even her mouth was in the shape of a little rosebud. To him and only to him she was Rosebud.

For some reason, Rie/Rosebud became the family's favorite. Everyone loved her and over the years she gave back that love without question. Rie attracted attention but if she was ever aware of it, it never showed because she was far too busy being an observer, a listener, putting everyone at ease by being sincerely interested in everyone she met. She viewed people and places with the eyes of a poet-artist. Color, race, or Creed did not have a place in her choice of friends. Respected by her peers, she was a peacemaker, well liked and loved.

Our family and friends found it impossible to be depressed or unhappy around her...she wouldn't allow it, her spontaneous musical laughter was our elixir to make our lives bearable. Rie was our sunshine. Just as the sun gives us warmth and lifts the gloom of night, so is Rie to all those who know and love her. Rie belonged to all of us.

Now holding the letter in my trembling hands, my soul felt my sister's pain at her daughter's illness. When Johnny came home that afternoon from work, I read the letter aloud to him. When I finished, I was crying.

Johnny, who is so sensitive to my feelings, put his arms around me to comfort and console me. He said, "Honey, would you feel better if you could be there?" I answered, "Yes," and the decision was made as simple as that.

As usual, my darling husband was trying in his gentle way to calm my fears. He was the one who made all the necessary arrangements, and in three days, I would be on my way home. I kissed my husband good-bye at our tiny airport and fought back tears. "Oh God, how I wish you were going with me," I cried.

Hugging me tightly, he replied, "Not half as much as I do. I'm going to miss you like hell but Rie and Sunny needs you." Then taking a deep breath, he rasped, "I love you." His words were spoken as a caress. "I love you too," I murmured. "I promise to call as soon as I have more news concerning Rie."

Our gaze held; unspoken fears lay in their depths. We both were desperately trying to maintain a calmness we were far from feeling. I think it's so much harder, sometimes, on those who are left behind and my heart was aching at the thought of Johnny's loneliness. I waved good-bye from the window of the plane. Good-bye my darling, Johnny. Good-bye my blue and green jungle…the jungle that had lured me into the false security of thinking I could escape reality or pain of the real world. I was going back to the real world… a world filled with uncertainty, but was I really prepared?

FEAR

The fear comes to tighten around me. It holds its hands around my throat while chilling my soul with its own.

Screaming from within, I try to find my logic, equally cold, to battle the shadowed adversary. But under the siege of fear it runs as a fugitive and I have nothing to fall on.

Tears slide down cold cheeks and the body trembles, but it is nothing compared to the inside.

Fear strikes the conscious and that is where the damage is done.

CHAPTER 5

Arriving at the New Orleans airport, I was met by my 26 year-old daughter, Dedo. Her real name is Marilyn Sue, but we always call her by her childhood nickname. Normally, she is always smiling, but now her face was serious. When we hugged, she held on as if she didn't want to let go. Finally she said, "Aunt Sunny suggested that you should take a couple of days to get over jet lag before going to her house. She's afraid you'll be too tired if you don't." As we walked through the terminal making our way to the car, Dedo squeezed my hand.

"Mom," she said, "it has really been bad for that little family."

"I know, baby, that's why I'm here. I came to help," I said, hoping in my heart that I could do just that. We had never experienced anything like this in our family before. My forty-three year old brother, Arthur, had died two years earlier with a massive heart attack in his sleep. That happened without any warning and I couldn't get back from the jungle in time for the funeral. I promised myself this would never happen again.

No sooner than I arrived at Dedo's house, Woody called to see if I had arrived safely. He also told of the pain that Rie had been going through, promising to meet me in Orange as soon as he could. He kept clearing his throat, trying to mask the tears. Underneath the tough outer veneer of a police officer was a very gentle and loving man. I have to laugh sometimes to think how many people have commented on the fact that Phil and Woody resemble each other through features and actions. The two are only related by marriage, but have been mistaken for brothers many times. Woody sounded very concerned over the toll Rie's illness was taking on the entire family.

I was very concerned for my parents, both in their early seventies, and both had heart problems. I knew they would have a hard time accepting Rie's illness if indeed it proved serious. My older sister, Marilyn, was keeping watch over them. I knew she could handle the situation with Mother and Daddy. Dave, her husband, would be just as helpful. Their job, trying to keep Mother and Daddy from learning the real problems about Sunny Marie would be one of the hardest. It was a real strain for everyone to appear normal under the conditions of Rie going back and forth to the hospital. If Marilyn could just hold down the home front with Mother and Daddy, then maybe I could be of some help to Sunny and Sunny Marie. I had only been at Dedo's house a short time when I received a phone call from Marilyn. When I heard her voice and how she was holding back tears, I panicked.

"Margie, they rushed Rie back to the hospital in Lake Charles again with severe headaches and nausea. All this time, they still aren't any closer to the answers for Rie's illness." As I gripped the telephone tightly, I remember saying, "Oh, dear God, Marilyn, we're on our way."

Jet lag was the least of my concern, my sister and her ill child were.

Dedo and her two little girls, Shannan and Leslie, drove me to the hospital, a drive that took four hours going as fast as we dared. We rushed into the hospital only to be told to our relief that Rie had been sent home already. Breathing a little easier, we drove to Orange.

On our arrival in Orange, Sunny met us at the door explaining they had just arrived back from the hospital and that Rie had been given an injection for her headache and nausea.

I entered the house and everything was quiet. It wasn't at all like the summer I had spent here. No rock band, no laughing teenagers. The joy that this household once shared was missing.

It was so hard after the first hug and kisses to mask my concern. I was shocked at the appearance of my little sister. The past three months of worry and concern had definitely taken its toll making her appear drawn and lifeless. She had even changed the color of her hair from blonde to dark brown making her skin tone appear shallow. This woman standing before me now was almost a stranger. Her voice was flat and her green eyes held no spark of life. She appeared ill herself, and to think, she was worried about me having jet lag.

Silently I prayed, "Oh God, thank you for making it possible for me to be here so I can take some of the burden from her shoulders. She looks so tired."

Sunny took us quietly into Rie's room. It was a beautiful room, fit for a princess. Any girl would cherish a room as pretty as this one. It was filled with red and pink roses on the off white curtains and bedspread— so like Rie to have her room decorated in roses, her favorite flower. Walking over to the white canopy bed, Dedo and I took turns kissing Rie lightly while trying not to waken this sleeping beauty. The pain injections enabled her to sleep in peace. As I watched her sleep, I was reminded of a glowing candle with that lovely red hair casting its glow over the stark white of the pillowcase.

Sunny pulled back the sheet to show us the ugly bruises caused from the arteriogram. The sight was shocking. The area was just as my sister had described it in her letter except now the bruises were starting to turn an ugly yellow and green. I heard Dedo suck in a shaking breath to keep from crying. My heart hurt from the pain our Rie had been through.

When Rie awakened, she was surprised to see us. Half awake, she smiled lazily and gave a soft exclamation, "Aunt Margie…Dedo? What are you guys doing here?"

"I couldn't wait until summer. I thought it was time I come see what was happening to you," I replied. "Your mother doesn't write me much these days."

Rie giggled softly and said, "Mom," she gazed lovingly up at Sunny, "has been too busy taking me back and forth to the hospital."

I kissed her check. "Well, I'll go back and forth with you two."

Rie's eyes lit up. "You're going to stay?"

"Until you get tired of me."

"Never," she replied, giving me a big hug. She held me tightly…almost too tightly. "Mom and I need you. I'm so glad you're here."

"Me too," I whispered. "Me too."

Rie shifted her eyes over to her mother, then back to me. Her eyes twinkled. "Maybe now that you're here, you can convince Mom not to wear that ridiculous wig."

I looked over at my sister and started laughing. "Oh, thank goodness it's only a wig. I thought it was real." Indignantly, Sunny admitted, "There are days I don't feel like fixing my hair."

I saw Rie try to hold back her laughter but it seemed to just bubble up. "She couldn't find a blonde wig so she bought that." She pointed to the wig in question. "Sometimes I wake up and see Mom with that thing on and I think it's a strange lady in my room. It scares me."

"It would scare me, too," I confessed.

"Oh, you two, honestly," Sunny declared before pulling the offending wig from her head. "Now, are you all satisfied?" She let her chagrin broaden into a smile.

"Yeah," triumphantly Rie smiled, "Now, you look like my mom."

"Now you look like my sister," I said, before laughing. We had a good visit, but Dedo and her girls had to return to their home in New Orleans. I kissed my daughter and grandchildren good-bye; making a pact we would take one day at a time helping this little family anyway possible.

The beginning of February saw all of us up one day and down the next. Rie would feel good for a while and then the pressure headaches would send her seeking the refuge and quiet of her bed. During this time, so she wouldn't get behind on her schoolwork, a homebound teacher was tutoring Rie. During the day, when Sunny was at work, I started taking Rie over to Mother's house. Because Rie couldn't see well enough to read her schoolwork, I read to her.

Shakespeare's tragedy, "Macbeth", was her required reading. Right from the start it was obviously not mine. Somehow, as I read it aloud to Rie, it turned into a comedy. I heard a soft giggle as I managed to massacre the written English language. I stopped and asked, "Rie, are you sure I'm helping you?"

Her smile was gentle and sweet. "Oh, Aunt Margie, you're doing great." She reached over and patted me on the arm. "Thank you so much for helping me." Mischievously she looked at me and replied just as sweetly, "Even if you don't quite sound like Orson Welles."

"Gee thanks, Rie, Orson Welles, my foot. I thought I was doing my best Richard Burton impression." She held her nose. That sent us both into peels of laughter.

As I spent days with Rie, sometimes I noticed her holding one hand over one eye when she watched television or tried to read. "Honey, are you feeling all right?"

"Yeah, just fine," she answered.

"What's this with the hand?" I held my hand to my eye mimicking her actions.

"Nothing really."

"Nothing?" I asked, raising my eyebrows. Her expression softened and her shoulders lifted in a small shrug. "I have a little double vision," she replied.

"Even with your glasses on?" She nodded her head slightly. "Don't you think we need to tell your mother?" She thought for a moment before answering, "I was hoping it would go away and Mom wouldn't have to take off from work to take me to the doctor."

"Sunny Marie, your mother wouldn't mind. She would want you to be checked out."

"I know," Rie gave a great sigh, "but, Mom, seems to be so tired and I feel as though I'm a burden sometimes. The doctors and hospital cost so much money."

"Has your mother or dad ever made you feel like you're a burden?"

"No, she and Dad never complain."

"You're dad has good insurance…doesn't he?" Rie nodded in agreement. "So, I don't see a problem. All the things your mother and dad do for you, wouldn't you do the same thing for them if they were ill?"

"Of course I would." She smiled. Her face shone with understanding. "I guess I didn't think about it that way." Together, Rie and I told Sunny about the double vision, Sunny made the decision to take Rie back to the doctor.

Rie's weight had gone from 96 to 115 pounds, but she was a long way from being overweight at five foot five. She couldn't wear any of her clothes so she wore gowns and robes. She went to the doctor's office wearing a pretty pink satin gown and matching robe.

It was during this time that I met Dr. Shamieh for the first time. I was surprised how young he appeared. It was obvious that Rie adored him. "You're gaining weight, I see," he said.

Rie laughed softly. "It's your fault, I'm eating like a horse."

"Good, keep it up." He checked Rie over. "So now you're having problems with your eyes." He checked her eyes. Rie nodded, explaining about her double vision. He listened with concern. "Just to be on the safe side," he explained, "I would like an eye specialist to test your eyes." He left the room for a minute. When he came back in he glanced over at my sister. "I want you to take Sunny Marie to the eye specialist." Surprised, Sunny asked, "Right now?"

"Yes. My office has already made you an appointment. Do you know the way?" Biting the corner of her lip, nervously, Sunny looked from me to the doctor. I could see the color drain from her face.

"No, I don't know anything about this town except how to get to the hospital and your office," Sunny confirmed. "Lake Charles is a lot bigger than Orange." Then making a quick decision, she said, "Just draw me a map, we'll get Rie there." After the directions were made clear, we took off. Sunny at the wheel, Rie in the back seat, and I was seated in front holding the hastily drawn map.

Rie patted her mother's shoulder. "Don't worry, Mom, Aunt Margie will direct us there without getting lost." I tried to exhibit confidence but lost it when Rie very gently took the map from my hands. I noticed the slight twitch of her lips. I expected her to giggle any minute but she didn't. But all she said was "Excuse me, Aunt Margie." Then turning the map around, she pointed her finger in the right direction. Even with double vision she could tell I held the map upside down and we were heading in the direction of the lake instead of the eye clinic. "I think we need to go that away," she directed softly.

"I knew that," I replied while I hurriedly grabbed the map back. She gave me a sly grin before settling back on the seat. Then I proceeded to tell Sunny what streets to turn on.

SIGHTLESS

I refuse to see. My world is opaque,
I am led by those who feel the need to serve someone like myself.
I listen and imagine. But imagination exists only as far as the encroaching darkness.
It nears me in clockwork heartbeats.
One day I will be totally immersed in that blackness, but do not feel pity for me.
I am not blind…I just refuse to see.

CHAPTER 6

After several wrong turns, we finally arrived at the eye specialist. The receptionist was waiting for us because the minute we walked in she ushered Sunny and Rie into see the doctor. I waited in the waiting room more than an hour before Rie and her mother finally walked out.

Rie was smiling. "Well, I seem to be all right," she said. "The specialist thinks the double vision is caused from a swollen optic nerve. He said had there been evidence of a brain tumor, it would have been detected in the test." A long sigh escaped her. "Boy, was I ever afraid there for a minute."

"Me too," Sunny confessed.

I answered, "Me three." I wasn't sure what they had been looking for but I was worried about the breakneck speed in which Doctor Shamieh sent us to the specialist. Evidently it had turned out to be nothing serious. Letting out a long held breath, I silently gave thanks to God. "Sounds like we have reason to celebrate," I said. "So now what do we do?"

Rie's eyes sparkled and she blurted out: "Eat!"

Sunny echoed, "Eat?" Sunny glanced at her watch. "Rie, you've got to be kidding. We just had breakfast a little over two hours ago."

"So?" Rie rolled her eyes. "That was over two hours ago. I'm starved now."

Sunny questioned, "Can you really eat again?" I was full to the brim, but one glance at Rie with her hands folded under her chin as if in prayer and her lips silently forming the word "please." I had to laugh. I couldn't let Rie down; I knew I had to agree to eat.

Reluctantly, I said, "I'm with Rie. Let's eat."

"Huh?" My sister did a double take giving me a suspicious look. "You, too?" Grinning, I nodded while Sunny gave a groan of mocked pain.

On the way to the car, Rie and I could hear Sunny mumbling, "This is absolutely ridiculous. I can't believe you two. Eating again this soon after breakfast…"

A few paces behind Sunny, Rie stopped me, kissing me on the cheek. She whispered softly, "Thanks, Aunt Margie. I know you're not hungry but I really am famished."

"Little girl," I pinched her on the tip of her nose, "you're going to be the reason I gain twenty pound and have to go on Weight Watcher meals."

She giggled softly. "How else are you going to become a fat little ghost?"

On the way home, we had to stop two times to buy Rie something to eat. It was amazing how this slim child could polish off food. The steroids caused her to be hungry constantly. We kept telling her we could actually see her putting on weight before our very eyes.

Laughing at our insults, she plopped her legs over the front seat. Then pulling up her satin gown, exposing her long slender leg, her voice teased, "You want to see weight? Well just take a gander at these legs. See how they've filled out." Her eyes twinkled. "Now, you want to see boobs?"

I yelled, "Nooo," while covering my eyes with my hands.

"Okay, just take my word for it, but I have boobs, too." She held her frail shoulders back, pushing her small chest out. "I can't believe it, this is all me. Look, no pads." She gazed down at her chest. "Isn't it great? I finally have cleavage, real cleavage," she said proudly.

It was great to see the twinkle in her eyes and hear the teasing lilt in her voice. Driving home, Sunny began telling me about a television movie she, Woody, and Rie had watched at the hospital. "It was a true story about a young woman who had a brain tumor. After the operation, the doctor said there was no hope of recovery and she would die.

The wonderful thing was the lady got better and continued on with her career as a singer."

"Good heavens!" I gasped. "How could you stand to watch a program like that when you weren't sure what they would find wrong with Rie?"

"Aunt Margie," Rie interrupted, "it was a lovely story. The woman survived against all odds," she glanced away reflectively, "but it was also sad. She didn't give God the credit for working the miracle. You should have seen us." She laughed. "Woody, Mom, and I cried through the entire show. The nurses had to bring an extra box of tissue."

After Woody left that night, I asked mom, "What if I have a brain tumor?" Rie stuffed another French fry in her mouth, chewed and chased it down with a loud slurp of cola.

I waited for her to finish. I watched Rie munching on her food. "Well?" I asked trying not to break up in laughter. "Aren't you going to stop eating long enough to tell me what your mother said?"

"Sorry," she shrugged waving a limp fry at me. "Mom said, 'We'll just face that question if and when it happens.'" Her eyes became serious. "You know, Aunt Margie, I think God wanted us to see that movie. I thought about that movie for a long time that night. It frightened me in away, but I did find out something about myself." She spread her hands wide. "I mean I could be like that girl and have a brain tumor," she shrugged, "who knows? But the difference between us is I have a God I trust. No matter what I have to face, life or death, He'll be there with me. He's there for all of us. I can't imagine anyone not having God in their life." She smiled that dazzling smile and rested her head against the back of the seat shutting her eyes.

How like Rie to say something like this. She always talked about God as if he was always with her. Most of her poems are about her relationship with God or supernatural happenings. She always reads the Bible and has even taught Sunday School classes. All her life, this child, now smelling of hamburger, onion rings and French fries, has been such a joy to the entire family. Such a soft-spoken little girl; she was the heart and life of her grandparents' life. The strange thing about this is; none of the other grandchildren seem to mind. Rie missed every chance of being a spoiled brat. It's been the standing joke in the family to say that Rie favored each of us in appearance. Her beauty isn't only outward but it seems to radiate from the inside out.

The days passed but the illness took a toll. Rie had always been active and now she was confined to home or her grandmother's house. Some days she was well and happy, while other days found her listless without the strength to get out of bed. A lot of this was caused by the headaches but most was caused by the uncertainty of what she had. The doctors still didn't have a clue. In-between bouts of happiness, depression could rear its ugly head and it was always a battle to overcome for all of us. Rie had never allowed the word gloominess into her vocabulary before now. Frown and expressions of worry replaced the pretty smiles we were use to.

One day when Rie was feeling especially sick and depressed, I said, "Hey Kid, God only chooses the strongest and most worthy to carry the heaviest burdens. Honey what He has in mind for you must be a biggy. He loves you more than we all do and He has a good reason for what He's putting you through. You have always told me to just let Him have complete control and He'll take care of everything. So maybe you better practice what you preach."

Rie closed her eyes and made a valiant effort to gain control of her emotions. She took a long trembling breath, "Sometimes I get so frustrated," she said passionately, "I feel so helpless, not knowing what I have. I see the pain in Mother's and Daddy's eyes. I don't want them worried about me. Sometimes when I feel weak and unsure I want to yell to God and ask 'WHY' and then I feel ashamed, unworthy of God's love."

"You not worthy?" I laughed in disbelief. "I've always been told that God is love, and baby, you have so much love for everyone that I feel you are truly one of God's chosen ones. I see in you what I could have been and what we all should be if we would only open the door all the way and let Him in. Don't you understand," I pleaded softly. "You're our sunshine and you reflect God's light. Without you our lives would have been shadowed and meaningless. You have taught us so much by your actions and deeds. Rie, you are not a coward or weak but one of the strongest people I know. It's only human to ask 'WHY', God doesn't love you less for it. He loves you more."

She listened quietly while I was telling her this and then she smiled that soft sweet dimpled-smile, that beautiful Sunny Marie smile.

Reaching over and hugging me tightly, she replied, "Oh, Aunt Margie, thank you for telling me that." Tears shimmered like diamonds in her eyes. "Thank you for the pretty words."

"God loves you. We all love you." Gathering her into my arms, I stroked her brilliant red curls trying to keep from crying. "Oh, my baby, God gave me the words to say. He knew you needed to hear them." That was a turning point for Rie. Depression wasn't seen again. Even though Rie was just as sick as before she became stronger, more talkative. It was as if she finally came to a decision that the illness

was not going to defeat her. This wonderful child would constantly tell us everyday how much she loved us. So many times I watched as she touched people's arm or face lovingly and in the sweetest voice, she would say, "I love you, I love you very much." This was a constant ongoing thing. We also assured her that we loved her.

After a lengthy visit at Mother's house, Rie and Sunny were leaving to go home. Mother and I stood in the doorway waving to them. Just moments after they had left, Mother turned to me holding her chest. Her face crumbled and she started crying. I thought she was having a heart attack. Placing my arms around her shoulders I comforted her. I worried about the pain she was experiencing and asked her if she needed her medicine.

Mother kept nodding her head no. Finally after her sobs quieted, she looked at me with the most terrifying expression I have ever seen on my mother's face, and asked, "Margie is my Sunny Marie going to die?"

The question caught me off guard. All I could do was remain silent.

Mother stood wringing her hands. "Rie always tells us she loves us but never like this. Have you noticed how every time she passes my chair, she reaches out her little hand and touches me? It's like..." Mother started to cry again, "it's like she's saying good-bye. Is she going to die?"

Was Mother having a premonition? I too felt like this, but I couldn't tell Mother and Daddy that I had these same feelings. They were already experiencing enough fears about their granddaughter without me making it worse.

For their sake, I tried to quince my uneasiness. I couldn't even describe it to myself why I felt a physical sensing that all was not what it should be, but it was there. That sixth sense again. Silently I waited, watching for the events to unfold, but always praying life would return to normal. Mother's eyes held mine. All I could say to my grieving mother was; "Mother, I don't know."

IN AGREEMENT

I awoke dreaming one night and greeted those ancient sages of philosophy as into my bedroom walked Jesus, Buddha, Confucius, Socrates, Plato, and many others from centuries past. They settled among themselves to impart to me the secrets of the universe and I quieted the excitement within me, hoping to catch every word.

They each lectured with a master's touch and spook about the wonders of all created and yet to be. They explained and pondered, agreed and argued yet each was genius correct. But soon before the dawn's first light they had to slow and stop.

All night long I had been a student of ages, full of wisdom, and as they stopped they searched my countenance to see if the knowledge had been well given.

I was startled by their stare, so intense and searching. "**WHY?**" was all I managed to ask?

Indeed, more startling was the look of shocked dismay displayed upon the features of one and all as they were standing, staring at me. The look so shared was disappointment.

Then suddenly, the force was true, and the light assaulted my mind's eye in understanding.

"**WHY NOT?**" I asked heartily and the thunder in my ears was a mighty applause from those who are yet immortal to me.

Early tests

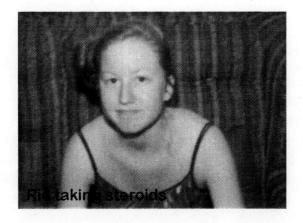

CHAPTER 7

The next morning glowed silver-white with new falling snow, but Rie was too tired to enjoy it. She was exhausted and was experiencing the pressure headaches again. I truly don't think she was ever without pain. She never complained so we really never knew how much she suffered.

While Rie stayed at Mother's house and rested, I begged Sunny and Phil to walk with me in the snow. The air was cold and the neighborhood yards were covered with a fresh white blanket of snow. Everything appeared new and clean. I thought it would be good for them to get out for a little while.

Sunny was dressed in a hooded red coat looking more like little red riding hood while Daddy helped me into his sheepskin-lined jacket that was miles too big and one of his hats he found in the closet. It made me feel proud to wear my daddy's coat and hat.

Mother took one look at me. "Oh, for heaven's sake, Margie," she said indignantly, "you're not going out looking like that. People will think you're a man."

Mother, always the proper lady, had hoped that her daughters would follow her example. My sister, Marilyn, had. She was always dressed to perfection, but Sunny and I were Mother's great disappointment. We dressed to please ourselves or our husbands, whatever was more comfortable or what the day called for. So it was to mother's humiliation that I left the house dressed like my father.

Outside was like a winter wonderland and in southeast Texas, when it snows, students are dismissed from school because it happens so seldom. Because the snow usually lasts no more than a day, everyone has to enjoy it fast before it melts.

Large downy, silver flakes of snow floated on the easy north wind, attaching themselves to anything standing still. The snow-layered trees and the frost-covered windows gave the neighborhood the appearance of a Currier and Ives print. It was beautiful beyond words.

After walking around the neighborhood admiring the handsome snowmen and taking pictures of the beautiful scene, we came back to Mother's. With nothing better to do, we built our own snow people on Mother's front lawn. Unlike the naked snowmen in the neighboring yards, we decided we were going to be different. So borrowing some of Mother's and Daddy's old clothes that were stored in the garage, we began to dress them. One snow person was tall and skinny while the other was short and chubby.

Maybe it was intentional, we were never really sure, but the snowwoman and snowman turned out to look exactly like some friends of Mother's and Daddy's, people whom Sunny and I weren't fond of…well, to put it bluntly, we didn't like them at all. It was Rie that always said she could find something good about everyone, but Sunny and I had a slight flaw, we found some people beyond our endurance to admire.

After only a short consideration, we decided to name the snow people, Margaret and Leo after our parent's friends. Sunny decided that to make Margaret come to life, she needed a scarf. Short Margaret always wore scarves even in the hottest weather.

Rummaging through the box of old clothes, Sunny found a lavender scarf and a square piece of lavender material. (Lavender was Margaret's favorite color.) There was even an old brown western hat and striped tie for Leo.

I dressed Leo in his fine duds while Sunny carefully wrapped the scarf around the neck of the snowwoman; tying it in front in the exact manner Margaret wore hers. We gave her a basket to hold, a lavender hat fashioned from the material, apple-wedge lips, and a carrot nose. The nose was only slightly longer than Margaret's real one. The nose topped off Margaret's perfection. We stood back and admired our creation and immediately started rolling with laughter.

We took turns posing beside Margaret for photographs. Daddy even posed by our snow people, laughing with us when we told him who they were. Leaving to go inside the house, he promised to send Mother out so she could enjoy our creations. We sat down in the snow waiting excitedly for Mother, snickering like silly children.

Mother came out of the house wearing a frown. Happily we yelled, motioning for her to come see our handiwork. She hurried over, but it wasn't to see our beautifully sculptured figures. Instead she wanted an explanation of our antics.

"I can't believe the noise all of you are making. Everybody in the neighborhood will hear you."

Phil, Sunny and I glanced around the empty yards, but we seemed to be the only people outside. We gazed at her questioningly watching her white, steamy breath sail up into the cold air.

"I care about what my neighbors think," she replied struggling to catch her breath, her voice high, and her face turning slightly red.

Spying the snow people, Mother demanded, "What is this? What are you doing?"

Believing she would join the fun, we introduced her to Margaret and Leo.

Needless to say, she didn't find it funny. Mother gave a small squeal before pulling Margaret's lavender scarf from the snowwoman's chubby neck. She made a sour face as she jerked the brown western hat from Leo's head, actually decapitating Leo as she pulled off his tie. We sat in stunned silence watching the destruction of our creation.

"How dare you make fun of my dear, dear friends!" she exclaimed, not bothering to lower her voice so the neighbors couldn't hear. "What if they were to drive up and see you making fun of them?"

"But, Mother," I said trying to keep from laughing, "they wouldn't have any idea the snow people were modeled in their image." Sunny and Phil agreed. "To anybody else the snow people appear like over-dressed snowmen."

Either Mother didn't care to hear our explanation or she was too busy berating us because she still continued stripping the clothes off the two snow people. When we sat there quietly watching her, like three bad children, Mother became exasperated. We were too big to spank and too old to intimidate. Throwing her hands into the air, she gave up. Making a loud huffing sound, she turned and marched military fashion across the snow-covered yard, loudly mumbling under her breath. The tie, the square piece of material and lavender scarf flew out behind her like flags in a gale. We watched her purposely slam the door behind her as she hurried in the house.

Silently, we looked at each other. Just as silently, we looked over at the nude snow people, one minus a head. As if on cue, all three of us collapsed into hysterical laughter, tears streaming down our faces.

It was so good to see the worry lines leave Sunny and Phil's faces for a short while. It was good to hear my little sister's bubbly laughter as we acted like children without a care in the world. We tried to get Rie to come out and play with us, but she only wanted to watch from the window, laughing as we entertained her. The love radiated from her eyes as she watched her parents playing and having snowball fights. We took turns throwing snowballs at her beautiful face behind the window glass. Every time we hit the mark, Rie gave us a thumbs-up sign, showing her approval.

February 21, 1980, Rie's birthday, found us at Mother and Daddy's house once again. We were to celebrate Rie's eighteenth birthday with a party as soon as Sunny and Phil came home from work. Rie's other grandparents, Helen and Euell (better known as Memaw and Pepaw), called from Port Arthur, wishing her a Happy Birthday.

Doug called from college. Rie's face registered disappointed when she found out he wasn't coming home until the following weekend. He informed her that his mother would bring her a pizza for lunch.

It boosted Rie's spirits when Doug's mother arrived with the pizza and Sunny and Phil arrived home from work. Aunt Marilyn, Uncle Dave, Philip, and Derek made up the rest of the party,

The next morning, February 22, was Daddy's birthday. Rie and Pawpaw always celebrated their birthdays together. But first, we were to take Rie over to Lake Charles for a simple check-up. It was understood we would celebrate in the late afternoon on our return.

But today there would be no celebration. Rie was nauseous. One could see the worry lines starting to form around Sunny's eyes. She whispered to me, "I don't like Rie's coloring." I observed Rie closely without her noticing me. Rie looked far too pale, almost colorless.

We made a bed for Rie in the back of the van. We placed a cool wet cloth over her eyes to reduce some of the pain. Before we were halfway to Lake Charles, Rie began to have involuntary movements of her arms and legs. First a leg would jump and then an arm would fly up at an odd angle. It was like someone pulling the strings of a puppet. We had never seen anything like this before.

Sunny was sitting on the bed with Rie while I was in the seat facing them. Phil was driving, trying to watch what was happening with Rie in the rearview mirror. The fear was visible in Sunny's voice as she asked Rie what was wrong. Rie replied softly, "I don't know why I'm doing this."

When the jerking became progressively worse, Sunny cried, "Phil hurry…get us there as fast as you can." Phil was already exceeding the speed limit, but at the fear in his wife's voice, he stomped the accelerator to the floor.

All of a sudden, Rie sat up in the middle of the bed, holding both of her arms to keep them under control. She screamed, "Mom, I'm sick at my stomach."

"Just throw up if you have to. Daddy will soon have us there."

"But I'll get us all messed up."

"Don't worry about that, honey," I replied. At this point who cared? Our minds were focused on getting to the hospital. We didn't care how we were going to look if Rie vomited on us. Placing our arms around Rie in a protective circle, Sunny and I held her close. In unison, we all began to say "The Lord's Prayer."

It seemed like hours before we arrived at Dr. Shamieh's office. While Sunny rushed in to inform the doctor of our arrival, Phil picked Rie up in his arms and carried her in. Without delay, we were ushered to an examining room where Dr. Shamieh quickly examined Rie. He kept repeating under his breath, "This is not good. This is not good. Take her immediately to the emergency room. We need a CAT scan as soon as possible."

Phil gathered up his daughter in a panic, trying desperately not to cause her unnecessary pain; he rushed her to the van. We rode across the street to St. Patrick's Hospital where the staff was already waiting outside with a stretcher. This made us more aware of the urgency of the situation. Rushing Rie inside, they instructed us to hurry and follow them to the third floor. There we were told to wait in the hallway until they could establish an IV.

Hurry and wait, hurry and wait, I chanted under my breath. We hurried, we prayed, but we waited in silence as the fear tightened around us. The overwhelming fear that surrounds you holds its hand around your throat while chilling the soul. It seems to burrow deeper and deeper burying itself in the deepest recess of your brain until you have trouble deciphering what is real. You become aware of everyone and everything around you. Oh, you manage to go through all the motions, trying to act normal, but breathing seems to be restricted, your heart beats out of sync, the body temperature drops, and your whole being trembles. Tears burn behind the eyes, but are held at check. You can't cry…you mustn't cry. Somewhere within the structure of your heart is a gnawing sickness that you can't swallow down. The body can conceal the effects of fear, but the eyes and face shows the strain.

Like three separate islands, Sunny, Phil and I waited in silence, keeping busy doing nothing. We inspected the cracked white walls and marble-grained floor, afraid of making eye contact with each other least we voice our unspeakable fear, least we see it reflected in the face or eyes of the other. We were afraid of breaking down...frightened if we did we couldn't stop the crying.

"Oh God," I kept praying over and over, "Please don't let this be bad. Why does it have to be our Rie? Why does this family have to suffer? Why can't You give this little family some relief from this terrible nightmare? Why, God, why? Can't you see we're drowning from all this fear? Please God, help us." I felt emptiness. In silence I screamed, "Where are you God?" But there was no answer.

THIS LIFE IS BUT A PLAY

The sleepy haze fall like a stage curtain dropping in front of a bevy of actors. (They are through performing and their portrayed characters are left on a table with costumes and make-up after the crowd goes home.)

Through the fog it is hard to make out familiar objects and every face becomes a stranger that one must hasten by in case the stranger be of the violent sort. (Scripts have been put away, each cast member, the unprepared actor in the impromptu of life.)

The heart beats fitfully when approaching cars slow their pace to crawl past, one's footsteps echo loudly alone on a concrete sidewalk. (Props are few and simple, but very real.)

One reaches home unharmed and forgets to thank the writer of the play that all is well. (The Director/Writer/Producer of life keeps this in mind for future reference in case He decides to make a tragedy out of the next act.)

Margaret   Sunny

Sunny   Marilyn   Margie

CHAPTER 8

Finally we were able to join Rie. She lay quietly in the hospital bed with a washcloth over her eyes. Two nurses were busily injecting medicine into the intravenous tubes that were protruding from each small hand. Thankfully the jerking movements subsided.

Sunny stood quietly at the end of the bed with tears rolling down her face. One of the nurses placed her arm around her. "Stay strong, little mother," she said. "As soon as Sunny Marie is stable enough you need to go across town so she can have a CAT scan made."

"But, my baby hates the noise the CAT scan makes," Sunny said.

A mischievous smile spread across Rie's face causing all her dimples to appear as she stated: "It reminds me of a big mechanical monster with its mouth open waiting to eat my head, The doctors say, 'Okay, open wide,' and then they stuff me inside."

We started laughing over her version of the CAT scan and that seemed to relax all of us. As we were waiting for word to go to the other hospital, Rie spoke out in a soft voice, "Mom, could you please see if I can be moved to another room?"

"Why, Babe?" Sunny answered with a frown, "Don't you like this room?"

Rie answered her mother in a strong clear voice, "No, I don't! This room doesn't have a Jesus Cross hanging on the wall."

Sunny slowly pivoted around searching the dark green walls for the cross that usually hung in all the rooms of the Catholic Hospital. "Oh, Margie, when we were here before there was a crucifix in her room and she loved it." Sunny kissed Rie on the top of the head. "Don't worry, we'll ask a nurse to bring us one."

"Thank you," Rie replied softly. "It makes me feel better when I have one."

As soon as Rie was relaxed from the medicine, the nurses said they would call for an ambulance to carry Rie to the other hospital. Rie smiled sweetly, "Thanks but no thanks," she said. "Daddy will take me in our van. I refuse to ride in an ambulance unless it's extremely necessary."

The nurses glanced at us questioningly for confirmation. When I gazed at Rie's stubborn set chin, I knew the decision was already made.

One of the nurses studied Rie for a long moment. "If that's the way you want it, I'll see if the doctor will agree." The doctor agreed, so once again we placed Rie back in the van, driving across town to have the CAT scan. This time we placed her on a pallet on the floor just inside the sliding door. Sunny sat on the floor between the captain's seats opposite the driver holding Rie in her arms to cushion her against any bumps. I sat if front next to Phil holding Rie's intravenous bags.

While staring out the window, Sunny began telling her daughter everything she saw as we drove to Lake Charles Memorial Hospital. No sooner than we pulled up at the hospital the nurses put Rie on a stretcher. As they were wheeling Rie away, we were kissing and assuring her we would be right outside in the waiting room.

We sat close together on a bench. All at once we looked at each other and started laughing at what Rie had said about the mechanical monster. We had a very vivid picture in our minds of what that monster looked like. Again our little angel had lessened the severity of the situation.

Nurses wheeled Rie out of the scanning room, giving us a sealed envelope to take back to St. Patrick's hospital. They said that the doctor would be waiting for the results.

At St. Patrick's we settled the now exhausted Rie in her room. She seemed to be resting nicely. Pulling a chair beside her bed, I stayed with her while Sunny and Phil, hand in hand, walked down the hall to talk to the doctor. I reached over and picked up the little hand that lay on top of the white blanket. Such beautiful long piano fingers. I kissed the back of the little hand, carefully, trying not to disturb the tube that was giving her peace. I had no idea how long Sunny and Phil had been gone when I heard the most heartbreaking sobs I have ever heard in my life coming from down the hall.

Oh, my God, someone's soul was being torn from their body. I stood up, walking quietly over to the door. I started to crack open the door so I could peer out, but like a bolt of lightning searing my heart, I knew who was in such agony. I grabbed the door handle as my knees gave way and I pressed my face against the wall taking deep breaths to keep from screaming out loud. My mind was screaming, "Oh God! They must have found something bad." After what seemed like forever, I made it back to the bed on shaking legs trying to act as normal as possible. I leaned over the resting child and whispered, "Little girl…"

Removing the cloth from her eyes, she stared at me long and steady. Swallowing a large lump in my throat, I managed to say; "Will you be all right for just a minute until I see if your mother and daddy are coming?"

I prayed inside, Please God, don't let her hear the crying.

But I knew in my heart she had because there was very little this child missed. Her eyes widened, but she didn't ask any questions. Wearing a serious expression on her pretty face, she nodded gravely. The movement was very slow.

REVERIE'
I understand deeply because its voice searches into my being.
Searching for the threads of my comprehension.
Tying them together, the woven pattern bespeaks my thoughts and the colors are self-ideals.

Meaning has become only a word, but feeling wraps itself around my soul and fills me with personal conviction.

I am one within.

I may now seek answers to the unspoken questions my logic ignores.

I have found my own Nirvana inside, and at peace

I will rest.

CHAPTER 9

Opening the door I glanced in the direction I heard the sobbing. At the end of the long corridor I could see Phil supporting Sunny. Her back was turned away from him and she was sobbing against the wall. I ran to where they were standing and grabbed her up in my arms.

She was shaking so hard from the sobs that racked her body. It was all I could do to hold her. I wanted to absorb the pain myself. "Phil," I pleaded, "go stay with Rie. I'll take Sunny to the pediatric playroom."

Phil hesitated. His face was pale and for the first time I noticed that his eyes glistened with tears, but he seemed to be in control. I knew if Rie saw him she would be more at ease. He hurried to Rie's room. Just before entering, I noticed him remove his handkerchief and wiped his face and eyes.

"Shhh," I whispered to Sunny. "Rie's going to hear you," That seemed to get her attention. She looked at me, becoming quieter.

"Come with me." I tugged Sunny's arm, pulling her along with me down the hall until we reached the door opposite Rie's room. We entered a large room filled with children's toys, small tables and chairs, and two sofas. I closed the big door behind us. I knew it would keep in any sound we made. We sat down on the nearest sofa. "Tell me what happened?" I said.

Sunny took a ragged breath trying to gain some control. Tears were streaming down her pale face, but she began to speak between out-breaks of sobs. "Oh, Margie, they found it. The doctor said all along Rie had symptoms of a brain tumor but nothing was showing up before now." She looked at me. She shook her head slowly. "It's huge," she said on a sob. "Oh God! It's deep seeded, right in the middle of the brain. Hiding."

I sat listening in shock, not moving, immovable. Now it was out in the open. Now the disease had a name. I was afraid to ask the dreaded question but I had to know. I found my voice, "Sunny, is it malignant?"

Sunny nodded a slow yes. "It's bad...real bad," she confirmed, "The doctor said this kind is always malignant. It's located in the third ventricle of the brain. He called it a Glioblastoma Multiforme...whatever that means." (Later we would find out that the Glioblastoma Multiforme tumors of the brain are known for their ability to grow rapidly into surrounding brain tissue. While these tumors rarely spread outside of the brain, they may send out tentacle-like projections to produce additional tumors. Rie's was located in the third ventricle of the brain, compromising both sides of the brain. It was malignant, unreachable, untreatable, and very uncommon for someone Rie's age.)

While she took an unsteady breath, I started hyperventilating. I wanted to know everything, but at the same time I didn't want to hear any more.

"Oh, my baby!" wailed Sunny while rocking back and forth. "All this time I was hoping it could be fixed. We did everything we were suppose to as parents to protect our children. Doctors are suppose to heal the sick...aren't they? This shouldn't happen in today's world. Why has this terrible thing happened? Why?" Her eyes beseeched me for an answer.

I had none. Silently I watched my little sister suffering. Everything in my body was ice cold. It hurt to breathe. I prayed to myself, "Oh God, remember me, I'm the weakest child you have. You must give me strength. Please don't let me fall apart; Sunny needs me to be strong. Put the words in my mouth that will give this mother comfort. Use me hold me together. I too want to scream and cry, but give me the strength not to." When I looked at Sunny, she held her trembling hands over her face. "Honey, what does the doctor want to do?"

Taking a deep breath, she dropped her hands into her lap. She leaned her head back on the couch as if she was very tired. Her voice sounded flat, "I don't know. He said something about talking to the doctors in Houston to see if they have any ideas what could be done. He's not optimistic. Right now it doesn't look good. The doctor said that this type of brain tumor is rare in someone as young as Rie. He kept stressing there is no cure. The tumor is embedded so deep in the brain that removal would cause Rie's death. DEATH!" Sunny emphasized the word, realizing for the first time what the outcome would be. Her eyes widened in alarm. "My God, my child is going to die no matter what they do."

A terrible spasm of pain screwed up Sunny's face, as though her mind was picturing something beyond comprehension. Suddenly she jerked up into an upright position and cried, "Oh, my God, my baby is going to die. I can't live without her…I can't. I can't imagine life without her. She's our sunshine," Sunny's voice quivered. "If Rie dies…I'll die too. I don't want to live without her."

Embracing her in both my arms, I rocked her back and forth as you would a small child while whispering to her. "Oh, Sunny, you can't die, the little boys need you, Phil needs you, we all need you."

Sunny pulled away from me. "Margie, Rie's the only daughter I have, the only one I'll ever have. She's my firstborn. What will I do without her?" She started crying again.

"I know honey, I know, but, Sunny, we have to be brave for Rie. She needs you right now. We can't let her suspect we have doubts about her coming through this."

Sunny seemed to call on some source of inner strength. Her face was so pale. The light sprinkling of freckles on her face, usually invisible, were now large dark blotches. Her swollen eyes glistened with tears. "I know that. Just give me a few minutes, I'll get it together." She gave an involuntary shiver. "I have to go back home right away. Now is the time to tell Mother and Daddy and my boys." She brushed angrily at the tears on her cheeks. "You know this is something I was hoping I would never have to do. Somehow I kept hoping the doctors were wrong and Rie was going to get better."

"I know. We all had those same hopes."

She nodded. "Can you go with me…back to Mother's?"

"Of course, that's what I'm here for, to do anything you want me to." Tears were streaming down our faces. Our hearts were broken, our fears engulfing us, actually suffocating us, and all the while my brain screaming BRAIN TUMOR!

Dear God is this real? Not Rie, not this beautiful child of love…this talented child. A monster brain tumor, lurking in the dark recesses of that brilliant mind, had just been waiting to make its presence known. Rie said it best when she had told us in August of the previous year, "I feel evil surrounding me. It's trying to get into my head." A premonition, I'm sure it was. Evil? Yes, what else can you call cancer?

How long we sat in that small room surrounded by toys and small chairs and tables, I don't remember. Some of the toys lay broken on the floor just like our hearts were. Was it just this morning that we came to the hospital? Oh! It seemed like that was ages ago.

After running cold water over our faces to reduce the swelling caused by tears, I asked, "Are you ready?"

"I think I can go back to Rie's room now," she said. She squared her shoulders as if she was marching into battle. We covered our heartbreak and masked our pain. We had to stay strong for Rie. We entered the dark room. Rie and Phil were very quiet. Phil was sitting next to the bed holding Rie's hand. He looked up.

I could see his eyes were shining with unshed tears, but he was still holding it together for his baby's sake. My heart hurt for this strong man and I knew he also wanted to scream and cry with the injustice of it all. His only daughter was hurt, but this was one hurt he couldn't kiss away.

I reached over and squeezed his shoulder, hoping to convey the love I felt for him and his family.

Making her voice sound almost normal, Sunny said, "Hey Phil, Margie and I are going back home to pick up some clothes. We didn't bring any with us and I really do need to check on the boys. We'll be back as soon as possible." She reached over to kiss him but instead she grabbed him tightly. Her face was buried in his shoulder while they held each other. Not one sound came from either of them as they stood in silence.

After a small hesitation, Sunny leaned over the bed and whispered to Rie, "Baby, will you be all right until we return? Daddy will stay with you and we'll hurry like the wind. I'll call Doug and tell him where you are. Is there anything you need before I go?"

The little hand came up and pointed to the wall. Rie gave a broad smile. "Yeah," she said softly, "I need my Jesus Cross."

Sunny and I glanced at each other. We got into action…fast. I ran down to the gift shop and Sunny went to talk to the nurses, asking for a cross for Rie's room.

In the gift shop, the first thing I saw was a silver and black crucifix about four inches tall. It only cost $3.95, but I felt it was just what she would want. I took it back up to her room and placed it in her hand. I said, "Honey, here is your very own Jesus Cross. It'll do until they bring you one for the wall."

She lifted a corner of the cloth so one little blue-gray eye could examine the object in her hand. "Oh, it's beautiful, Aunt Margie. Thanks." She closed her fingers over it, turning it first in one direction, then turning it in another direction. "Yep, it fits just right." Holding it up to the light she scrutinized it closer. Her angelic face looked puzzled. "What is that?" she asked, tapping the bottom of her cross.

We all rushed to the bed to study her cross. On the bottom of Jesus' feet was a skull and crossbones. It looked as though He was standing on top of it.

We all agreed. We did not know what it meant. Sunny ran out into the hall and came back with Sister Barbara, a nun who was young and petite and had the most enchanting smile. Most of the nuns at St. Patrick's Hospital came from Ireland, but Sister Barbara was Louisiana French. We showed her the crucifix and asked her to please explain the meaning of the skull and crossbones.

Sister Barbara smiled and said, "Sunny Marie, the skull and crossbones means that Jesus has victory over death."

"Thanks. I love Jesus, but I've never seen Him standing on the skull and crossbones before." She gazed over at me. "I love my Jesus cross."

Closing her long beautiful fingers around that inexpensive little cross, she placed it next to her cheek. Unbeknown to any of us at that time, it was to play a big roll in all our lives in the next few days.

Sunny and I walked out of the hospital into a day filled with blue sky and sunshine, into the city sounds of ambulance sirens, the roar of car engines, and pedestrians laughing. The world was going on about its business as if nothing had happened. Sunny Marie was gravely ill.

Suddenly the sound of people laughing seemed alien to my ears. Would we ever laugh again? Even the blue sky and sunshine wasn't as bright or as pretty as I remembered. Everything around me appeared different. Maybe because our world was now bleak, filled with sadness and heartbreak. It was still the same world, only Sunny and I had changed, our spirit had changed, our perception of life had changed.

I felt dazed. I couldn't believe the sun was still shining. I expected it to be dark outside. We had just lived a lifetime in one day…no, not a day…just hours.

I started to get behind the wheel of the van to do the driving, but Sunny placed a hand on my shoulder stopping me. "Let me," she whispered in a despondent voice. "I've got to keep busy if I am going to make it."

Sunny and I drove to Orange to break the news to the rest of the family. We had so many calls to make to friends and family members informing them of the nature of Rie's illness. For the first twenty miles, we rode in silence, lost in our own thoughts. We were both suffering from an aching weariness that is mental as well as physical called hopelessness. I felt an aching desire to say something to help my sister with her pain, but I kept my silence. No words could stop her from suffering. For the first time in her young life, she was facing mental and physical pain beyond description. Nothing a doctor could heal and all the medicine in the world couldn't give relief from this type of agony. Suffering is one of the downsides of living.

Gazing over at my sister, I watched her profile while she continued chewing on her bottom lip. The knuckles of her hands were white as they gripped the steering wheel. Suddenly I wondered if she was really up to this? It was going to be rough. My heart cried inside for what we were going to face at home. Into her silence, I asked, "Sunny, are you all right?"

For a moment I didn't think she heard me. Then her expressionless eyes met mine. The luster was gone, her face was a solemn mask, "No!" she answered. "I'll never be all right again."

She was right. None of us would ever be all right again. Our life as we knew it would never be the same again.

VISION
I see people of all races kneeling. There is
> no one

listening to false protestation. There is
> no one

vying for the favor of dead gods. They are kneeling.
Kneeling in front of a rather roughly constructed object.
> Oh, nothing

that would equal the pyramids in grandeur.
> Nothing

that could stand up against the Acropolis in proportion.
> Nothing

that would reach the Taj Mahal's idea of majesty.
That roughly constructed object so simple in shape
was a cross.

The cross?

Just a cross...
Only a vision—what could it mean after all?

CHAPTER 10

Today was Daddy's birthday and we were on our way home to tell him and Mother that the light of their life had a malignant brain tumor, and the doctors were not even sure how they would treat it.

Mother and Daddy had been such a big part of Rie's life since the day she was born. They had even sold their farm in East Texas to move two blocks away to be near her as she grew up.

Daddy had always been such a gentle man, loving, and easy going. He carried a quiet strength and we knew we could always run to him with our problems. But how would he handle this problem?

Mother had always been domineering and headstrong. She had a Scotch-Irish temperament. She could fire up fast, never forgetting an argument, but we loved her in spite of this. She was a perfectionist—a take-charge person, only wanting the best for her children and grand-children. Mother loved spoiling her children and grandchildren and we enjoyed spending as much time with them as possible. There was never any time in our lives we didn't know our parents loved us. Now I cringed from the thought of hurting them.

As we drove into their driveway, Daddy was finishing spreading a load of topsoil. He rushed to the window of the van and smiled at us shaking his head. "You lazy girls, you're too late, I'm finished now."

Our daddy was always joking and laughing with everyone. He was the type to throw back his head, laughing at his own jokes. He kept a twinkle in his eyes and never seemed to be down. This time he looked at his girls and realized we were not laughing. No happy birthday wishes. No smiles. No, "how are you."

Climbing down from the van, Sunny took his arm and said in a soft slow voice, "Daddy, come inside the house, I have to talk to you and Mother." He stiffened slightly and the laughing expression died on his face.

Mother dressed in a brightly colored purple dress came to the front door wearing a smile of greeting. She was a pretty woman, with a soft cap of brown curls framing her creamy face and very clear blue eyes. She was young looking for her seventy years. When she didn't spot Rie in the van, a stricken expression appeared in place of the welcoming smile. Instantly she started wringing her hands in her flowery apron. "What's wrong?" She voiced in puzzlement. "Sunny, where's Rie? Why isn't she with you?"

"Rie's at the hospital, Mother," Sunny replied. "We need to go into the dining room so we can all talk."

The thought crossed my mind, "Yes, come into the dining room so we can talk and break your hearts. Happy birthday my darling Daddy." I prayed, "Dear God, give us the strength to break the news."

"Margie," Sunny asked quietly, "please call Marilyn and Dave. They need to be here too."

I hurried to the bedroom phone making the call as fast as possible. I was so thankful that my sweet sister had the presence of mind not to ask any questions. She simply said they would be here as soon as possible. I called Doug, explaining that Rie was back in the hospital. I couldn't bring myself to tell him about the brain tumor. He said it would be Sunday before he could get a ride from college, and I knew we would have to tell him at that time.

In the dining room, Mother and Daddy sat like mechanical dolls around the table that held Daddy's birthday cake at one end. Now with the news we had to impart the pretty bakery cake appeared cheerless, even though it was decorated with bright flowers of red. Dear God, this would be one birthday for the books, none of us would ever forget.

Sunny and I took seats across from them. Sunny took a deep breath before she said in a pained voice, "The doctors have concluded their test. They now know what Rie has." No one said a word. Mother and Daddy waited motionless, their eyes glued to their younger daughter. Their faces were blank. Only their eyes showed the distress they were in. "Mother, Daddy…Rie has a brain tumor."

"Oh no!" Mother moaned. Her fingers fluttered helplessly on the tabletop. "Oh, God, no!" Daddy let out a trembling breath. He clutched his long fingers tightly together.

"Please try to be brave," Sunny pleaded. "I need you both so much right now…more than I ever have before. We have to draw strength from each other." She began to tell them what had transpired since we left home early that morning, leaving out nothing but trying to make it sound as positive as possible. Leaving room for hope however slight as it seemed at the moment.

Mother became impatient with Sunny's explanation. "Is my baby going to die?"

The room was quiet as if everyone was holding their breath. Her question echoed through our hearts setting up a vibration through our soul.

Slowly Sunny stood up from her chair and walked over to mother. She gathered her into her arms as if she was our Mother's mother. I wasn't sure if she was giving comfort or wanting to be comforted. Her voice cracked on a sob as she replied, "I don't know. I truly don't know."

"Rie can't," Mother blurted in a tone bordering on panic. "She just can't. Not our baby. She can't die. I don't want to hear any more…" Her voice broke off in a hysterical sob. In Mother's frustration leaving the table, she pushed Sunny away as she hurried into the kitchen. Unsure who to lash out at, she started slamming cabinet doors and throwing dishes around the counter. The jarring sound of a couple of pots falling to the floor sent our nerves off the Richter scale.

Daddy took off his glasses, running his hands over his eyes. He kept his hands covering his eyes as he spoke, "What about the little fellows?"

"Daddy," I said, "Philip and Derek have to know the truth." With his hands still covering his eyes, he nodded, Marilyn and Dave, and Philip and Derek arrived about the same time. We went through all of the information again. Sunny stayed strong for her children as she told them about their sister.

Philip asked, "Does Rie know?" Sunny shook her head no.

"Well, when are you going to tell her?" Derek demanded.

"As soon as we go back to the hospital."

Their little faces were so pale and they really didn't know what a brain tumor was. They questioned and Sunny answered the best she could. Marilyn also tried to explain. None of us had ever known anyone with a brain tumor. Things like this didn't happen to people you know, let alone, people you loved. We were all afraid for Rie, but the boys were petrified with fear. Derek kept asking what was going to happen, but Philip rolled his mind and heart into a quiet shell. He slowly got up, leaving the room. He had heard all he could take.

Hurrying into my room, I began grabbing the first objects of clothing I came to, cramming them into a flight bag. Before we walked out the door to go to Sunny's house, Sunny held her boys tightly in her arms. "Hey guys, I don't know what is going to happen next or when I'll return," she said quietly. "Promise me, you'll behave for Mawmaw and Pawpaw."

Both nodded their agreement. Derek placed an arm around his mother's shoulders. "We'll be okay. Tell Rie I love her."

"Yeah," Philip mumbled, "tell her for me, too.

"Rie already knows how much you love her," Sunny assured her boys.

"Yeah, but tell her anyway," replied Derek.

Before saying good-bye we assured them we would call daily to keep them informed. We went to Sunny's house. From there we called Phil's mother and father. They too were shocked. Sunny promised to let them know daily what was happening. They asked how they could help and Sunny asked them to call Dinah (Phil's sister), and her family, and Kelly (Phil's brother in New Orleans.) "Right now just pray for all of us," she told them.

In darkness we drove away from Orange. I thought about the ones left behind. I prayed out loud, "Please God, give these people courage and faith. Hold them in your arms." Our trip back to Lake Charles was quiet. Sitting in the darkness of the van with just the green dashboard lights reflecting off our faces, neither one of us said a word. We had neither the need nor the desire to talk. We were literally talked out. My sister never took her eyes off the road, again gripping the steering wheel in a death grip. It had been a stressful day. We were both trying to deal with our thoughts in our own way. We had left behind shattered hearts. But they were going to have to deal with their pain and grief without us. Rie needed us now.

We found a parking spot near the back door of the hospital and unloaded our small bags of clothing. We were here to stay.

The night was cold, wet, chilling us to the bone. We walked under the carport into the busy part of the hospital. The bright lights assaulted us. My nose twitched at the sterile odor. It's funny how hospitals always have the same smell. We hurried, almost ran to the elevator, Other's did the same. When the doors finally closed, we were just two in the horde of people inside. It must be visiting hours, I surmised. As the elevator stopped on each floor a few people began getting off only to be replaced by more. Sunny and I were shoved into opposite corners.

Under normal circumstances, Sunny and I would have been friendly, talking with the people nearest us. But now with the burden-weighing heavy on our hearts, we stayed mute. I glanced at my sister's face across the elevator and wondered if mine appeared as drawn and as pale. Probably. Her eyes were focused on the numbers beside the door. Every time the elevator bell rang, announcing the floor before the door would open. Sunny's body jumped.

Glancing around at the many nameless faces wedged into the small confines of space, I was curious if any of them were experiencing the panic that I was beginning to feel. Most of them were visiting loved ones too. How many were going to impart bad news to their ill ones? It wasn't going to be easy for Sunny and I to tell Rie the same thing we told our loved ones at home. But because all of it was happening to Rie, she had a right to know. It was her life that was going to be affected, but it was also ours too.

When the elevator doors opened onto Rie's floor, we excused ourselves through the cluster of expressionless people. We headed in the direction of Rie's room. This time our steps faltered, our breaths became shorter, and reality struck us like lightening. It was obvious that neither one of us wanted to face the ordeal of breaking the news to Rie.

Just outside the door, Sunny stopped me. She sagged against the wall drawing in a deep breath. A dozen emotions registered on her face: fear, panic, sadness, pain, uncertainty, and those were only a few. I knew my face must have mirrored everyone of those emotions and more. I picked up her cold hand, giving it a reassuring squeeze. She squeezed back. She studied my face. My heart was somewhere in my throat.

"Dear God," she whispered in a trembling voice, "now we have to tell Rie."

RELATIONS

We breathe in syncopated harmony as we walk awkward by, toward the same goal.
We choose different paths but ultimately reach the same conclusion.
Do not stray too far away lest we lose communication.
Do not come too close, there is the fear of being moved off course.
I am moving straight. I'll expect you to follow the

parallels.
If you fall from the tight-wire do not think I shall reach for you.
I do not wish to lose my footing, too.
You can not walk my journey nor I yours.
So we remain alone, judging the distance for ourselves...

CHAPTER 11

Swallowing the lumps in our throats we opened the door of Rie's room and walked in. Phil was sitting at the side of Rie's bed; almost in the very same spot he had been when we left. He was talking softly to her.

Praying I could conceal my emotions, I said in a loud voice, "Well kid, we're moving in!" I showed her my flight bag. "Nobody leaves until you do." I bent over her bed, kissing her on the top of her red curls that cascaded over the white pillowcase like liquefied lava.

Rie smiled that gorgeous tender smile and replied, "It's okay, Aunt Margie, Daddy has already told me everything." Sunny and I both glanced questioningly at Phil. With a gradual nod of his head, he confirmed Rie's statement. Relief was evident in our faces.

Sunny's fingertips caressed her daughter's cheek. In a soft voice, she said, "Remember that television movie we saw about the girl with a brain tumor?" She swallowed hard to hold back her emotions.

Rie regarded her mother in silence giving her a nod. "Well, God in his way was trying to prepare us," Sunny replied in a voice that was barely audible. Then more loudly, she said, "Baby, we'll see this thing through…all of us."

Rie smiled that enchanting dimpled-smile at her mother and her eyes became filled with twinkling lights. Reaching out her hand to touch her mother's arm, she whispered, "Oh, Mom! I love you and Dad so very much. Both of you must always remember how much."

Sunny made a small sound before gathering her child into her arms. Her voice became thick with emotion. "And you must always remember that you are our heart and soul. You are our silver lining in a storm. You're the birds that fly and the flowers that grow. You're the mountains, the cliffs, and the oceans. All these things, God sent to us in you. Oh, my sweet baby, you are everything to Daddy and me."

Rie put her arms around her mother's neck and held her close saying, "You are all those things to me too, Mom." All the while that Rie was hugging her Mother, her little hand held firmly to the cross and with those mystic gray eyes devoid of tears, she said, "I want all of you to know, I'm not afraid like I thought I would be."

Slowly her eyes traveled around the room until her eyes touched each of us. Her eyes didn't reflect fear. They were clear and knowing…too old for one so young. "It's hard to explain, but I feel as though God is protecting me physically, emotionally, and spiritually. I've felt like that long before Daddy told me what the doctors found but I cried today because I've never heard my daddy cry before." She glanced around her mother at Phil. "I'm sorry, Daddy."

"It's okay, honey," Phil whispered.

Rie's face took on a glow, her lips parted in a soft smile. "Mom, when you and Aunt Margie came in just now I was trying to explain to Daddy. I feel God's presence so very strong around me and those beautiful voices I told you I could hear back in August, well now I can tell you about them. It was the Holy Spirit talking to me, preparing me."

She pushed a stray tendril of hair behind her mother's ear. Her eyes beseeching her Mother's understanding. "Mom, you and I know that God doesn't make mistakes. The doctors will do whatever is best." Her face reflected a look of sweet ecstasy. She showed her mother her cross. "See, I have Jesus. I don't want any of you to ever doubt it for one second. He's with me whatever the outcome. I believe in heaven and nothing will ever separate me from God's love. Life or death."

Rie stopped talking. Her forehead wrinkled in a frown. Reaching up to her mother's face, she wiped away a tear with one long slender finger.

"Oh, Mom," she scolded. "Why are you crying?"

The dam opened. Tears poured down Sunny's face like small silent rivers, but she seemed to simulate a control I didn't think possible under the circumstances.

"Why I'm I crying!" Sunny shouted, stunned by the question. "Where does it say that mothers can't cry? My gosh, Rie, mothers...especially this mother has to cry once in awhile." Little quirks around the corners of her full lips appeared.

Rie was enjoying her mother's dramatic outburst. "Cry!" she exclaimed just as dramatically, "but just don't overdo it, Mom." She surprised us with a big wink. "All of you can cry sometimes, if you have to, but only a little. Okay?"

"Oh, all right," Sunny mumbled, rubbing away the remaining tears.

Rie glanced over at Phil and me. "Is that okay with you two?" Phil and I both agreed.

Rie's smile showed through her weary features. She was tired. It had been a long heartbreaking day for all of us. Rie slipped lower on the bed resting her head on the pillow and once again placed the cloth over her eyes. We all stood around the room in stunned disbelief. I thought, oh, my precious child, if you only knew how we all are holding back buckets of tears. But you know that, don't you? This is your way of helping all of us, getting us through the tough times.

My little girl, look how strong you have become. Have you always been this strong or is God accelerating your growth for reasons unknown to us? To me it was obvious Rie was much older than we were. We were the children and she our teacher. I stood back in awe of this woman child. Like she said, God was present around her and it was becoming more evident daily.

Suddenly, removing the cloth from her eyes, she started talking excitedly about a visitor she had while we were gone. She began to tell us about a Catholic priest by the name of Father Constanza. Passionately, she said, "Daddy was standing in the corner crying when he thought I was asleep. I asked him, 'Daddy, why are you crying?' and he started telling me about my brain tumor. Daddy was crying so hard, I started crying too. Then Father Constanza walked in and demanded why we were crying. Daddy told him," she exclaimed in her husky voice, her eyes shining.

"Mom, Aunt Margie, I wish you could have seen him. All at once, he held up both his arms to the ceiling and in a deep melodious voice he called to Jesus. He said, 'Oh, my Jesus, hold these children in your loving arms and keep them safe. Be with them in their pain and suffering.'" She shook the little cross at us. "He said the most beautiful prayer I've ever heard." Her eyes became dreamy. "I felt the presence of Heaven right here in this room and the light of Jesus was shining down upon us. Daddy and I immediately stopped crying." She gave her father a big smile. She snapped her fingers. "Just like that we

were completely at peace. As sure as I'm looking at all of you, I'm that sure that God sent Father Constanza to us. After hearing Father Constanza, I knew that God would be there for me no matter what the outcome. I hope you can meet Father Constanza soon. He's really a nice man."

Rie appeared happy as she finished telling us about her visitor. Phil agreed with his daughter. "It was really something, wasn't it, babe?" They exchanged smiles. "We really needed him at that moment. It was really rough going for a time," his voice quivered with held in emotion.

I saw the pain on Phil's face. He was crushed. Nothing else mattered, except his child's life. He had always been called "Big Dad," by his children and now here was something besides a broken toy or skinned knee to fix. Big Dad was helpless, just like the rest of us. My heart cried, but my eyes stayed dry. God was answering my prayers by holding me together. Emotions lay at the surface for all of us, but I made up my mind to stay as calm as possible for Rie's sake. If she could do it, I had to do it also. We all had to do it for her.

One look at Rie with her cross in her hand and her shining eyes, I had the feeling that she had enough strength and courage for all of us.

I propped Rie up in bed on several pillows. She smiled and kissed me. Then she gazed over at her mother sitting near by.

"Mom, from now on when the doctors want to talk with you and Dad, do it right here in my presence where I can hear what they say. Please don't try to keep anything from me again. I'm the one involved." Her big gray eyes were very serious. "You have to promise me." When Sunny and Phil gave her their solemn promise that nothing would be kept from her again she lay back on the pillows. Just before she closed her eyes for a nap she gave us a thumbs up.

Because Rie was having intravenous dips around-the-clock, the nurses told her to use the bedpan since she had to go to the bathroom so much. Rie was a very modest person, so this didn't sit well with her. She refused the assistance of the nurses so we had to place her on the bedpan ourselves. Sunny and I were inexperienced, nurses we weren't but we did our best.

The first time we placed Rie on the cold metal bedpan, it literally took her breath away. "Gee, some spastic nurses you both are," Rie complained. "You're trying to torture me, aren't you?" She mockingly stretched her hand out. "I can just see it now in the morning headlines, child tortured to death on cold bedpan by spastic nurse fiends posing as mother and aunt."

"Was it that bad?" I giggled.

She raised an eyebrow, a bemused expression in her eyes. Then very innocently, she inquired, "Wanna change places?" A slight smile made her lips curve. "You and Mom want to see how it feels."

In unison Sunny and I nodded no and then started laughing. Sorry, Rie," I told her, "from now on I'll run hot water on it for you."

"That would be wonderful," Rie exclaimed, "Why didn't you think of it before you froze me?

I shrugged. "I guess we're just dumb spastic nurses."

"You said it." Her deep throaty laughter was infectious. The warming of the bedpan with hot water became a regular ritual. Occasionally Rie would get tired of the bedpan and insist on getting up, walking to the bathroom. We were like a parade. Because Rie was light headed and weak, Sunny held her arms while I brought up the rear with the stand and IV bottles. Rie would march, singing "Jesus Loves Me" at the top of her voice.

Sunny jokingly said, "Oh, Rie, you can't sing that song on the toilet."

"Of course I can," Rie insisted.

"You can't," Sunny argued.

Rie stopped in her forward movement. Like "The Three Stooges" we bumped into each other, one, two and three. Rie slanted her mother a questioning look, "Why not?"

"Because…" Sunny appeared dumbfound, "because it would be sacrilegious."

A softness appeared in Rie's eyes and she replied, "But, Mother, it's not sacrilegious. My Jesus goes everywhere with me."

Sister Barbara was standing in the doorway listening to our conversation. Sunny looked over at the little nun and asked her opinion about the song being sung in the bathroom. Sister Barbara chuckled, "I go along with Sunny Marie. It isn't sacrilegious to sing God's praises. Jesus goes everywhere."

Rie gave her mother a smug knowing look, and said, "See, I told you. Sister Barbara is the voice of authority."

Sister Barbara left the room laughing. She said over her shoulder, "Please continue with the singing."

The singing continued and "Jesus Loves Me" was to become our favorite song. When the headaches were absent, Rie enjoyed singing. Those were the times our hearts would sing. At night Rie slept with her

Jesus cross held tightly in her hand. For safety reasons, some of the nurses would try to pry it from her hands only to find out she was not to be separated from it. Rie would come awake uttering a cry of alarm. She would instinctively fight to hold onto her cross. The nurses found out fast, this was not some meek child, but a very determined young woman.

The nuns, priests, ministers, family, and friends that came into the room would usually ask Rie, "How are you feeling today?" Rie would hold up the little silver cross and say, "I'm just fine, thank you. I have my Jesus."

You cannot begin to know the effect this had on everyone who heard it. Father Flynn, the resident priest for St. Patrick Church, and Father Constanza would say, "Praise the Lord. What a witness for our Savior."

We had to wait until Sunday night when Dr. Milan returned from Houston to know exactly what we could expect. So from Friday to Sunday was like a month instead of three days.

In Rie's room we had a couch and a chair that made into beds. Sunny and I would take turns sleeping on them when we could sleep. Phil slept in the van in the parking lot of the hospital. We all joked and laughed as much as we could to keep Rie's and our own spirits up, but on the inside our silent screams continued.

Phil was really beginning to worry us because he was feeling so badly. One of the nurses took his blood pressure and found out it was extremely high. He was deteriorating right before our eyes.

When we got to the point where we felt we couldn't keep up a cheerful front, we took turns going across the hall to the children's playroom. It was only there in the confines of that isolated room that we fell apart and did our crying. The nurses took turns sitting with us. They were so helpful and took such good care of Rie and us.

Sunday morning arrived with family visitors. Marilyn and Dave came first. Mother and Daddy brought Philip and Derek. Rie was so excited that her family was here.

The minute Mother and Daddy walked in, Rie jumped up in bed giving a soft squeal of joy, "Oh, Mawmaw, Pawpaw, you look beautiful." Then when she saw their concerned faces, she asked, "Are you okay?"

When they could only manage a nod, Rie didn't push it. She seemed to know how close to tears they were.

Rie spotted her brothers. "Hey guys," she grinned acknowledging her brothers, "thanks for coming to see me. I love you all so much. This is absolutely wonderful. My whole family is here," she cried as she bounced on the bed. Derek went around the bed inspecting the IV tubes while asking questions that made Rie laugh.

"Hey, Rie, is this fluid filling you up like at a filling station? Can you unplug yourself anytime you want to?"

"Will you just shut up and let me hug you two? Her little face lit up with love for her two younger brothers. When she hugged Philip, he clung to her while kissing her cheek. "I've missed you, Red."

"I've missed you...too much." Philip held onto her hand as he told her about friends at school.

After awhile, the boys went down to the gift shop coming back with flowers for her. They checked out her bed by raising and lowering it. They both took turns lying beside her to see what it felt like going up and down. They had her laughing until tears rolled down her face.

Pastor Brock (Sunny and Phil's Methodist minister) and his wife came to visit. The room was now filled to capacity. Laughter and love filled the room and it felt and sounded good...almost normal. Oh, how we needed this.

As Sunny stood gazing out the window, she saw Doug drive into the parking lot. She called Pastor Brock aside. Doug hadn't been told about the brain tumor. Sunny wanted Pastor Brock to meet with Doug and explain to him before he saw Rie.

Pastor Brock and I met Doug coming down the hall and asked him to go into the playroom. We broke the news to him and told him we were waiting to hear what the doctors were going to do. He broke down and cried. My heart went out to this young man. Sunny Marie was his love; security; his future and we were telling him about a malignant brain tumor that was going to change their life together. We were trying to say all the right things like, "be brave, don't cry, and keep up a front for Rie," things that would be hard for us to live up to.

Bless his heart, Doug pulled himself together before going into Rie's room. He hugged and kissed her as he usually did. Playfully he told her she better get well or she was going to be the reason he failed college.

We were all holding up well. Mother and Daddy were in good spirits. Rie decided to take a short nap. She covered her eyes with a damp cloth. We continued sitting around her bed talking softly, but not talking about the issue…no, never the reason why she was here. We were being strong in many ways, but not strong enough. Ever so often we could hear different ones sniffling.

Without taking the cloth from her eyes, Rie's asked, "Aunt Margie, are they crying?"

I had a lump in my throat, but I answered, "Yes, baby, they are."

Rie lay still and put her hands on top of the sheet and asked, "Why?"

How could I tell her that everyone in this room was so afraid for her? What did I mean, AFRAID FOR HER? We were afraid for ourselves. Afraid we might have to go through life without her.

Instead, I frivolously answered, "They're all jealous because they aren't getting that good stuff out of your IV bottle like you are."

Her soft pretty lips curved into a big smile. "If that's the only reason, then it's okay for them to cry, because I don't think the nurses will let me share it."

Doug was holding her hand when he suddenly lost control. He began sobbing. Rie threw the cloth from her eyes. Sitting up in bed, she gathered him into her arms. "Oh, Doug!" She rocked him back and forth quietly crooning to him. "Please don't cry. God is in control. He's with me. His strength is with me." She kissed his cheek. "Let God be with you. Believe me, I'm not afraid so…please don't you be afraid. You have to put your faith in God. I have, now you need to."

This beautiful child gave us all comfort that day. Not once did we see fear or one small tear from her. She was so calm it was unbelievable.

After Doug took the boys down to buy some candy the room became quiet. Phil was sitting by his daughter's side. He bent over and gently kissed her cheek. Placing her arms around her father's shoulders Rie held him. For a long moment they embraced. When Rie pulled back in his arms, she sighed, "I love you Daddy."

"I love you, too, babe," he uttered softly.

"I've always thought myself so lucky to have a Father like you. You're the best."

I watched Phil swallow a few times before he could answer. "Thank you, but I've always considered how blessed I was having you for my daughter."

Rie hugged him briefly, and then giggled. "Even when we argued?"

Phil smiled remembering how she loved to debate an issue. Any issue just as long as she could take the opposite stand. After long arguments on the pros and cons, just after he would finally concede to her, she would immediately do a turn-a-bout taking the opposite side again. She was never belligerent or angry. It was done in fun. He laughed. "Even then," he stated with absolute assurance.

"I didn't drive you crazy?" She stared up at him a little suspiciously.

He shook his head no. "Never."

Her face brightened, her eyes crinkled at the corners. "Good," she grinned. "I use to love arguing with you. I had to keep you on your toes."

Phil chuckled, "You certainly did that. For awhile I wondered if you were going to be a lawyer when you grew up and drive the judges crazy."

At first we noticed a small twinge of discomfort on Rie's face. Then suddenly she grimaced in pain. She touched her head, running her fingers over her forehead. They shook.

"Daddy," she cried, "my head hurts." Phil motioned for Sunny to get the nurse. His face was now paper white. Hurrying to the other side of the bed, I gently picked Rie's head up, positioning the pillow under it so she could lay flat. She groaned in pain. Phil and I exchanged glances. This was going to be one of the bad headaches and we both knew it.

Dipping the cloth in cool water, Phil twisted out the excess water before placing it on Rie's forehead. He was hoping this small action would give her needed relief. "Hang on, baby," Phil said breathlessly. "The nurse will be here in just a moment."

"It really hurts," Rie grasped as she took a labored breath. Her teeth bit down hard on her lower lip. Sunny came flying into the room with a nurse on her heels.

The pain injection was hurriedly given. We all took a deep sigh of relief, silently counting the minutes before the pain would be lessened. We stood in silence watching for any visible sign of relaxation on Rie's face and body. Finally the blessed relief came. Her hands and face relaxed. The nurse smiled. "Sunny Marie, next time don't wait so long in-between pain shots."

"Thanks," Rie grinned. "Believe me, I won't." Still with the cloth covering her eyes, she blindly waved good-bye to the nurse.

"Honey," Phil leaned forward, "I'm trying to visualize what your headaches feel like. Can you explain them to me?"

Rie drew back the damp cloth from her eyes, touching his arm urgently. The expression on her sweet face changed instantly to a look of sheer horror. "Oh no, Daddy!" she cried. "I can't! I won't!" Her lips trembled. "It's my secret, and God willing, none of you...." her eyes gazed at each of us with a sadness I had not witnessed before, "I pray that none of you will ever have to know."

DISCUSSION OF A DEPRESSION

I feel tears start to fall inside, but I refuse to let
them fall on the outside.
It's much more painful this way, but I guess it's my way of
being brave.

I struggle to survive, but inwardly there is little to save except the remaining fragment of a torn soul and spirit.

I wonder if I can rebuild and bring to life the dead parts of my feeling.

I close my eyes and in darkness of thought I realize this must be what death feels like.

I encompass myself in my own muted blanket of emotion and stare out at the world through the worn areas of fabric.

CHAPTER 12

Dr. Milan came into the room with news that surgery would be early Monday morning, explaining that shunts would be placed into Rie's head to relieve the pressure on the brain. He assured us this would give Rie instant relief from the headaches and the operation would only take about thirty minutes to an hour…no more.

The operation had nothing to do with the brain tumor. That would be faced later when Rie was stronger. We all felt so much better. At last they were going to do something to help the pain. Family and friends went home assuring us they would return to be with us tomorrow. Sunny told Mother and Daddy not to bother coming back since it was going to be a simple operation and let the boys continue going to school. She promised to call as soon as the surgery was over.

Doug wanted to be with us, but Sunny begged him not to miss any more college. He had already missed too much. So kissing Rie good-bye, he held her tightly saying he would see her Monday night. Marilyn and Pastor Brock said they would be over, planning to stay until surgery was over. With hope running high, we kissed everyone good-bye.

After the gang left, Phil, Sunny, and I were sitting around Rie's bed talking about the impending operation. Very seriously Sunny said, "Just think Rie, maybe after they place the shunts in your head you can play the violin. I've heard that strange things happen when they fool with the brain."

"Hold it," I said. I walked over to the phone and asked, "What is Doctor Milan's number?"

Momentarily stunned Rie and Sunny both looked at me as if I had just lost my mind. "Why do you want Dr. Milan's number?" Sunny asked frowning.

"I want the same operation Rie is having so I can play something too. It's not fair," I stated indignantly. "Rie can already play too many instruments. I want some talent too." All of us burst into laughter. I said, "Poor Rie, when would you ever find time to play the violin with everything else you do? If we could have one tenth of your talents, little girl, we would think ourselves fortunate."

Stephanie Radke, Rie's best friend, and her mother came to visit. The girls had been best friends since the second grade. Stephanie's mother had been Rie's piano teacher.

Rie's face brightened the minute Stephanie walked into the room. They gave each other a big hug and finished it off with the piggy salute (touching one finger to the end of their nose and making a pig sound.) Only they knew what it meant.

Stephanie was tall, dark headed, her clear green eyes were dark fringed, and a soft natural blush colored her cheeks. Just one look at her pretty face and dancing eyes made you smile with happiness. To my knowledge, Stephanie was always full of merriment. The girls could laugh at everything and did. They could find joy in most situations and shared the same jovial sense of humor, but today laughing Stephanie was on the quiet side, her concerned eyes regarded Rie.

Stephanie's lightning-quick warmth instantly covered her shock and started cheering up Rie. She began to relate some of their antics over the years and the room was suddenly filled with laughter. Stephanie said, "Do you remember the day we saved pink bathroom tissue for a month and sneaked it to school? We decorated the girls' bathroom in large pink bows around the toilets? We ran the paper through the door pulls, around the mirrors, and even taped pink bows on the waste paper baskets.

"We would've gotten away with it too, except for a teacher coming down the hall. When Coach Nugent saw us leaving the bathroom, she called to us to stop, asking us why we were out of class." The corners of Rie's mouth curved slightly, then the grin grew wider.

"We really tried to keep a straight face but, Rie, you started giggling and naturally I fell apart and started laughing also. Then Coach Nugent demanded we stay in the hall until she could take a look in the bathroom. She immediately came out wearing a stern face. We really lost it when she told us it was the prettiest bathroom she had ever seen. We thought she was enjoying our joke but then, she said, 'Okay, Ladies, you have exactly five minutes to clean up your mess or be sent to the office.'"

Rie's face reflected her happiness, forgetting momentarily her headaches and up coming surgery. With eyes bright, cheeks flushed, she leaned forward in bed wrapping her arms around her knees. She giggled softly, explaining, "We nearly broke our necks cleaning up our beautiful handiwork. We heard Coach Nugent laughing all the way down the hall."

Stephanie nodded. "Lucky for us she didn't send us to the principal."

"I know," Rie wiped tears from her eyes. "It was a close call but it was fun. We always had fun."

"Yeah, we did," Stephanie agreed. "It wasn't our fault that crazy things just seemed to happen to us."

"I know." Rie rolled her eyes. "Just like the time when John Ennis came to the house wanting to show me a new dance. After we practiced for a while, we called Mom into the room to show her the new steps.

"That guy could dance out of this world," Stephanie confirmed.

"Boy, could he!" Rie nodded. "Just as he jumped up to do a split, we all heard his pants rip and then his face turned a beet red." Rie fanned her hand into the air. "Remember...?" she giggled, "How at first, when he didn't move, we thought he was hurt. Mom asked him if he was hurt but John only turned a deeper red and replied, 'No, Mrs. E., I'm not hurt exactly, but my pride will be if I make a move.'"

"Mrs. E.," Stephanie pointed over at Sunny, "you just stood there."

"I didn't know what he was talking about," Sunny replied. "It wasn't until he pleaded, 'Please, Mrs. E, I can't hold this position much longer without exposing myself. My pants have ripped from front to back.' Then I finally understood."

"We tried to keep from laughing, really we did," Rie replied, "but it was impossible to hold it in. I saw Mom swallow the grin on her face before she finally said, 'Right, just wait there, John, until I return.'" Rie rolled her eyes. "Wait there?" Rie exclaimed. "I mean what else was the poor boy going to do? But my Mom saved the day by bringing in a pair of Dad's pants. She made us leave the room while John made a quick change. We laughed even harder when Dad's pants kept falling down because they were too big!"

"Yeah," Stephanie agreed, "but it never slowed John down. He was such a great sport about the whole thing. He still continued to dance holding his pants up with one hand." She pointed over at Rie, "When he lifted you on his shoulders and spun around, your mom and I shut our eyes, expecting to see a sight we weren't planning on."

"You, too?" Rie giggled. "My eyes were shut, also."

"I'd forgotten about that incident," Sunny replied. "You two girls were forever doing something."

"Oh, Mrs. E., I remember how you, Mom, and the teachers weren't too happy at some of the things we pulled," Stephanie insisted. "Just like the year the teachers wouldn't let Rie and I sit together at school because they said we couldn't control our talking. Our report cards were sent home with straight A's in all subjects but F for talking in class." Both Mothers nodded in agreement.

"We still managed to get notes to each other," Rie confirmed, "and then giggled in class over our notes." Rie glanced at Sunny and Stephanie's mom. "The teachers were always calling both of us to con-ferences. They weren't quite sure what to do with us."

"Short of taping your mouths shut," Sunny replied, "we didn't know how to stop you two from giggling. We tried every type of punishment known to man. Finally, I think even the teachers gave up."

Stephanie and Rie continued to reminisce. Girlish giggles filled the room. When Stephanie and her mother started to leave, the two girls held on to each other like this was the last time they would see one another. From laughter to tears these two girls had shared so much, but this, Rie was going to have to do on her own. Stephanie promised to see her as soon as the operation was over. After praying together, they quickly said their good-byes.

Phil sat with Rie as we walked Stephanie and her mother to the end of the hall and answered questions concerning the tumor. Stephanie had been brave for Rie. She had even been funny and cheered Rie up but now tears were rolling down her face. She was so very concerned for her friend's fate.

Sunny assured them that she would call after the operation was over. Stephanie promised to keep everybody at school up-to-date on what was happening. In the mornings, before school, they were already having prayers for Rie. Everyone at school was waiting for word and there was talk about different ones coming over to visit.

"Stephanie," Sunny said softly, "you be Rie's spokesperson and keep the students and teachers informed. Tell them how much she loves and misses them, but try to let them know, without hurting their feelings, that now is not the right time for visitation. Tell them you'll let them know when things are better. I'll keep in touch with you as often as possible. Thank you both for coming, she needed you very much today." With hugs and kisses and a lot of crying, we watched them leave the hospital. By the time we went back to Rie's room, it was already getting dark outside.

A nurse met us in the hall and informed us they would be washing Rie's hair for surgery. At this time they still were not sure if all her hair was going to be shaved off or not. Sunny wanted to know how they were going to wash Rie's hair if the doctors didn't want her out of bed.

The nurse patiently explained, "I'll use a flat tray that fits under the head. This way I can wash her hair without getting water on the bed. It's very easy on the patient."

My sister pulled me aside, "Margie, you and I are going to wash Rie's hair. I don't want the nurses to do it. If they cut her hair off for surgery tomorrow this may be the last time I'll get to touch her hair for a very long time. I have taken care of her hair for eighteen years and I won't stop now. We can do it…I know we can."

Sunny asked the nurse if we could do it with them supervising the job. The nurse agreed, telling us she would be right back with all the things we would need. I watched the determined expression on my sister's face and knew the nurse had seen the same look. "Oh, dear God, hold us all up," I prayed silently. "This is rough but I know You put me here for a reason. This little mother is determined to keep things as normal as possible for her baby. Please! Please keep her strong, keep us all strong."

Rie was resting when we went into the room. She smiled up at her mother and me. "It was nice seeing Stephanie and her mom. I've missed them."

"It was good to hear you laugh," I said.

"It was good to laugh and remember the good times Stephanie and I shared. Steph could always make me laugh." Rie grinned but her words faded to a whisper, "She's a great friend."

There was sadness in Rie's eyes. So before Rie could become teary eye, Sunny gave a quick run down on how her hair was to be washed. Rie listened patiently to her mother. Then as soon as she was finished, Rie cried out, "Wash my hair in bed! You've got to be kidding."

"The doctor doesn't want you out of bed." Rie continued to stare questioningly. "It's not such a big deal," Sunny exclaimed. "Really it isn't."

Phil asked, "Do you really know how to do it?"

"Sure," Sunny replied without a moment's hesitation. Then she looked over at me and raised her eyebrows with an impish grin. "There's nothing to it."

Rie gave a nervous laugh. "Well maybe not for you, but it is for me."

"Oh, give me a break," Sunny replied indignantly. "All you have to do is just lie there while I wash your hair."

Rie lifted one brow inquisitively. "Why do I have this overwhelming feeling in the pit of my stomach that this will end up the same as the bedpan," Rie said, a little worried.

"Okay, let me put it in plain English," Sunny stated. "It's either me and Aunt Margie doing it for you or some strange nurse washing your hair and getting it all tangled up."

Rie watched us in silence. "Well?" Sunny asked.

"Hold on," Rie snickered, "I'm weighing my options."

"Don't take all night, you only have two," Sunny snorted.

"Oh, all right!" Rie grinned. "I would rather have you and Aunt Margie wash my hair." Then Rie asked point blank, "Are they going to shave all my hair off?"

Phil and I glanced at each other while Sunny firmly said, "Honey, they probably will." Sunny's lip trembled ever so slightly but she managed to hide it from her daughter.

Rie smiled up at her mom and squeezed her hand. "It's okay, Mom. This long hair bothers me when I have headaches and really gets in my way when I stay in bed so much."

That was all she said, a child that had long hair all her life except for a time in junior high school. Rie wanted her hair short just once and her mother had cut it to her ears. After that, she let it grow back out. Her mother only cut the dead ends off twice a year.

Eighteen-years-old, no tears, no vanity, no fears, only acceptance. All that beautiful long red dancing hair, a soft glowing candle. It hurt my heart, but I said, "Rie, maybe it will grow back real curly this time."

She threw back her head and chuckled, "Maybe it will come back blonde and then I can sit out in the sun. I've always burned in the sun as a red head." She shrugged. "Anyhow, blondes are supposed to have more fun. Yep, maybe it would be fun to be a blonde next time." Her eyes sparkled with the thought of being a blonde.

A nurse, we did not recognize, came to the door and asked, "Could I please meet the girl with the cross." Sunny introduced the nurse to Rie. The nurse walked up to the bed and took Rie's hand in hers. "So you're the one." Rie looked blankly back at her. "Did you know you're the talk of this hospital and everyone knows you by name? Even visitors of other patients ask about you."

"Me?" Rie said. "I don't understand. Why?"

"Because, you're the only girl in this hospital that carries your cross and faith like a shield. Even the nuns are impressed. When people ask the nuns or nurses that have met you, how you are, they say, 'Oh, Sunny Marie is just fine…she has Jesus.'"

"They're right." Rie smiled broadly. "I do." She showed the nurse her cross clutched tightly in her hand.

The nurse examined the cross closely. "So, this is the cross."

Then for a long moment the two young women studied each other in a soul search. Evidently, they approved of each other because they both smiled softly. "It's true, isn't it?" replied the nurse, "You truly believe, don't you?"

"Yes, it's true," Rie said matter-of-factly.

"And you're not afraid?"

"I'm human." Rie's expression suddenly turned somber. "I would rather be well." She gave a slight shrug, then quickly added, "Everyone fears the unknown, I'm no different. But faith abolishes fear. The two can not abide together." Rie's eyes brightened and her lips turned into a radiant smile. "You know, I have always had this feeling of God's presence for as long as I can remember. Maybe that's why I'm not shocked at this illness or loaded down with fear. It's like…" she searched for just the right words, "it's as if God has been preparing me for this moment."

She laughed and rolled her eyes. "That sounds heavy doesn't it?" Her eyes sought her mother's face. She nodded over at Sunny, whispering to the nurse, "It frightens Mom when I talk this way, but it's the way I feel. I live in the present now, but I have this feeling that I need to be somewhere else in the universe. Suddenly I'm comprehending the meaning of all my poems I've written and all the strange emotions I've experienced. I'm more at peace now than ever before." She smiled showing all her dimples. "Weird, huh?" The nurse assured Rie that she didn't think it weird at all.

"I trust God. God is my strength and He promised to be with me." Smiling, Rie gestured with both hands. "Oh, not just on the good days, but also on the bad days as well. That's why I hold my cross. Jesus knows about suffering and he knows me. So you see, I'm not alone nor am I afraid. I have faith in my Lord."

The nurse seemed deeply moved. "I envy you your belief. I don't believe if I was in your place I could be as strong."

"When you place your faith in God, he gives you strength."

"He certainly has you." The nurse's eyes blurred with tears. She squeezed Rie's hand. "You know, you have really done something to this hospital, to the people, even to me." Then giving Rie the kind of embrace family receives, she whispered, "Just remember, we're all praying for you."

"Thanks, it's been nice meeting you," Rie replied. "Thank you for coming." The nurse started to leave, and then turned. "Oh, by the way, just between us girls, how old are you?"

I turned to the cute, petite, nurse and said, "Sunny Marie is eighteen going on forty-five. If we get to heaven and find out there is anything to the belief of reincarnation than I believe her soul is much older than ours. She has wisdom and talents far beyond a mere eighteen years. We are her students." I pointed to Sunny, Phil and myself. "Can you imagine for one moment what it's like to stay up with this child and her beliefs? She blows us away."

"No wonder everyone in this hospital is impressed with you, Sunny Marie. I've never met an eighteen-year-old as wise as you are. I wish I could read your poems," the nurse said.

The nurse's words brought to mind a poem Rie had written while she was in school, it was called "Wise Man" and it flashed in my mind: "I am a wise man rich with life's answers…though I have no money. Full with knowledge…though I have no food. Friendly with life's puzzles…though I have no friends, and faithful in an unseen God…though I have no idol." After the nurse left, Rie glanced around the room and said with a smug expression, "You know, I am getting older. I feel older. Have you noticed how fast I've grown up since I've been in the hospital?"

Laughingly, Sunny poked her daughter on the chest. "Oh yes we have Miss Smarty-pants, but just look what you're doing to us? We had no intention of growing up so fast. We thought we had a lifetime to age, nice and slow. But noooo!" Sunny chided. "We don't have your knowledge, your faith, your serenity. It's not fair. You're forcing us to grow up before we're ready."

Oh, dear God! Was she ever? I looked around that small room at Sunny and Phil. We were not the same people we were just a week ago or even a day ago. Oh yes, we were definitely growing for some reason unknown to us, but I wasn't pushing for answers not yet. I didn't want to know what the future held for us. Just living each day was all we could handle for now.

Finally the nurse brought all the paraphernalia to shampoo Rie's hair. As we washed that lovely hair, we kept up a constant chatter as though we were afraid not to laugh and talk lest we would fall apart. I watched my sister, so efficient, taking care of her daughter. Her fingers were tangled in the russet tresses of hair; its thickness spilled into the large flat pan under Rie's head. Sunny worked the scalp and massaged the neck. She knew Rie's every wish before a word could be spoken.

Once while we were pouring the rinse water over Rie's head, she squealed out, "Mom! You just poured water in my ear!"

"I'm sorry." Sunny looked into her daughter's eyes for a moment and very seriously said, "You've heard that people climb Mount Everest because it's there, well all at once this powerful urge came over me to fill this small opened cavity because it was there."

"I knew it was going to be like this. Cold bedpans, now water in my ear, what next?" Rie mumbled under her breath. Louder, she said, "Forget Mount Everest, Mom. You're showing tendency of modeling yourself after one of the Three Stooges."

Sunny snapped her fingers in Rie face. Then she patted the top of her head in a poor imitation of Curly. "It could be worse," she mimicked. Sunny dried out Rie's ear.

"Ha!" Rie raised her eyebrow. "Worse for who?" Rie shook the rest of the water from her ear. Then sticking her fingers in both her ears, she ordered her mother to pour the rest of the water. "Just make sure you don't fill any of those cavities that's called a nose or a mouth."

"Then maybe you should just keep the biggest cavity shut," Sunny replied. Rie quickly closed her mouth.

As I dried her hair with a towel, I said, "Rie, if they have to shave off your hair would it help if your Mom and I would have ours shaved too. Then we could all grow it back together."

"You both bald?" Rie wailed, eyeing both of us. Then she closed her eyes. "I'm trying to picture it." She gave a soft chuckle. Opening her eyes, she directed her gaze at me and started laughing. She gave my long braid a pull. Her eyes lit up with twinkling lights. "Oh, Aunt Margie, I wouldn't want you and Mom to go around bald. Uncle Johnny would never give his consent for you to cut your hair."

"Your Uncle Johnny loves my hair long, but he would just have to love me bald."

"No," she dimpled. "I don't think the world is ready for all of us to be bald-headed at one time…especially not you two.

"If it made Yul Brenner a sex symbol just think what it could do for us," her mother replied.

"Somehow," Rie snickered, her eyes dancing merrily, "I don't believe it would have the same effect on both of you."

SPECTATOR

The day is as calm as a windless ocean scene that promises nothing but deep quiet stillness. Scarce cumulus clouds float peacefully in an azure sky that compliments the budding spring greenery of trees and blooming flowers of every color. There is a light warmth in the air excluding the nip of a dying winter that more than likely is already dead. Rain fell the previous night, but no traces of it can be found in the dry-cleaned afternoon.

Chronic with spring fever, children and adults alike take to the outside and walk, jog, ride and run throughout the neighborhood laughing. Friends greet friends and the sky remains blue in the ever-changing world of a day in my life.

I stand back and watch as a spectator might do. Memories are being made, stored somewhere deep in the recess of my brain. This moment of life has been recorded for future playback.

THIS IS MY LIFE! I AM HAPPY.

Chapter 13

Phil kissed his daughter goodnight confirming that he would see her tomorrow early, we settled down to our routine of the night. I began rubbing her legs and feet with a skin-care oil. Applying it to each pretty shaped toe, I said, "This little piggy went to market, this little pig stayed home, this little pig had roast beef, this little pig had none, but this little pig went wee, wee, wee, all the way home." I tucked that little foot under the sheet and before I could walk away.

Rie pushed the other foot out and said, without a smile and in a very serious voice, "You forgot to do little pigs on this foot." We laughed. Laughter kept us sane.

Everything became quiet. I started to flip off the light switch when I heard Rie's voice..."Aunt Margie, promise me you'll make Mom wear her make-up." A mischievous grin spread across Rie's face as she looked over at her mother.

Thumbing through the Bible, Sunny lifted her head and asked, "What's this? Why must I wear make-up?"

"Because, Mom, if the doctors see you without make-up they may think you're the one that needs the operation." Rie looked over at me and winked. "Aunt Margie, this is fact. I make Mom put her make-up on every morning so she doesn't look sicker than me."

Sunny gave an indignant snort. "I have you know I wear my make-up most of the time."

Rie smiled a loving smile at her mother. "Just kidding, Mom."

Sunny replied, "You better be, kid."

Rie's smile faded and she became serious. "I love you. Mom, you know it?"

Sunny smiled back but her eyes filled with tears. "Yes, my doll, you've told me and showed me in a million ways." Lovingly, Sunny adjusted the sheet over her daughter, and then just as lovingly she ran a finger down the pretty face as she said, "I love you, too, pumpkin, more than life itself. More then there are stars in the heavens. I love you up to the sky, down to the ground, all around the world and two trash cans full." Sunny kissed Rie's cheek before hugging her tightly.

I was wrapped up in the moment. All at once the statement hit me. "Two trash cans full? Where did that come from?" I shook my head not believing what I had heard. Sunny giggled and said, "That's something Memaw, Phil's mother, always told the kids when they were little. We use it all the time to express how much we love each other."

We constantly joked and laughed. Strange how easy Rie made it for us, no complaints, no tears, no outward show of fear on Rie's part. She would smile so serenely at our crazy antics. We really wanted to grab this child up in our arms and scream and cry and ask God, "Why this child?"

During this weekend Rie had constantly asked her mother to read the Bible to her. I listened to this mother read in a voice so clear and calm…page after page. Everyone that came to visit talked about how God was in this room. God was so strong around all of us that each of us was beginning to change. The painful process of growing up. Aging if you will. We were Christians, with faith in our Lord, but we have never put our faith to the test. We talked the talk but never walked the walk. In the last few days we were living our faith. We had a living example before our eyes…Sunny Marie. We could not sleep thinking what tomorrow would bring. I watched Rie sleep and I quoted "Intellect" one of her poems out loud, "I am the wise man, hear me think. Hear my brain whir with cosmic awareness and thrive on intergalactic thoughts of space in a sea of reality. Watch me think. Watch my eyes close to concentrate on the more immediate matters to be pondered—do not bother me with your daily problems of crime, injustice, and politics. I am the wise man. I must first climb my personal ideas to their extent; you cannot fathom my meditation. Do not awaken me until the war is over—then we shall compare notes."

Oh baby, I wish we could be awakened after the operation is over. All your beautiful poems, you seemed to write one for every happening in our life.

Monday morning arrived with Doug calling, saying he was coming over after all. He claimed there was no way he could go to college while Rie was being operated on. He was adamant about being there for Rie.

Phil arrived from sleeping in the van. He was barely holding himself together. The strain was visible on his face, the mounting dread mirrored in his eyes. "Daddy," Rie inspected her daddy up and down, "are you all right?"

"Yes, baby," Phil forced a smile, "I'll be just fine when you're feeling better."

Rie had not been allowed food and water since midnight. She was due for surgery around 11:30 A.M. Father Flynn came in bright and early. He asked if our minister had arrived. When we said no, he informed us he would send the Methodist minister on staff, just in case our pastor didn't arrive before Rie went to surgery. Moments later, Pastor Mark Meier came hurrying into the room out of breath. I'll never forget that young Pastor's reaction to Sunny Marie. They shook hands and he sat close by her bed continuing to hold her hand as they talked. Still holding her cross, she assured Mark, as she had everyone else, that she felt no fear and God was taking care of her. I'm not sure how long this young man had been a minister, but you knew by watching him he had never met a young person like Rie. He, like everyone who came into contact with her, became emotionally involved. Before he left, we all held hands saying the Lord's Prayer in a circle of love. Rie's voice was clear and the strongest in the room. Pastor Meier promised Rie he would return everyday.

Marilyn, Doug, and Pastor Brock arrived and the waiting began. We all sat around Rie's room keeping the talk as light and cheerful as possible under the circumstances. Rie talked very little. She kept a damp cloth over her eyes, only smiling when something funny was said.

We were talking about different movies (anything we could think of except the surgery) when Rie surprised us all by stating, "Pastor Brock, did you know my Aunt Marilyn goes to see dirty movies?"

Marilyn let out an outrage shriek. "Rieeee, you know better than that!"

Everyone in the room cracked up with laughter. We all knew better. Marilyn, to our knowledge had never attended a dirty movie in her life. She was very religious. Her son, David, was a Lutheran minister.

"Ha, ha," Rie chuckled. "Guess I really got you that time, Aunt Marilyn."

Marilyn hung her head in mock embarrassment and said, "Now you've ruined my reputation." Pastor Brock threw back his head in a hearty laugh.

Doug was holding on to Rie's hand. She asked, "What's wrong with you, Doug, you're practically breaking my hand."

Gently he kissed the tips of her fingers and asked, "Is that better?" We could see tears in his eyes. He was trying so hard not to let her know he was crying.

Rie smiled. Blindly she pressed her fingertips to his lips, "Much," she whispered.

Eleven thirty came and passed and now it was twelve thirty. Rie sat up in bed taking the cloth off her eyes. She looked around the room with big wide clear eyes. I whispered, "What's wrong, little girl?" She looked up at me very steady and all she said was, "I'm a little disturbed."

I turned back to everyone in the room. "Okay, up until now, Rie, has held us all up and made it as easy as possible, never complaining. Now it's our turn to do everything we can to keep her from being 'a little disturbed.'"

Everyone stood up surrounding her bed. Placing our hands on her, we kept up a constant chatter to help pass the time. Smiling, Rie settled back down in bed, covering her eyes with the cloth. After a long time, Rie gave a loud sigh.

I decided some action was needed. "All right, this is it. I'll go see what's holding up our show. If Uncle Johnny was here, he would say, 'I'll kick some doors down if they don't get on the ball.' So since he's not here, I guess it's up to me to kick down those doors."

Eyes still covered by her cloth Rie smiled with pleasure. She stuck up her thumb. "Go get'em Aunt Margie."

I went searching for someone to tell us why we were having such a long delay. I found out that there had been more activity in the operating room than expected. I explained to Rie that it would not be long now. We all stood by her bed with our hands on her, still trying to keep her from being a "little disturbed," when she took the cloth again from her eyes. She looked down at all the hands lying on the white sheet.

Smiling that serene gentle smile as only she could do, she said, "Oh, I love my hands. They must go everywhere with me."

Marilyn grinned and asked, "How would we explain to the doctors about all those lumps under the sheet in the operating room?"

Rie waved her hand in the air, taking in all her hands in question and replied in a syrupy southern accent, "Well, it's like this doctors and nurses, I just can't go anywhere unless all my loving hands can go with me."

Giving Doug a quick kiss, Rie turned toward me and asked, "Aunt Margie, could Doug have a cross like you gave me? He needs Jesus in his life."

"Oh yes, my baby." I ran as fast I could and bought Doug a cross that looked exactly like Rie's. They held their hands together with their crosses touching. Finally, at one o'clock, a nurse arrived with Rie's injection to get her ready for surgery. Then the stretcher came to take our baby away. The silence in the room became deafening. Our hearts cried…no, please not yet. Don't take her away yet. We wanted it over, but oh, the fear gnawing at our hearts. Finally the silence was broken as we all took turns kissing and saying all the things we needed to tell her.

Doug's hands clutched tightly to Rie's face. With tears falling like a cascade over his hands, Doug told Rie how much he loved her. He broke into hard sobs. Pastor Brock put his arms around Doug, gently pulling him away.

When it came my turn to tell Rie good-bye, I kissed and hugged her, whispering, "Go with God, my baby." That soft little smile appeared and she whispered back, "Oh, Aunt Margie, God goes with me." She waved that little cross at me as they wheeled her down the hall to show me she still had Jesus.

Sunny and Phil continued to walk with her as far as they could go. At the door of the elevator the nurse told Rie to leave her cross with her mother. Reluctantly, Rie handed over her Jesus Cross to Sunny, and stated to the nurse, "It isn't big. I don't understand why I can't take it with me." But the nurse insisted it should stay behind. Rie gave it to her mother. "Mom, please keep my Jesus Cross safe."

Sunny assured her she would hold it for her until she came out of the surgery. She reached over and kissed the top of Rie's forehead. "I'm sorry, baby, they won't let you take it to surgery."

"That's okay, I have Jesus in here," she said pointing to her heart. Then her face became concerned, "Mom, are you going to read the Bible while I'm in surgery?"

"Yes," Sunny nodded. "Daddy and I both will read it."

"I would like you to always read the Bible...and Mom, you and Daddy never...never lose the Faith. Remember, you two are the best." She lovingly touched her mother's face. "I love you with all my heart and soul."

"I know," Sunny replied. Sunny and Phil were crying as they kissed and hugged their precious daughter good-bye. She held Rie in her arms and in a very soft voice recited their special love poem. "You are our heart and soul. You are our sunshine and rainbows. You are the wind and rain. You are the silver lining in the storm. You are the birds that fly and the flowers that grow. You are the mountains, cliffs and oceans. All these things God sent to us in you. You are everything to us. We love you, little girl, more than words can say."

"You both are all those things to me, too," Rie whispered. With that the nurses rolled Rie into the elevator with tears rolling down their faces, also.

Everyone that came into contact with this family was affected. You could see God touching everyone's heart through this special child. It was one of the hardest things in the world watching our baby being wheeled away to a place we couldn't go.

I'm sure everyone goes through the same feeling as they turn their love ones over to surgeons. It's frightening but necessary. Always in the back of your mind you pray that the doctors know what they're doing, that they'll make the right decisions. That the doctors and nurses surrounding your child know God personally and that God will guide their hands through the intricate operation, but most of all you just pray that you have enough faith to get you through the fear that manages to steal into your conscious thoughts of reason.

I marveled at Rie's faith, so strong, so sure. To her fear and faith couldn't abide together. So where were we going wrong?

PEACE

As if a giant stone had been dropped in the middle of the lake, the vibrating surface of the water laps against the sandy shore unceasingly with the force of the wind behind it.

The dark line of trees across the cove reveals little of the life beneath them.

Water-soaked logs roll slightly in their sand trenches in shallow water.

The resonant hum of a boat is heard among the bird calls and the tree frogs throaty pitch.

Occasionally a pinecone will fall with a hollow thud to the
ground.
Sunlight is streaked on the ground when it breaks through the
foliage of branches and green spring buds.
I lay here meditating, soaking in my surroundings.
I am at peace.

CHAPTER 14

We gathered in the waiting room that was already filled to capacity with people clustered in small separate groups waiting for friends and family, each little group an island in a sea of turmoil. It's funny how one perceives his surroundings at a time like this. You're conscious of everyone and everything around you, but yet you feel detached as well.

Some people were talking loud while others talked in whispers. Somewhere in the corner a television was on, muted music building up a scene of chasing cars and screeching brakes. No one was watching.

Someone was laughing. Laughing seemed out of place and I wanted to reach over and turn it off with a knob. Someone was praying...no not someone, but me. I was praying out loud. Phil's Aunt and Uncle were visiting. They wanted to help and give comfort. But all any of us could do was wait.

Unconscious of others in the room, Sunny and Phil were holding on to each other reading the Bible as they had promised their daughter. Sunny was holding onto the little cross as if her life depended on it. Sunny whispered loudly to Phil, "I don't want to be here. I don't want to walk this road."

I know I wanted to shout to my sister. I can see the pain in your eyes. My heart cried in silence, "If I could walk the road for you, I would in a heartbeat, but God chose you and all I can do is be there for you."

"I know, honey," Phil's voice was strong as he consoled Sunny, but a pulse throbbed in his forehead. "Rie's in God's hands now. All we can do now is read the Bible. That's what she wanted us to do."

"I know it is," Sunny whispered back, "but I don't like this waiting around while my child is being operated on. Head surgery! My God, how many people do we know has had head surgery?" He tried to smile but failed.

"None," he confirmed.

"Exactly. That's why I don't like any of this." Her voice rose slightly. "None of this is real. Why can't this be a dream and we can wake up to a normal life?"

"Shhh," Phil quieted Sunny. "It will be over soon."

I, too, wished it could all be a dream. We all were sitting through this day with a sense of unreality of this time and place. As time passed, doctors appeared at the door calling out a family's name. People would jump up, hurrying to the door to hear what the doctor had to say. Little groups of people began to leave as their loved one's came out of surgery. These nameless people, strangers we would never see again, but yet for just a moment of time we were able to touch each other's life, feel each other's pain. We wished each other subdued farewells. We continued to sit, waiting, knowing that our time would come.

One hour stretched into two. Two hours became three. How could this be? This was to be a simple, operation, just to place the shunts, not the main surgery. Sunny and Phil were beginning to show the strain. Doug was falling apart and crying in Sunny's arms. Pastor Brock sat with Phil talking quietly. Phil's aunt and uncle had gone home. I didn't remember saying good-bye.

Marilyn and I looked at each other afraid to say anything. Four hours now, our group was the only one left. Someone had thankfully turned off the television. We had stopped talking and everything was quiet...too quiet. Had they forgot about us? Phil called the nurse's station. Rie was still in surgery.

We took turns pacing in the waiting room and outside in the green-colored hall. Every hour on the hour Phil, Marilyn, and I alternated calling home to let the family know what was happening, but mostly what was not happening.

It was time again to call home. Sunny wanted to talk to her boys. Marilyn and Sunny walked out into the hall to call. Suddenly with the force of a physical blow, I had this overwhelming urge to be with them. It was like someone shouting to my senses, "Sunny needs you." I jumped up and followed. I peered anxiously around the corner. I wasn't going to disturb them if they were on the phone. I just needed to assure myself that Sunny was all right.

Marilyn and Sunny were standing right outside the double doors of the operating room only a few feet away. Marilyn was turned away from me facing Sunny. I couldn't see her face. Sunny was turned toward me, her eyes were glazed and she had the most horrified expression on her face. She was deadly white and looked like a statue, not of marble but of milky wax.

Hurry, my mind screamed. It was the longest few feet I've ever ran. I rushed to Sunny and grabbed her moments before her knees gave way. She just crumbled against me. "Sunny!" I cried. "What's wrong with you?" She looked right through me, down the hall to the operating room. In a tortured defeated voice, she moaned, "My baby's dead."

Shaking her hard, I screamed, "How do you know that?" When she didn't respond to me I turned toward Marilyn. "What is she talking about?"

"Let's just get her inside the room and I'll tell you all about it," said Marilyn in a stricken voice.

Held between the two of us Sunny was like a rag doll in our hands. Her body was limp while her head rolled from side to side. She started crying deep painful sobs, shaking and mumbling over and over, "Oh, God, my baby is dead!"

Sunny was so limp…so cold. Life just seemed to drain right out of her, almost as if she didn't have any bones left in her body. It took Phil,

Marilyn, and myself to half carry half drag her back into the waiting room. Placing her in a chair, I sat on the floor in front of her holding on to her cold clammy hands while Marilyn and Phil sat on each side holding her up. Sunny continued to moan softly.

"Honey, what's wrong?" Phil pleaded. His face was lined with concern. He hurriedly pulled his handkerchief from his pocket gently wiping the tears from his her face. He gently brushed the hair from his wife's forehead.

I don't believe Sunny was even conscious of any of us. Sunny said in a strangled voice, "Rie's dead."

Marilyn looked up at me with tortured eyes and explained, "Just as we were going to call the boys, a man dressed in a green surgical suit came out of the operating room crying and muttering to himself. That's when Sunny thought Rie was dead."

Glancing into the hall, we witnessed two men walking back to the operating room. One was dressed in green; the other dressed in white. They were talking as they passed our door. The one in green said, "I've tried everything I know and nothing is working, but I think I know of a new way to proceed." He kept repeating, "I've got it now. I know I can do it." I asked Marilyn if that was the same doctor and she nodded her head yes.

"Sunny," I screamed. "Don't give up. That doctor isn't giving up yet, he's going back in there to do what he has to do for Rie. No one has come out to tell us she's dead. Remember what Rie said, 'Hold on to your faith!'"

I watched my sister go into a shell. I remember saying to God, "God, don't do this, you can't do this!" We sat huddled together so afraid…so very afraid. Where was our faith now?

At six thirty, Dr. Milan and his nurse, Janie, came into the waiting room. I don't remember any of us moving or speaking. We all sat just waiting…watching.

He appeared looking harassed, totally exhausted, and emptied of emotion. He hung against the doorframe. In a tired voice he said, "Well, it's over and she's okay for now."

Sunny straightened up and in a very shaking voice, she asked, "You're finished? Rie is all right?"

He nodded. "Yeah, she's out of surgery."

Color came back into Sunny's face, and she murmured softly, "Thank you. Oh, thank you." Then she must have taken notice of his appearance. "I know you must be tired."

"God!" Dr. Milan's voice became angry. "It was rough going and it took longer than we anticipated...much longer." The doctor leaned heavier against the doorframe. "Sunny Marie will be kept in ICU tonight and you'll be able to see her in a little while. We had to place the shunts about ten times before we had success. Nine times, she rejected the tubes and would push them back at us." He ran his hand over his eyes. "It was a real fiasco in there."

We didn't ask any more questions. The doctor had done everything he knew to do. There is no way I can adequately describe my feelings and I'm sure no one else could describe theirs. God had given Rie back. She was alive. The shunts would give Rie a fighting chance now. Her headaches would be under control until the doctors could find a way to get rid of the tumor.

"Thank you, God," I prayed, "forgive us for our lack of faith. Forgive us of our fear."

After Phil found out they would only let him and Sunny in to see Rie, he told us to go home and be with the family while they stayed at the hospital. Phil said they would sleep in the van in the hospital parking lot. The hospital would be able to get them in a hurry if they were needed for Rie.

Marilyn, Pastor Brock, Doug, and I rode the elevator down to the first floor. We grabbed each other in a football huddle and were jumping up and down saying, "Praise God, we won, we won. She's alive. Rie's going to get better." People saw us. They stopped and stared. We were like lunatics in our happiness. Thank God, we could take good news home.

Forty-five minutes later when I walked in the door at Mother's, Sunny called from the hospital. "We just saw Rie."

"Wonderful," I replied, excited that my sister got to see her baby. Silence filled the telephone line. "What's wrong, Sunny?"

"She doesn't look good." Her voice was deep throaty and had taken on that flat far away sound. Sunny didn't sound good.

A shadow seemed to fall upon my joy, causing me to feel a chill. A pulse throbbed in my temples and I swallowed back bile.

"Rie's…" Sunny said in a stricken voice, "Rie's jumping almost off the bed." She started to cough. "I…I asked the nurse if this was normal after a shunt operation and," there was a moment of silence, "she said I would have to ask my doctor. Margie," a sob shook her voice. "Rie has machines and tubes everywhere on her. Her face looks so swollen. It doesn't look too good. I don't think the doctor was telling us the truth."

My legs nearly collapsed from underneath me. Rie was supposed to be better after the operation, what was going on. I gained control over my aching heart and asked, "Are you and Phil going to be all right tonight?"

Again there was a long silence, then she answered, "I…we'll make it…I mean what else can we do? They won't let us see Rie until morning." She gave a great sigh. "Who knows? Maybe there'll be some improvement then."

"Do you need me to come back tonight?" I felt like I needed to be there. Phil and Sunny were alone and frightened.

"No," Sunny gave another deep sigh, "just stay with Mother and Daddy. Don't tell them how bad it is."

"I won't. Call us tomorrow as soon as you see her," I begged.

"Honey, we love you. We'll be saying prayers."

"Yeah, say a lot. Rie needs them right now." She hesitated. "Phil and I do to. Bye."

I slowly hung up the telephone. With anxious faces, Mother and Daddy stood hovering by my elbow, waiting for Sunny's words. "Why did you hang up?" Mother scolded. "I wanted to talk to your sister. I haven't got a chance to talk to her all day."

"Mom, Dad," with an enormous effort I swallowed the urge to weep before I could say another word, "Sunny wanted to talk with you, but she had to hurry off the telephone." I lied. "The doctors are keeping Rie in ICU to keep a close watch over her tonight."

Mother's voice shook. "But why ICU? I thought the shunts were going to make her feel better."

"Mom, you were a nurse. You know how the doctor's want to be sure, especially since Rie's surgery took longer then they anticipated." I patted her shoulder reassuringly. "Don't worry, Mom and Dad, as far as Sunny knows, Rie will be all right. The doctor doesn't seem to be alarmed." I prayed that wasn't another lie.

How I prayed that night, "God, let your will be done. You have carried us this far. Please continue to watch over your children. We need you! Oh, how we need you! Forgive us for forgetting you are still the Master. In your hands you hold our soul…you hold our Sunny Marie."

TRANCE
I sense awareness through the dim-lit corridors of thought.
I do not ask to understand, comprehension prevails alone.
I speak not and hear less.
I remain in my own little controlled dream where night rules
      in utter darkness.
A night, black yes, but transparent.

CHAPTER 15

Early the next morning the phone rang and I jumped up wanting to be the one to answer. I heard Sunny's frantic voice. She was weeping. "Margie, you and Marilyn, come as fast as you can. It's critical, Rie is in a coma and I need you both with me. Oh, please, please hurry!"

"Honey, just hold on. We're coming as soon as possible." Then I saw Mother and Daddy sitting outside on the patio, they were having their morning coffee. "Do you want me to tell Mother and Daddy?" I asked.

Sunny took a deep breath in the attempt to calm herself. "Not yet, Margie. Not yet. They probably would want to come over and I don't want them to see Rie like this. Doug needs to be told before he comes over."

"Don't worry about anything, I'll take care of it." As soon as I hung up the phone I shifted into action, all the time praying Mother or Daddy wouldn't come in the house and hear my conversation. I hurriedly called Doug, told him we would be by to pick him up. I refrained from telling him any details. He would find out soon enough. Next I called Marilyn explaining to her everything that Sunny had told me. Marilyn simply said, "Be ready, I'm on my way."

I told Mother and Daddy that Sunny called and said Rie was still in ICU but all was well as far as she knew. Mother had washed and ironed Sunny and Phil's clothes and asked me to take them when I left. I told her that Marilyn and I would relieve them so they could shower and change. At least that part was true. Somehow we left Mother's house without her and Daddy realizing we were in distress. They thought we were hurrying out of the house to spend our usual day at the hospital.

I don't remember too much about the trip to Lake Charles except reaching over and grabbing Marilyn's hand, which was so cold and clammy. I tried to explain to Doug the condition Rie was in. It was hard because I had no idea myself.

As soon as we arrived, we went searching for Sunny and Phil at the hospital. We found the ICU waiting room but we didn't see Sunny and Phil.

The main room was empty so we sat down to wait. There were several doors leading off the main room and all of them closed. One door in particular had a white piece of paper taped to it. I walked over to see what it said. The words read, "The Phil Eppler Family."

I turned to Marilyn and Doug, my legs felt like jelly. "Oh, my God," I cried, "They gave Phil and Sunny a room. Rie must be dead." Marilyn and Doug's face was chalk-white.

We opened the door slowly not knowing in what kind of condition we were going to find Sunny and Phil. They were both sitting on a couch talking to a nun. They were still in the same clothes they had worn the day before. They must have slept in their clothes because they were full of wrinkles. Sunny's face was void of make-up. Both looked tired, as if neither one had been able to sleep the entire night. Sunny jumped up and hugged us as we came in.

Our faces must have showed our shock because she quickly explained, "Rie is still alive, but in a deep coma. The doctors can't tell us anything, yet." She indicated the nun and said, "This is Sister Margarita. She found me crying this morning in the waiting room. I told her about Rie and she immediately gave us this private waiting room for us to use day and night. We can only see Rie twice a day for ten minutes at a time."

Sister Margarita was one of the sweetest, most gracious people I have ever met. She told us if we needed anything day or night to let them know. She said she would bring us pillows and blankets for the sofas.

Sunny and Phil went to talk to the doctor. Doug was in a state of shock. He didn't say a word. He stayed in a corner suffering by himself. Marilyn and I sat by the window, gazing out at the cold gray curtain of winter outside and felt as if this curtain of cold despair had also wrapped around our hearts. My heart felt as if it was in a vice slowly being squeezed of all life. Marilyn kept brushing away tears trying not to break down.

When Sunny and Phil came in, their faces were devoid of normal color and they were leaning on each other for support. In a trembling voice my little sister repeated what the doctor had just told them. "The doctor thinks when they did the surgery on Rie's head, the pressure from the tumor caused the brain to explode." Her body shuddered. "He doesn't think there is enough brain left to keep her alive for very long, maybe around 5% brain function." She hesitated for a long moment unable to speak.

Finally she cleared her throat of tears and in a strangled voice she continued, "He doesn't give us any hope of her coming out of the coma or any hope of her living out the week even with the machines on her. As far as he is concerned, Rie's brain dead."

The words BRAIN DEAD echoed around the room. I felt it in every part of my being. Pain gnawed in my stomach.

I saw Doug jump. He inhaled a deep trembling breath. Marilyn slumped against the chair covering her eyes. I heard her murmur a soft, "Dear God!"

Brain Dead! I wanted to yell to God. How could this be? Why did You let such a thing happen to our Rie? This was the kid that was so brilliant; her brain was so active. She gave love without strings, a gift from her heart. Why Lord? Why our Rie?

Sunny stood up, looking at us with tears running down her face, all hope gone from her eyes. Like a mechanical doll she stood before us, with gestures stiff and unnatural. In a leaden automated voice, she informed us, "You'll be able to see Rie, but you need to be prepared for a shock."

Looking over at Doug, she said, "If you can't handle it, don't go in. Rie's hair is all gone, her body is in constant violent seizures, and she has tubes and machines everywhere in that small room."

Inhaling deeply, Sunny began clasping and unclasping her hands. "The tumor is affecting the thermostat of the brain. Because her fever is so high, they have her packed in ice." Her voice softened almost to a whisper. "Doug, she doesn't look like your Rie anymore. Decide what you're going to do.

If you do not want to see her like this, we'll understand." Doug started crying again. Phil placed his arms around him to hold him up. After a long agonizing moment, Doug made up his mind. Through sobs, he said he wanted to stay with the family so he could be close to Rie.

Sunny's voice rose slightly. "Honey, we now have to be brave for Rie. She needs us right now to keep our faith and be strong," Sunny hugged Doug tightly. Phil too, enclosed him in a three-way hug. The three of them stood holding on to each other while the moments ticked by and sound became substance in a silent void. Tears became rivers running down our faces, and we waited in that small room that measured ten feet by twenty feet.

In the strained silence, we waited for the time to visit our Rie. Sister Margarita and Sister Barbara came into the sitting room, off and on all day to help in any way they could. Oh, what comfort these soft-spoken little nuns gave us. Father Flynn and Father Constanza came by and said prayers. Pastor Mark Meier stayed with us most of the day. The whole hospital opened its arms to us in every way possible.

Nurses from ICU and from the fourth floor came by to talk to us and ask if there was anything they could do. They suggested that each time we visited Rie to talk in a normal voice as if she could hear us. They told us doctors aren't sure how much the unconscious person can hear and understand when they are in a coma. The ICU nurses said they talk to all their coma patients as they work on them. One sound or one word may work its magic making the patient want to return to the real world.

"Oh, please," I prayed to God. "Let it be so." Our little room had several sofas and chairs that made beds. We had a telephone in the room so we could keep in touch with family and they could call directly to our room. This room became our home away from home.

Once again we moved into this hospital. From this room I made telephone calls and sent Telexes to all my family. "Sunny Marie is in coma. Critical! Pray for Miracle." This went to my youngest son and his wife, Art and Sherri, in South Africa; my middle son, Benny, who was on a ship off Japan; and my husband, Johnny, in Indonesia. I called my daughter, Dedo, and her husband, Hank, in New Orleans and my oldest son and his wife, Woody and Sylvia, in Houston.

Time came for us to go in and visit with our Rie. We stood outside double doors with about twenty other people. We took turns going in. Sunny and Phil went in first, Doug and Marilyn went next, and I went in last.

The first thing I saw was a small room, big enough for a bed and machines…a lot of machines. One wall was covered with a beautiful mural of a lake with red and golden trees dressed for fall.

In the bed our Rie lay entangled in tubes. Several IV tubes in each arm, breathing tubes down her throat, and a catheter tube. Sensors that constantly affirmed functions and response of that small delicate body that lay in the elevated bed against the gold colored wall, blinked, vibrated, ticked, and clicked.

I looked around at all the life support machines the many bags of IVs filled with medicine, heart monitors, and a breathing machine. Massive doses of Valium were being pumped into Rie's body to keep the seizures down. Nurses came in to turn her. Every time they touched her, Rie would nearly jump off the bed.

Everything I saw seemed over dramatized. "Please God," I prayed, "this isn't real. This is not Rie with the dancing hair. This isn't our Rie that loved to be touched and kissed." What I saw was in no way the same soft smiling eighteen-year-old we said good-bye to only yesterday. Her eyes were closed and that horrible sound of the breathing machine made it sound like some heavy breathing monster instead of this dainty little girl. She had incisions on her neck and the surgery on top of her head was shaped like a horseshoe. A nurse placed a dainty little white cap over the top of Rie's head. It resembled a nightcap.

Rie's frail little body was packed in ice and her body was quaking in convulsive seizures. I leaned over and kissed her porcelain cheek and said, "Hi, honey! It's Aunt Margie. Little girl, you've run off and left us for a little while. I'm sure it's something you have to do, but we'll be waiting right here until you return. Don't stay away too long, little darling. We love you and we know God is taking care of you."

I stood there for a minute with my hands on her long slender legs trying to absorb some of the rigors into my own body. "Oh, God," I prayed, "there isn't one among us that wouldn't do this for her if it was possible. Father, you have a reason and we love you, but it is so hard...so very hard to cope with this. Help me; give me strength to help this child's mother and father."

I ran from that intensive care room out into the now familiar hospital corridor. I leaned my head against the wall and let the tears fall. "My Jesus, what do we do now?" I cried. My jaws were clenched against the mounting dread, the hollowness that filled my heart, the pain that racked my body. "What do we do now?"

By afternoon, our little waiting room was overflowing with family and friends, Phil's mother and daddy, Helen and Euell, and his sister, Dinah. Pastor Brock and his wife and Pastor Meier were also there. Church friends were constantly coming in and out. We would greet each new visitor and tell them about the operation. Everyone was in a state of shock, wondering how so much could happen in such a short time. The telephone was forever ringing and we would take turns talking to the callers.

During visiting hour we all took turns going in the ICU room to talk to Rie. When Pepaw and Memaw Eppler went in, they sang Rie's favorite hymns to her, all the nurses and doctors gathered around to hear their sweet clear voices fill the small room. The nurses and doctors commented that they had never heard singing in ICU before.

It was my turn to talk to the sleeping beauty and I sat down beside her bed and lifted the graceful hand that was holding a tightly clutched washcloth. Bless the nurse that remembered to fold one in Rie's hand to keep her long fingernails from cutting into her palm as she clenched her hands in seizures.

"Hello, baby, Aunt Margie is back to tell you just how much you are loved by so many people. This whole hospital, friends, and family are all praying for you to get better. We're all staying at the hospital until you wake up. Remember I told you we wouldn't leave here until you do. Don't worry about your mom and dad. I'll take care of them until you wake up. But please, try not to be too long on your soul-flight, little girl. We really do need you back."

My throat began to tighten up so I kissed the sleeping beauty good night. While I was standing at the foot of her bed it dawned on me, Rie's head was on the opposite side of the hall wall.

I placed my back to the side wall and counted off the steps from there to her bed...twenty. Two more steps brought me even to Rie's head. Then I went out into the hall counting off the exact amount of steps there...twenty-two. I kissed the wall exactly where I believed Rie's head rested against the opposite wall. I didn't need an X to mark the spot; my lipstick left a big red lip print. I smiled. I didn't care if people saw me do the deed. I was proud of it. It didn't bother me that the wall could be crawling with germs. I didn't bother to wipe it off but left it for all to see. Later I showed our family.

"This is the spot where Rie's head is," I said proudly, "just on the other side."

It was only done for the moment but as it turned out it became our "kissing wall." In the days that followed, none of us would pass that spot without reaching out and placing our hands there or pressing a kiss on the wall. It was our gathering place. We prayed there, we cried there, and we would stand there for hours sending love messages through that solid wall to our Rie. It became our twenty-two steps of love.

MEDITATION

The turbulent soul within me is calmed and soothed by the inner melodies of my heart. My logic remains apart and aloof, choosing to have no part of emotion and human weakness. The clockwork of beating veins within the shelter of my skin functions by its own timed intervals. Through the involuntary act of my breathing I inhale and exit the act in contented slowness. My mind, siding with logic and the reasonable, tends to look at things without bias and personal judgment. Unfortunately, the heart throbs stronger and the term "level-headed" does not exist.

So, I am sitting here experiencing the life of my body and nurturing the thoughts and debates between heart and mind. My soul is peaceful now and sits back to referee between emotion and logic.

Chapter 16

Sometimes it became unbearable in that tiny waiting room. Stuffy, hard to breath, impossible to rest or sleep, nowhere to hide in body or mind, too many tears and too little laughter. Sometimes we drowned in our own sadness.

The crowded small room spilled over into the main waiting room. Both were always filled with people that knew Rie or people that wished they had known Rie. Sweet, loving, caring people. Old, young, middle aged people. They wanted to be there, needed to be with us and we needed them, but at times it was like Grand Central Station.

Everyone wanted answers: What happened? Why was Rie in a coma? Would Rie get better? What were the doctors telling us? What is the prognosis? What are the diagnoses? Questions...always questions, but what was worse, we had no answers.

When I needed time to myself I would walk down to ICU and stand quietly by the kissing wall, talking to Rie and telling her how much I loved her.

Hundreds of lipstick marks soon appeared on the wall to mark the location. Not just mine, but others as well.

After visiting the kissing wall, I walked quietly into our small waiting room, Sunny was standing there by herself; everyone else had gone downstairs to the cafeteria. Usually everyone would go down together for his or her meals. The hospital was noted for their Creole Cuisine.

Sunny stood like a statue at the one window gazing out at the now darkened sky. She wasn't aware I was there. In a tortured voice, she cried out, "Dear Jesus, please don't let my Rie die. I can't live without her." She collapsed in sobs.

Completely lost in her agony, she jumped when I placed my arms around her shoulders. I tried to take the place of mother, father, sister, and friend. I opened my mouth to speak, but then said nothing.

I had no words right now that I could say to help this frightened young mother, so I just held her. As great as my pain was, I was not walking in her shoes. This was her first born…her only daughter.

In silence, I raised my eyes to the darkness beyond the window, staring at the moon that had started to rise and thought, like the moon…life has a dark side, too. Would the sun never shine on our hearts again? When would our time of darkness be over?

Apprehension of the unknown started to gnaw at my insides while the gasp of my breathing made my fear grow bigger. I wanted to take my sister, her daughter, and run away as fast as we could leaving our problems behind us.

But that wasn't rational, that wasn't real. A monitor somewhere on the inside of me screamed, "But there's nowhere to run."

Through my tears, I spotted more flowers in the corner. Red carnations? I wanted to laugh; I wanted to cry. Thank goodness they weren't roses. Rie wouldn't approve roses being picked for her.

Since Rie had been in the coma, so many flowers were being brought to the waiting room and no place to put them. ICU wouldn't allow flowers. We asked the nurses to please give them to people who had not received any. We informed the nurses to tell the patients they were sent with love from Sunny Marie. Rie would have loved sharing her flowers with others.

Cards were stuck on the walls around the room with tape. She received hundreds of cards, letters, telephone calls and visits from students, strangers, nuns, doctors, ministers, family members, and hundreds of friends. Anyway possible, All were giving their comfort.

It was during this time that we notice that some of our visitors had special qualities. To these we referred to as angels. We didn't know what else to call them. They were different from our regular visitors, but they came in all shapes and sizes. They brought messages and small gifts of love, requiring nothing in return. All were people we didn't know and never saw again, but oh, what they left behind will be remembered for a lifetime.

A small elderly, bent gnome of a woman came hurrying into our waiting room Tuesday morning. She moved with the ease and energy of a child. She was dressed in a tattered, green thin coat and run down black shoes, that at first glance, you wondered how cold she must get outside in the damp frigid air of the February winter.

Like a small bird, she fluttered from chair to chair searching the faces of the people sitting on the sofas. She had one of the most contagious smiles I've ever seen. She looked around the room, asking in a musical voice, "Where is she? Where is she?"

Believing the lady was lost and confused, I asked, "Who are you looking for?"

The elderly woman studied me for a long moment, her eyes clear and steady. They penetrated my soul. Suddenly I had the feeling I had known this woman all my life. Then her face lit up like a light had been turned on. She actually beamed. In her sing-song voice, she replied, "Why, the mother of that beautiful little red headed angel. I've got to find her mother?"

I thought how odd that she should call our baby redheaded. Rie's head was completely shaved. Anyone looking at Rie now wouldn't know that she had red hair.

By now the room had become absolutely still. All eyes were glued to the elderly woman. Everyone waited, wondering who this stranger was and why she was here.

In the corner of the room, Sunny rose off the sofa walking over to this petite woman. "I'm Sunny Eppler," she answered. "I have an eighteen-year-old daughter in ICU. Is she the one you're speaking of?"

The little lady stepped forward looking up into my sister's face.

She affectionately placed a small wrinkled hand on Sunny's arm. Searching my sister's face, she gave a dazzling smile, and said, "Oh, yes, of course you're the one. I can see you're her mother. I just had to find you and give you a hug and kiss for that lovely child."

The lady continued to hold on to my sister's arm as she spoke quickly, and said, "Now, God knows what He's doing. Your baby isn't dead so you keep talking to her. She hears you, she does. Everything will be fine." Reaching up, she hugged and kissed Sunny. "Remember, don't you give up. God isn't through with her yet." She patted Sunny's hand. "Honey, you just keep praying. God hears every word."

With that she turned to leave. Sunny touched the woman's arm to stop her. "Would you like to sit with us?" Apologetically, she said, "I'm sorry, I didn't catch your name."

"Oh, no. I must go." Her smile became radiant. Once again she gave Sunny a big hug. With a last good-bye, she left as quickly as she entered still wearing that big smile on her aged face. I watched her walk through the door expecting to see someone waiting for her. Had she had wings she couldn't have moved faster. I sat back down feeling lightheaded and suddenly breathless.

Sunny turned slowly around looking at all of us sitting in the room. She glowed like the woman. Her face wore a peaceful expression for the first time since we came to the hospital. I asked her, "Are you all right?" I knew I wasn't. She smiled a touching smile that lit up her eyes, and said simply, "I've just touched an angel."

The entire room was quiet not a sound could be heard. I think at that moment that everyone in the room felt the same way. "Thank you, Jesus, for our visitor," I prayed. "My little sister needed that...we all needed to hear those words. Thank you for sending your messenger." Later that day, the doctors wanted another CAT scan. The hospital informed Sunny it would be our choice as to which ambulance we would use. Opening the large phone book, she looked up ambulance services.

142

In utter confusion, Sunny asked, "Which one do we use? I don't know anything about ambulances in this town."

"Just pick one," I told her. "God will take care of the rest."

She called a number and told them what she needed. They told her they would be at the hospital within five minutes.

True to their word, the ambulance came to pick up our Rie. Two young paramedics explained to Phil that we could ride over to the other hospital with them. Sunny rode in the back of the ambulance with Rie and one of the paramedics, while Phil and I rode in front with the driver.

We were thankful that both young men were caring and compassionate. While waiting for the CAT scan, they wanted to hear everything they could about why this sleeping beauty was in a coma.

After our return, they came back to our waiting room informing us they were going to pray for all of us.

After reading the CAT scan, Dr. Milan came in to see Sunny and Phil. "The situation is critical," he said. "Sunny Marie is a vegetable. She is showing no sign of any response."

We sit there in numb silence. Maybe we were waiting for him to soften his tone of voice. Maybe we were waiting for him to say, "But this is what can be done." But whatever we were waiting for wasn't his next words.

Straight out, he said, "Your daughter is dead except for her heartbeat. Her heart is strong and with the machines there is no way of knowing how long she will live." He shrugged and for just a moment I caught a glimpse of sadness cross his face. His professionalism extinguished it in a second. "I'll inform you of any change in her condition, but I can assure you it doesn't look good." With a grim expression, he expressed his sympathy and left.

What do you say? What do you do when you're told your child is a vegetable with no hope of getting well, no life in that marvelous brilliant brain. No glow in those beautiful eyes, no smile on those soft lips.

You fall apart, you're angry, you cry heartbreaking tears, you hurt, and dear God, the pain...always the pain. You go down on your knees and cry out, "God! God where are you? I love you, God, but please don't take our Rie away. She's so good we need her. Please God, don't let it end this way." Doug's mother and father came to take him home. His mother and father loved Sunny Marie believing that one-day she would be their daughter-in-law. They were taking it hard, too, but they needed time to hold their son. Like us, they needed time to cry together.

When we gathered ourselves together into some semblance of sanity again, Sunny asked, "Margie, would you and Marilyn go break the news to Mother, Daddy, and my boys? I can't leave right now and I don't won't them to learn about this over the phone."

Her words hit me like a bolt of lightening from a clear blue sky.

I stood as if turned to stone. I started arguing with God. "Me!" I screamed silently to my Lord. "Me be the one to break this kind of news? Oh, God, remember me. I'm the weak one. Why have you chosen me? My little sister believes me to be strong, able to do anything, but You know and I know she's wrong. She's putting her trust in me and I'm just not strong enough. God, this is a biggy. If I do it, You're really going to have to give me strength…a lot of strength." I wanted to say no. I meant to say no, but to Sunny, I said, "Honey, I would do anything to lighten your pain or your grief." I swallowed a softball size lump. "Yes, we'll go and tell them."

Marilyn drove us to Orange on Interstate 10. I watched the beautiful landscape pass by before my eyes as I would a movie. The afternoon sunlight was softening the countryside scenery. Even the power lines, gas tanks, and refineries were pretty in spite of their ugliness. Most of the trees were dressed in winter brown which made the big live oaks stand out in the fields because they still had green leaves. These grandfather trees stood as guardians of the land with their limbs reaching down to embrace the ground.

Some of these trees were two hundred years old and older. This is all river country from Lake Charles on the Calcasieu River to Orange,

Texas on the Sabine River…Cajun country. We came to the Texas and Louisiana State Line in the middle of the Sabine River.

Looking down into the chocolate waters below the bridge, I could see through the brown feathery leaves of the cypress trees a swampy jungle of vines and lily pads. It was a primitive world of forgotten times. The Spanish moss hung down like gray veils concealing an undiscovered secret garden.

We crossed two bayous. Along the mud banks were large stately white cranes and small dainty egrets feeding at the feet of cypress knees. Even on this drape cold winter day there was beauty to behold. But with all this beauty around me, I felt a mounting dread of hollowness. I wished I could stop time and not face what we had ahead of us.

We arrived in Orange before the boys were home from school. Very carefully we broke the news to Mother and Daddy first. More pain…more tears.

"Honey," Daddy cried in his anger and pain, "why doesn't God take me instead? I'm an old man…I've lived my life."

I placed my arms around him. "Daddy, God wants Rie, our time will come. Don't you see that God has a time for us all? Right now Sunny needs you more than she has ever needed you in her life. Please don't give up. We have to believe God knows best. We have to pray for strength and courage. Rie has these things and she tried to pass them on to us." Daddy just sat with his head in his hands. Beautiful hands. Long fingered hands like our Rie.

We had never seen our daddy cry and it was hard to stand there hearing him sobbing as if his heart had been broken in a million pieces. This was our happiness man, the man that brought us so much joy and laughter.

Mother stood against the wall crying, moaning Sunny Marie's name.

"I can't take this. Why? Why has this terrible thing happened to our beautiful baby? She has never done anything to hurt anyone," she screamed out in her anger, venting her frustrations. "We haven't done anything to deserve this from God. Why? Why does He allow such a thing to happen?" Encircling her in my arms, I said, "Mother, there is no one to blame. No one did this to Rie…she didn't do it to herself. Please don't be angry with God. Rie wouldn't want us too."

Mother's body was limp in the circle of my arms. I placed her in the nearest chair and knelt in front of her. Her chin rested on her chest while she cried softly.

"Oh, Mother, how many times has Rie told us to trust the Lord and live our faith? She's lived her faith. Now it's our time to live ours."

Everything and everyone sit in a strange composed silence. Each lost in his or her thoughts. "Mother…" I said after a moment. She raised her eyes looking at me through her sadness, but she had recovered her composure. "Sunny needs you," I said quietly. "You have to give her your full support and understanding in what she is going through. Your loosing one of your granddaughters, but Mother, she's loosing her only daughter. It's not easy watching her daughter die before her eyes and not be able to do anything to help save her. You above all people should know how she feels. You lost your only son. Don't you see that all we have left is faith that God knows what He's doing?"

"Oh, Margie," she murmured barely above a whisper. "I knew…I knew deep down Rie was going to die. I had that feeling when she would tell us so many times how much she loved us. What will we do without our sunshine?" She stood, walked to her bedroom and throwing herself across her bed she sobbed helplessly.

Daddy came over to Marilyn and me. In a low-pained voice he asked, "How are my flappers (a name he had always called his three girls) holding up." He took a deep breath. "Thank you for taking care of Sunny Rie and her mom. If you need me, I can be there."

"Oh, Daddy," I laid my head on his shoulder and cried as I did when I was a child. "It's so hard sometimes. It hurts so much. Sometimes I feel like my heart is going to come right out of my chest from the pain and then I look at Sunny knowing how much greater her pain must be." Daddy patted my shoulder.

"You and Marilyn have to stay strong for your mother and me." His voice cracked, his lips trembled. "You have to take care of our Sunny for us. We can't. It's out of our hands now."

"Daddy," Marilyn whispered softly, "we're all in God's hands now."

"I didn't think I would ever live to see one of my grandchildren go before me." Gently he patted me on the back with those loving hands that could always fix our broken toys and childhood injuries. He hugged both of us while we all wept tears that we had held back.

MY FAIRY TALE BOOK

We had no money, poor were we.
Our wealth was judged by the holes you could see,
But I had a treasure so rich to me,
The book Mama read me while I sit upon her knee.

It freed me from our world so small,
Now filled with tiny fairies and giants so tall.
Through winter, spring, from summer to fall,
The land of magic to me would call.

When our stomachs were empty and days were cold,
Me into her lap mama would fold.
Into her hand the book she would mold,
And reading softly the tales were told.

As I grew older her lap grew cold.
My father was dead, my mother old,
And youth, the tale always foretold,
Seeks the world eager and bold.

I decided to leave when mother died.
On a cold, wet night after I cried,

I packed my bags and in town I tired
To live a life before, I too, died.

Now that I'm older I have expensive books.
My home is guarded and safe from crooks.
I have a butler, a maid, and a cook
But my treasured possession is Mama's Fairy Tale Book

CHAPTER 17

Mother and Daddy decided to leave Philip and Derek to our care. Both were emotional drained and decided to lie down for a nap.

Sitting down for coffee gave Marilyn and me a chance to pull ourselves together before Philip and Derek came home from school.

Like always, both boys came in with smiling faces. They had no idea what we were going to tell them. During coffee, Marilyn and I decided that I would explain to Derek and she would tell Philip.

When Marilyn mentioned we wanted to talk with them, they exchanged glances with each other. Like a light being turned off, their smiles disappeared. Just by the expressions on their faces they already knew it wasn't going to be good. Before we could say anything, Derek said he needed to do homework first and headed for his room, something any other time would be the last thing on his mind.

Marilyn suggested to Philip that they walk out to the backyard patio. Without saying a word, he placed his book on the dining table. Together he and his Aunt walked out the patio door. He was as tall as she was. It was cold but neither seemed to notice.

The patio was a scene right out of HOME AND GARDENS magazine. Mother had baskets of green plants hanging from the top of the awning. Around the bottom edge of the patio flowers bloomed in spite of the cold weather. Red tulips, yellow daffodils and pretty face pansies were growing profusely everywhere in the flowerbeds. It was a joyful place, not a place for bad news.

As they sat down in the big oak swing, Marilyn began explaining to Philip about Rie being a vegetable and how she was being kept alive by machines. Not a muscle moved, not an eyelid blinked as he asked her point blank, "Are you telling me my sister is going to die?"

Taking a deep breath, Marilyn replied, "Yes, Philip, she is."

"I don't believe it," he said in quick denial. Out of sheer frustration, he plucked the head of a red tulip shredding the tender blossom into hundreds of pieces. Muscles worked in his firm jaw while he kept his eyes downcast.

Marilyn covered his busy fingers with her own. "People are like the flowers here in Mawmaw's garden. They have a certain time to grow and a time to bloom. Some are beautiful and fragile but filled with wonderful fragrance. That's the kind of flower Rie is. She was placed on this earth to grow, bloom, and now be picked by God."

She hesitated allowing her words to sink in, afraid to say too much but more afraid not to. With Philip it was hard to judge how much he was allowing to penetrate. His only movement was the twitching in his jaw. Tentatively she continued. "We'll always have the memory of having the most exquisite flower living in our garden and how we enjoyed her as she bloomed." She touched his arm to gain his attention. Finally he gazed up at her with his wide-set almond shaped green eyes.

"Philip," she said softly, "none of us will live forever, our time will come just like Rie's and we'll also be picked by God."

Philip spoke emphatically, "Mom and Dad should be here telling me this. They should be the ones doing this." He threw the last remaining shredded petals to the ground. "This is screwy." He shook his head in confusion. "I've been without Mom and Dad since Sunny Marie has been in the hospital. Now you're telling me I'm going to be without Sunny Marie forever." His face twisted with emotion but he held it in check. "I don't want my sister to die…she can't."

"Honey." Marilyn placed her arm around his shoulder for comfort. "I know this is hard on you with your mother and dad spending so much time at Rie's bedside, but they would do the same for you if you were ill. I know how confused you must get sometimes. They love you and want to be with you, but right now they have to be with Rie."

Not a tear fell. His chest gave a great heave. "I know that," he said. He became silent, almost brooding. Leaning his head back, he gave the swing a push with the toe of his scuffed up track shoes. The swing made a squawking sound as it moved forward and backward through the cold air.

After the swing came to a complete stop, he said in a normal voice, "Thank you for telling me about Sunny Marie, Aunt Marilyn." He gave a noncommittal shrug of his strong young shoulders. "I never thought of life being a garden before," he said quietly. "I know Mom and Dad are having a bad time. I always took for granted the times we spent together." He paused. Taking a big gulp of air he exclaimed in a husky voice, "I miss being a family." He stood up staring a long time at his Aunt. "It won't ever be the same…will it?"

Unable to speak, slowly Marilyn shook her head no to his answer. "I think it sucks," he replied in anger. "I have the best sister in the world and God's going to take her away from me. She isn't wild or a dope head like some kids at school." He hit his fist against the chain on the swing sending the swing rocking erratically. Anguish throbbed in his voice. "She's good and kind. She doesn't deserve this, so why is all this happening to her?"

When Marilyn couldn't answer him, Philip walked into the house disappearing into his bedroom he shared with Derek. We heard the door close softly.

I hugged Marilyn and we cried together. "It was rough," she mumbled. She looked exhausted.

"Oh, God, I wish this day was over," I replied. When I could finally pull myself together, I went searching for Derek. I found him in Mother's kitchen finishing a glass of milk. "Hey, guy, I need to talk to you."

"Philip just kicked me out of our room," Derek said. "He isn't happy."

"No," I replied. "Philip isn't very happy right now."

His big round green eyes impaled me. "I'm not going to like this...am I?"

"No, it's not good." I took Derek on my lap and told him what the doctor said. He didn't say a word but tears flowed down those beautiful freckled cheeks. I talked to him a long time and then I left him alone to get himself together. I was sitting at the kitchen table when he came up to me.

"Aunt Margie doesn't God still work miracles?"

"Oh, yes, my darling!" I answered. "All the time."

"Well couldn't he work a miracle now and make Rie well again? Couldn't it happen like it does in the Bible?" He was so sincere as he asked these questions, staring straight into my eyes...my heart. I gazed into the face of this young boy, watching the tears rolling down his cheeks. I knew I had to find the right words to answer his questions.

"Derek," my throat threatened to strangle me. I took a deep breath before I could continue. "With God, all things are possible...and yes, He could make Rie well again. What God is asking us to do now is to let Him have His way. We have to accept God's will, loving and trusting Him...no matter what that will is."

"But I love Rie," his voice quivered. "I don't want her to die."

"Derek, God loves Rie so much more than we do, but He loves us, too. We must let God decide what is best, but, sweetheart, Rie has been a miracle for 18 years. Don't you see how much God has loved us by letting us keep Rie this long."

Weighing my statement, he gazed at me for a long time. The expression on his freckled face became thoughtful. Finally, in a trembling voice, he stated, "Then that's what God will do. He'll work another miracle and make her well." Drying his tears on the back of his sleeve, he gave me a big dimpled smile, satisfied that God was going to take care of the miracle.

Oh, the trust of a child. Meeting the broad smile with one of my own, I said, "Okay, kid, you're right. Now is the time to tell God we're ready for a miracle."

His face looked at me questioningly. "Exactly how do we do that, Aunt Margie?"

"We pray."

"Oh, yeah" he grinned, "I can do that."

The rest of the day, we kept busy answering the phone. Dr. Jones called to say he was going to Lake Charles to see Sunny and Phil and to confer with the neurosurgeons in charge of Rie. Marilyn's two sons, David and Ron called, saying they were on their way home. Art and Sherri called informing us that it would be impossible for them to come from South Africa since they had just arrived to start a new job. They asked me to kiss their Aunt Sunny, Uncle Phil, and Rie for them and tell them they were praying. Benny called from off his ship in Japan. "Mom, there is no way I can be there. Please put your arms around Rie and kiss her for me. Tell her…" he sobbed brokenly, "tell Rie I love her." Like the rest of us, his heart was broken.

Johnny called from Indonesia informing me he would be home on Sunday. Dedo and her family were coming Thursday and Woody and his wife were coming tonight to stay a few days.

Marilyn, Dave and I took the boys to the hospital to be with Sunny and Phil. Philip and Derek were going to see their sister for the first time since before the operation. The family would once more be together in a circle of love, but also they would be united in a circle of grief.

God's love enfolded us and we, with His help, would face this terrible ordeal together. We would stand united in His loving grace.

TRANSFIGURATION

Only through me do they live.

Yet, because of my eternal thoughts they are immortal.

My body may be as frangible as glass, but as of yet

there has been no wind to disperse the crystalline
essence reflected within me.
They have evolved from mere thought and breathe on
their own accord.
I am the house in which they dwell.
You ponder about the soul…how basic indeed is mankind.

CHAPTER 18

Not only were we bringing Philip and Derek to see their sister but we were also bringing Rie's graduation pictures that had been mailed to Sunny's house. There were over a hundred wallet size photos of six different poses of Rie. They were to be sent out in her graduation invitations at the end of her school year.

When we arrived, Sunny and Phil were in the family waiting room talking to friends from Phil's plant. They both jumped up when we walked in with the boys. The little family reunion brought tears to my eyes as I watched this family hold on to each other. Sunny and Phil sandwiched the boys between them with their arms around their sons' shoulders.

Phil asked, "How's school?"

"It hasn't changed," Derek replied.

Sunny looked over at Philip. "Are you behaving at Mawmaw's?"

"Yeah," Philip answered disinterested. "Can we see Rie, now?"

"I need to explain about your sister," Sunny replied.

"Aunt Marilyn has already explained," Philip said.

Sunny quickly replied, "Hey, guy, just listen to what I have to tell you...okay." Both boys nodded in agreement. The boys fell silent while their mother began telling them what to expect when they went in to visit their sister. They listened quietly as their mother softly explained as gently as possible the hard cold truths concerning Rie's condition. Quietly they digested the information.

How do you explain to children…children that have never seen anyone seriously ill before? The last time they had seen their sister she was laughing with them. Now they were being told that their sister scarcely resembled the Sunny Marie they knew and loved.

At the end of the explanation, Sunny asked, "Any questions?" Derek always had questions but this time he shook his head, no. Philip diverted his attention to the wall in front of him, shutting everyone out.

Dr. Jones came to tell us he was now going to talk to Rie's doctors and that he would see us later. We all sat in silence. Only the inhaling and exhaling of breaths could be heard. Everyone was waiting…waiting for the time to visit our Rie.

For want of something better to do, Phil took his sons to the cafeteria. Sunny became restless. She walked aimlessly around the small room. Marilyn put her arms around her, asking softly, "Honey, would you like to walk down to the kissing wall?"

"Yeah, that might help," she agreed. At the door Sunny turned toward me. "Are you coming with us?"

Needing a few moments to myself, I replied, "I'll stay here for a little while longer." They were only gone for a few seconds when an urge came over me to be with them. It was like the time Sunny was outside the operating room when she thought Rie was dead. Again my senses took a jolt. I was compelled by an overwhelming need to follow them.

Just as I caught up with them, I glanced down the corridor. An extremely tall man stood leaning against our kissing wall, crying. He had his back to us, but his head rested in the exact spot on the wall where our lipstick kisses mark the spot. Marilyn and I exchanged glances. We stopped not knowing exactly what to do. To tell you the truth, I don't believe we could have moved even if we wanted to. It was as if we shouldn't intrude, only watch. So we stayed where we were.

Not so with Sunny, she continued walking on ahead until she stood opposite the tall stranger. Placing both hands on the man's arms, she asked if she could be of some help.

As the man turned his face toward Sunny her body gave a small jerk. The expression on her face was that of surprise. The man never stopped crying as he watched her. Again, she asked, "Is there anything I can do for you?" He stared at her in a searching manner. He didn't try to hide his tears or his distress, but allowed the tears to flow. "Do you have someone in ICU? Do you need some help?"

In a deep voice, the man answered, "Are you the mother of the eighteen-year-old girl in ICU?"

"Yes," she nodded proudly, "I'm Sunny Marie's mother."

"I've heard of her courage and faith and how she holds onto her cross. She has Jesus." It wasn't a question but a statement.

"Yes, she does," Sunny agreed.

The man nodded in total agreement. Tears still rolling down his tanned cheeks, he replied, "I had to come tonight to bring her a gift."

He inclined his head. "I travel all over, tracing stories of miracles that involve the Virgin Mary. There's a church in Flushing, New York where bouquets of roses are placed at the feet of the Holy Mother. The petals of the roses never die or wilt. The church places the petals on cards. I've brought one for Sunny Marie."

He reached for Sunny's hand, placing the small card in her palm. Tears were still streaming down this big man's face and I wondered how such a big man could hold so many tears. Stranger still, never once did he wipe them away, but held onto Sunny's hand explaining, "Place the card to Sunny Marie's lips, touch it to her head, and leave it close to her on the bed. God will work His miracle," he announced with conviction.

Sunny radiantly smiled up into the face of this man. Warmly, she said, "Oh, thank you so much for coming, sharing with us the knowledge of this card, and the story of the of the Virgin Mary."

Reaching into her pocket for a picture of Rie, she asked, "Would you like to see a picture of my daughter?"

He shook his head. "No! I know all I need to know about Sunny Marie." He turned and disappeared down the hall. No name, no good-bye, no see you later. He just walked away still crying.

We rushed to our sister's side. "Are you all right?" The expression on her face held that same tranquility we had seen once before. It was the time the old woman came to her in the waiting room telling her not to give up hope. Sunny's face glowed.

Turning her hands over and inspecting them, she calmly spoke. "Did you see what happened?"

"No, what?" Marilyn and I spoke in unison.

Her smile lit up that drab hallway. "That man was sent by God. He was filled with the Holy Spirit and I felt it as an electrical shock?"

"We should be ashamed for not asking him his name," Marilyn stated.

"But of course we know him," Sunny replied staring at us as if we had lost our minds. Our confusion must have showed on our face because she answered, "God's messenger. He was on a mission from God. That's all we need to know about him."

Of course another messenger sent by God? If we recognized some of these wonderful earth angels, how many angels were we entertaining unawares. We were grateful that God had put us in their keeping.

Sunny looked down at the small card still clutched tightly in her fist and spoke in a composed voice, "You know, my Rie, is just like this card. When she dies, she'll live in heaven, and be like this rose petal. She'll never wilt, nor die, but will always be beautiful in God's light."

She gently fingered the card holding the rose petal. "If this card doesn't do any more than show us that God will work His miracle by taking her to heaven. That will be blessing enough."

Sunny knocked on the door of ICU. As the nurse appeared, Sunny quickly explained what the man had requested. Without farther questions, this precious nurse found a safety pin and pinned the little card, along with the silver crucifix, to Rie's hospital gown, promising to tell the other nurses to do the same.

When we walked into the silent waiting room, Dr. Jones was sitting by Phil. Phil was lying down on the leather couch. He was so out of it. His color was bad and he didn't look good.

"What's wrong with Phil?" Sunny quietly asked Dr. Jones, "Is it his blood pressure?"

Dr. Jones pulled Sunny into the corner of the room before whispering back. "It's everything. He's grieving himself to death."

"He sleeps like this all day now," Sunny explained. We all glanced over at Phil and saw that he was in a deep sleep.

Dr. Jones knelt down beside Phil and said, "Hey, buddy, wake up and talk to me." Phil kept his eyes closed, shutting out his friend, Jimmy Jones, Sunny, and all the rest of us.

When it became time to walk down to ICU, Phil finally got up and walked down with his mother and father beside him. Sunny walked down with Marilyn, Dave, Philip, Derek, Dr. Jones and me. Sunny said, "Dear God, Phil's shutting me out. What am I going to do, Dr. Jimmy?"

Dr. Jones put his arms around Sunny's shoulders. "Right now he wants to blame someone for Rie's trouble. It's easier to take it out on you. He'll be all right, just give him time to come to grips with the situation."

"Dr. Jimmy," she stated in an unsure voice, "we may not have time for him to get himself together." Dr. Jones' face deepened in a frown. He continued walking declining to comment.

In front of the ICU door, we were all wedged against the wall as we waited to get into Intensive Care. It seemed as if there were more people than usual.

Sunny was busy talking to a woman next to her asking her who she was visiting. They seemed to be in an animated conversation.

In a whispered voice so Sunny couldn't hear, Marilyn asked, "In your opinion, Dr. Jones, how long does Rie have to live?"

He didn't hesitate but said, "It's not good. I don't think she'll survive more then twenty-four hours."

Marilyn was standing against the wall as he told her this. I was shocked by his answer. I was standing looking at Marilyn waiting for her to comment on Dr. Jones statement. If she wasn't I was.

She started to say something, at least her mouth was working but no sound came out. She closed her eyes and then very slowly slid down the wall.

I watched her not believing my eyes. My first thought was, What does she think she's doing at a time like this? Then Sunny screamed Marilyn's name. At the same time, Dave grabbed Marilyn's arm to keep her from falling. Everything was happening in slow motion. My sister was dying right before my eyes. Suddenly I came to life. I grabbed Marilyn's other arm, giving her a hard shake. I screamed, "Marilyn, stop this! Sunny Marie is dying…you can't die, too. Oh, please don't die."

I glanced over at Sunny's concerned face and asked, "Is she dead?" I couldn't look for myself. "Marilyn can't die like this. Make her get up."

Dr. Jones moved me out of his way. He let her slide down to the floor as he straightened her legs out, laying her down on the floor.

A lady came running from the back of the crowd pushing Dr. Jones away. She screamed out in a shrill voice, "Help! Help! Get a doctor! This lady is dying."

"I am a doctor," Dr. Jones very calmly stated. He tried to position himself between Marilyn and the hysterical woman. "Please," he pleaded, "give me room to work."

He again tried to render aid to Marilyn. Again this same woman (all two hundred and fifty pounds to Dr. Jones's one hundred and fifty pounds) literally pushed him to the side. She proceeded to grab Marilyn up by her arms trying to drag her forward. We were never sure what she was planning to do with Marilyn.

A tug of war broke out between Dr. Jones and this strange lady. Finally in desperation, Dr. Jones raised his voice and said very professionally, "Lady, leave her alone. I'm a doctor." Momentarily startled, the woman stopped her forward movement and dubiously eyed the man standing in her way. Confusion reigned on her expression, but she was still determined to hold onto Marilyn's arm just in case he might be lying.

Dr. Jones disengaged the woman's hand from around my sister's arms. "Really, it's true! I'm a real, certified doctor. In fact, I'm her doctor," he said as he pointed to Marilyn.

Sunny looked over at him and said under her breath so the lady couldn't hear, "Evidently you don't fit her image of what a doctor looks like."

"Evidently not," he whispered back.

The lady covered her emotional turmoil by giving a loud sniff before walking back into the crowd of people.

When Dr. Jones pushed the crowd back to give Marilyn air, she finally opened her eyes. She was confused and unsteady. She eyed the crowd of onlookers. "Dave, why is everyone standing around looking at me?"

Dave lifted her up gently. Placing his arm around her waist, he walked her back to the family waiting room until she could regain some color in her cheeks. I was so afraid for Marilyn. Sunny asked Dr. Jones what was wrong with her. "It was just shock, too much stress." He didn't elaborate and thank God. Sunny didn't press for a better answer.

We thought Marilyn was so strong and could handle anything. Even she thought she was the strongest in the family. This was the sister who was the nurse. When Dr. Jones told her that Rie only had twenty-four hours to live, she fainted. I was happy she was better, but worried how pale she appeared. One thing was certain; we were all suffering from shock, each in our own way.

ALONE

The candle cast a warm glow over the room, the guitar plays softly into the dark corners resounding into the flame. The pillows are soft underneath my head and moonlight is faint through the windows.

Everything is as it should be, but without presence.

My identity is lost and the candle burns alone. The music plays on hollow ears for there is no one to attune me to it.

Within the darkness of the room there is deeper blackness. An emptiness that, I, alone cannot fill.

To occupy a mood, a person must own a heart, a mind and a soul. Mine are no longer with me. What I have known as "my life" no longer exists.

So, I sit here, alone, only with memories and the beating of my remembrance to hold. I wait. Not just for another person, but for my heart, my mind and my soul to become one.

CHAPTER 19

As the doors to ICU opened, we once again took turns going in to see Rie. Phil, Helen, and Euell went in first. Sunny, Philip, Derek, and I went in next. This was the first time the boys were seeing their sister since the operation. Her room was the first room to the right. Derek walked in and stood looking at all the machines that were attached to his sister. His young freckled face paled, as his eyes found Rie in the midst of the many apparatuses that were keeping her alive. Kissing her cheek, he said, "Wow, Rie! Look at all these machines. How can you sleep with them making so much noise?"

The tremor in his voice was obvious, but he was determined to be brave. "We miss you. You have to get well." He swallowed a lump in his throat. "Please get well." Laying his hand on Rie's arm, he gently rubbed it. "If you don't hurry and wake up, I'll…" he choked back a sob, "I'll read your diary."

Giant tears rolled down his baby face. Stepping back, he motioned for his brother to take his place.

Philip stood quietly against the far wall watching his sister. His throat was working, but he wasn't making any sound. He pushed himself away from the wall, and ever so slowly walked over to the bed. Placing a finger on Rie's porcelain cheek, he slowly, almost reverently, traced the contour of her delicate cheekbone. He whispered, "Rie, please get well.

Come home. I miss you," his voice cracked. "You know it's not the same without you. I need to talk with you."

I saw tears in his eyes, but he refused to allow them to fall. He was fourteen years old, soon to be fifteen in June, and was holding back tears like a man...trying to be strong.

I was in agony, powerless to help this brother as he grieved for his sister. The mother in me wanted to reach out and tell him, "It's okay to cry...just let go," but I knew he had to cry in his own time.

Sunny put her arms around both her boys, and together they walked from the room.

I sat beside the sleeping beauty, lifting the graceful hand that was holding a washcloth clutched tightly. As I sat watching Rie breath, an older nurse came in carrying a fan. She placed it on the other side of Rie's bed. Glancing over at me, she smiled. "I know about these little red heads," she said. "They get hotter than other people do..." her bottom lip quivered. "I found a fan to keep her cool."

I walked over to this kind nurse and hugged her neck. "God bless you for thinking about our baby."

It was strange, this lady had no way of knowing that Rie always slept with a fan on, winter or summer. Rie claimed she had to have the gentle hum of the fan to sleep. No one knew this but her family.

I witnessed the nurse wiping tears from her eyes while she busied herself hooking up the fan. If Sunny had been here, she would have called this sweet lady one of her angels. She was one more of those special people, sent by God.

It was late when I returned to the waiting room. Most of the people had left. Sunny walked up to Phil and put her arms around him but he turned away. He walked over and sat by his mother.

She stared at him baffled. She turned toward me, "What can I do?" She asked humbly. "He won't let me near him. I do the talking to visitors when they come and he tells me I talk too much. I take care of all the business at home and make the decisions at the hospital, because he is unable to make decisions right now." Defeat clouded her eyes. "Where is he? Where is the man I love and respect? Where are those strong arms I could always run to when I needed comforting? With a stricken expression on her face, she said, "Look at us, Margie. Will things ever be the same again between us?"

All I could do was hold her in my arms as she cried softly. I knew they needed each other, but I was completely helpless. I could see Phil withdrawing. I knew his pain was great. Phil loved his family, as much as a daddy could. He had always been a good husband. Sunny and him always had a strong, happy marriage.

Phil walked from the family waiting room. Sunny followed. A few minutes later she came back in, shaking her head. "He won't have anything to do with me. He told me to leave him alone."

Later Phil and his two sons came into the room and everyone settled down for the night. Derek cuddled up to his mother and asked, "Mom, is Rie really going to die?" Before Sunny could answer, Philip jumped to his feet, slapped his brother on top of the head and started shouting, "Man! Don't talk like that. She's not going to die...she's not. Do you hear...she's not." His eyes searched blindly around the room. "No matter what anyone says, my sister is not going to die," he choked back tears. He took off running from the room with his daddy running after him.

"What's with him?" asked Derek innocently.

"He's suffering heartbreak," I replied. Much later Philip and his dad returned. Neither talked. The boys made a bed on the floor with their sleeping bags. Sunny and Phil were at opposite ends of the room. It was as if a wall stood between them.

We turned the lights off and the room became quiet as Derek said his prayers out loud. "God Bless everyone I know and love and my animals at home. Fix my brother's heartbreak." Silence then a sniffle. "God, please make a miracle. Make my sister well again. You're the one that makes miracles, so I know You can make one for us. Please," a broken sob, "please, just this once. Amen."

Out of the mouth of babes…this was all our prayer that night.

Much later, in the darkness, a cold hand awakened me. Sunny whispered, "Margie, get up. I have to go home."

"You've got to be kidding." I looked at my watch and it showed 4 a.m. I whispered back, "Now? Do you know what time it is?"

"Yeah. There's something I have to take care of. Are you going with me?" Her voice was determined. Too determined for four in the morning.

"Sure, I'll go with you." I wasn't sure what we were going to do but after seeing her face in the light from the small table lamp, I knew it must be important. I didn't ask any more questions.

Sunny woke both boys and told them she had something important to do at home. After grumbling and complaining, they were full of questions, but she told them she would tell us all about it on the way home.

By this time everyone in the room was awake and asking question. Sunny continued getting ready. Her only answer was, "I have something very important to do at home."

Phil was put out. He glared at his wife with a disapproving expression. "You know, it's not a good idea leaving the hospital at this time of morning. Anything could happen to you." He rubbed a hand over his face, and then he almost shouted. "You shouldn't be leaving the hospital. After all you're Rie's mother."

Sunny met his gaze, long and hard. "And you're her father," she replied in the same tone of voice.

"Just what in heaven's name are you going to do that's so important?"

"I'll tell you later," she replied.

"Tell me now," he fumed.

"Listen to me, Phil." Her voice softened. "You and your mother will just have to take care of things here until I return. Call me at Mother's house if you need me."

Phil stood looking so confused. He had always been the strong one of his family. Now the roles were reversed. He was depending on Sunny more and more to make the decisions. He lay back on his bed and mumbled, "Well, I hope you know what you're doing because I sure as hell don't?"

"Believe me...I do!" she screamed back. Philip, Derek, Sunny, and I left the hospital. It was still pitch-black outside. The boys curled up in the back of the van, covered up with a blanket, and fell asleep.

No sooner than we crossed the Calcasieu River Bridge, Sunny calmly said, "The Lord spoke to me last night." She had my full attention. "You mean in a dream?" She shook her head. "No, in a voice as clear as you are talking to me now."

As I remained silent, she explained, "Someone called my name. I didn't move because it was dark and I was afraid. Then all at once I felt this love all around me. It was like a light had been turned on in the room, almost like the voice was light itself."

She deepened her voice to imitate how the voice sounded to her. "This voice said, 'Sunny Carole, you must go and find Sunny Marie a resting place.' The voice was filled with such love. I knew the voice had to be the Holy Spirit. The voice repeated, 'Sunny Carole, you must be the one to find Sunny Marie's resting place.' At that moment, I thought of Abraham. You know the chapter where God talks to Abraham, and tells him to take his only son and sacrifice him as a burnt offering. Well to make a long story short, Abraham did as he was told. Lying Isaac on the altar he started to plunge in the knife. Then God shouted to him from heaven, saying, 'Do not hurt your son, for I know that I am first in you life...you have not withheld even your beloved son from Me.'" She looked over and confessed, "I always had trouble believing that chapter. I couldn't conceive how a father could kill his own child for the love of God or why God would want him too."

I reached over and squeezed her hand on the steering wheel, and said, "But honey, what does that have to do with Rie?"

Her eyes watered with tears. "Oh, Margie, when the Angel called my name, I realized it wasn't about Abraham killing his son but about faith and obedience to God. In that moment, I too, knew I trusted the Lord in all things. He wants me to let go. I have to trust Him, unconditionally. I have to let Him have His way. Rie no longer belongs to us…she never did. God has been good letting us have her for eighteen years. Now it's time we give her back."

As I watched my sister, I couldn't believe my eyes. I had seen times when the old lady and the mystery man with the rose petal caused her to have a glow around her but now it was more pronounced. Now she was radiant with a new confidence.

"Will you come with me while I make the necessary arrangements?" she whispered.

Not comprehending what she was talking about, I said, "Necessary arrangements for what?"

"For Rie, so everything will be exactly the way she wants them to be. Over the years, Rie and I talked about so many things. Rie told me how she wanted to be buried."

"Honey, why don't you tell us how you want everything and I'll take care of it for you when the time comes."

"Oh, don't you see?" She replied. "This is the last time I can plan anything for my Rie and I want to do it while I have the strength and courage. After she dies I'm not sure what kind of state I'll be in."

I understood what she was saying. After Rie's death I wasn't sure what state any of us would be in.

Dropping the boys and me off at Mother's house, Sunny went home to shower and dress, promising to be over at Mother's around 11 a.m.

Woody, David, and Ron were at Mother's house when Sunny came in. She told everyone about her experience that morning, explaining she had to take care of some business.

Daddy and Mother tried to talk her into staying with them but she assured them she was fine.

I told Woody and David Lee where we were going and both said they wanted to go with us. Woody drove and David Lee sat in front while I rode in back with Sunny. We didn't talk driving out to the cemetery. I kept looking at Sunny and holding her cold clammy hand in mine. I prayed for God to give us all the strength needed for what we were about to do.

The cemetery is on the outskirts of Orange, and is located in a wooded area. We were not strangers to this place. Our brother was buried here.

What seemed strange now, was to remember that Rie had been the last person to kiss him before he died. He was on duty, as a constable, at the High School football game. He was the one that always opened the field-gate to allow the marching band onto the field at half time. Rie was head twirler and on this one occasion, she actually held the band up while she took time to run back, and in front of hundreds of people, she kissed him. Few knew it was her uncle.

That night when she came home from the game she told her mother that an overwhelming need came over her to tell Uncle Arthur how much she loved him. That same night he died.

Woody parked and the four of us walked into the small trailer type office. Inside were two men and one woman. Sunny asked them to please show her some grave plots. She explained to them how her child was expected to die at any time and that she wanted to pick just the right place for her baby.

These people stood with shocked expressions on their faces because they never had anything like this happen before. Here was this brave little mother taking care of things before her child was even dead.

One man kept asking her if she wanted to wait. She became annoyed with him. "I have to do it now before she dies! That way I won't have to walk this way again, blinded by tears." David Lee was a Lutheran minister, 6'3" tall. He never said a word but held on to his Aunt Sunny's arm while he walked the graveyard with her.

Woody held on to me, as we searched for just the right spot, for Sunny Marie. The man showed us all he had available in the new area, but Sunny wasn't happy with any of them. She walked over to the older sight where our brother was buried.

"Here." She pointed to the ground right across the street from his grave. "This is where I want Rie to be buried."

"Bbbut," the man stuttered, "I...I'm not sure we have any available space right here."

"Please check," I requested. He hurriedly consulted his book of charts and maps, thumbing through countless pages. To my relief he found several opened plots exactly where Sunny had pointed.

Sighing deeply, Sunny turned her face up to the tall pine trees that bordered this area. Sunny signed the necessary papers. Before leaving she gave each of the people a picture of Rie. Needless to say, this was a day they would remember for a long time.

As we drove closer to town, Sunny told Woody, "Now I have to go to the funeral home." Woody turned around with a shocked expression on his face and asked, "Sorry, what did you say?"

Very distinctly, she repeated her request. Wood and David Lee exchanged glances, but neither said a word. Sunny gave Woody directions. We didn't try to talk her out of it. She had a mission to fulfill. All we could do was be there for her.

As we walked into Claybar's Funeral Home, a man came to meet us. Sunny had called earlier and made an appointment. She recognized the man that greeted us because his daughter and Rie had been friends in school. Sunny met the man's smile with one of her own and thanked him politely. The man looked perplexed. "What can we help you with?" Sunny patiently explained about Rie and her condition. Then she said, "I need to make Sunny Marie's arrangements."

The man patted her hand warmly and replied, "Oh, but surely you don't won't to be bothered with that right now? You can do that after her death."

"No, I can't," she said in a sweet lilting voice. "God is giving me the courage and strength at this moment to do this job. It has to be exactly the way my Rie wants it done and I am the only one who knows."

The poor man looked at me for help. I nodded and said, "It's all right. She knows what she's doing."

Sunny gave him all the information about the pallbearers, flowers, and music. Her voice was very steady. There were no tears.

I kept thinking, "Oh, God! Please don't let me break down. It's so hard to keep from crying." I looked over at Woody and David Lee, seeing the heartbreak in their faces, and the effort it was taking them to keep from crying. The man asked Sunny if she wanted to wait until later to pick out the coffin.

"No! It has to be done now!" She took a deep breath, "Tell the florist I also want a blanket of spring flowers for the coffin so this can represent all her loving hands. It will be from all the family."

As we started into the room that held the coffins, Woody grabbed my arm and held me back. "Mom," his voice trembled, "I'll do anything for Aunt Sunny and Rie, but I can't go in that room. I'm sorry, but I can't."

I searched my son's eyes and saw the tears building up, and said, "It's okay, honey, we understand. You wait here for us." I too, didn't want to go into the room, but knew I couldn't let my sister down.

David Lee very quietly went into the room with us. His face was set in a stern mask, his deeply tanned features were several shades lighter than before, but he kept his eyes glued on his Aunt Sunny the whole time as we walked through the rows of caskets. His hand was locked on her elbow.

We were holding our breaths least we broke. This was so hard on all of us and I prayed with each step we took. Earlier, I had given Sunny the same kind of crucifix as I had Rie and Doug. Now she was holding tightly to hers as we walked through each row.

Oh, that walk through the caskets. Nothing had ever prepared me for it. I always thought when it was my time to die some of my children would take care of this end of it for me. But now here I was walking with my sister.

Sunny held the cross with one hand while the other reached out, softly touching the material inside, feeling, inspecting, comparing the lace to the silk, or velvet. I was beginning to hyperventilate. My heart hurt so badly, but what about her? I kept telling myself, if my sister can do this…I can do no less.

Sunny continued to talk as we walked down each row. She said, "Rie always thought it was sad for anyone to spend a lot of money on caskets. Rie told me two years ago, 'Mother, I want to have a very simple coffin, nothing fancy or expensive…just pretty.'

"I remember laughing at her and saying, 'How can a casket be pretty?' She became upset with me. Her words were, 'When my eyes close for the last time, I don't want my love ones to see me in death. I want to be remembered, as I was when I was living. Uncle Arthur had a sad funeral. Please don't ever give me a sad funeral with sad songs. I want to be buried like I lived…happy.'

"I laughed and told her that she would be doing these things for me when I die because mothers are suppose to die first." Sunny took a deep breath. "Rie told me that no one in her family could die before her. When I asked why, she said 'Because, Mom, I wouldn't be able to stand the sadness.'" "Did you know she couldn't even go to her Uncle Arthur's funeral, because, she said, 'It's going to be too sad.' I asked her if she wanted to walk up to the casket and say her last good-bye, and she told me very firmly, 'No! I said my last good-bye at the football game the night he died. Mom, take a long look at Uncle Arthur. No one is in that house anymore. The soul has flown…the house is empty.'

"Margie, to my knowledge, that was the first time I had ever heard her say anything like that. Isn't it strange how she talked about so much concerning her death? It never occurred to me to talk about my death to anyone…not even to you." Sunny made her choice. No sooner than we were inside the car, Sunny leaned back against the seat and said, "Well, thank goodness that's finished. I've taken care of everything just like she wanted me too."

With those words said, Sunny broke into the most heart-breaking sobs. Thank God for the breakdown. All this time Sunny seemed so

strong while Woody, David Lee and I stayed on the verge of near col-
lapse. We couldn't show any sign of breaking. All this day, we followed
Sunny's lead. Our hearts breaking silently while watching this determined mother carry out her mission. When she broke down…we all
broke down with her. We sat huddled in the car crying. We went
through an entire box of tissues. No one spoke or even cared too. It was
the time just to let go. It was now over and we could share the pain.

By the time we arrived at Mother's, somehow we had ourselves back
under control. I looked around at Sunny's, Woody's and David's faces
and realized we were all wearing masks to hold back the tears that were
still lodged in our hearts, As we entered Mother's house, Sunny turned
to Woody and said, "I'm going to ask another favor of you."

Color draining from his face, he lost his composure, "Oh, no! Don't
do it, Aunt Sunny," he cried. "Don't ask me to sing at Rie's funeral."

"No, honey," Sunny quickly replied, "I know Rie would love you to
play your guitar and sing, but I'm not going to place that heavy load on
you. I would like you to wear your police uniform. Rie is so proud of
you and thinks you're so handsome wearing it. Also, I'm going to ask
Dedo's husband to wear his Louisiana State Trooper's uniform."

Woody gave an audible sigh of relief and said, "That I can do, gladly."

Mother and Daddy never asked what we had accomplished on our
trip. It was better they not know. At the moment, Mother was upset over
Philip and Derek. While we had been gone, Philip and his brother had
driven Rie's car to McDonald's. Philip was too young to have a license
and had been stopped by a policeman. The city policeman only pointed
out that one of the taillights were out. He didn't check Philip for a
license. One of the neighbors had called Mother and told her about
them taking Rie's car. Mother was in a terrible state, ranting and raving
about how the boys couldn't be trusted.

Sunny took her boys to the side and asked them if it was true. Both
the boys said that it was. "But why Philip?" Sunny cried. "What would

make you do something like this? You know better. You're not allowed to drive…you're too young. Any of us would have taken you."

"Rie always took us," he challenged. "We don't have Rie anymore. It's up to me. From now own, I'll be the oldest. I have to do things now like she used to do."

"Oh, baby, I know." Sunny sympathetically replied. "But Rie wouldn't want you to get into trouble or have a wreck. Please don't to that again. Mawmaw and Pawpaw don't need to be worried. It's hard on them keeping both of you. Promise me, Philip and Derek, that you will try and be good while I'm gone."

"I promise," Philip declared, his pride still a little bruised.

"All right," he gritted between his teeth, "no more driving the car."

Sunny held her boys and told them any time they wanted too, they could come to the hospital. They agreed to call her everyday. We went by her house to feed the dogs and pick up more clothing.

Walking into Rie's room, Sunny lovingly touched everything on her dresser. She flipped through several loose notebook pages until she spotted one she was looking for. She picked up the poem and read it to me:

IT'S EASY

It's easy to say, "I love you." It's easy to say. "I care."
It's easy to laugh when I'm with you, enjoying the things we share.
It's easy to hide my fears in your loving arms so strong.
It's easy to turn to you, love whenever things go wrong.
It's easy to talk about our future but words just make me cry.
It's easy, my darling, to kiss you, but it's so hard to say good-bye.

"That had to be written for Doug. Can you believe all these beautiful poems?" Turning to face me, she placed the stack of paper in her purse and asked, "How many weeks have we been at the hospital?"

"No, baby," I answered, "not weeks…just days. Only six days to be exact."

She had a confused expression on her face. Her voice sounded sad as she said, "Days? Funny, it seems like months…doesn't it?"

REFLECTION

As if in a dream, I wander in slow motion through
my realities.
I sense others around me only through vision, but spiritually
unaware of their presence.
There is no voluntary control over such an experience,
for how can you awaken the subconscious that demands to sleep.
On the days when half of me refuse to awaken, I simply go about
dazed and let the weaker conscious side, take full responsibility.

CHAPTER 20

As we arrived in the parking lot, we felt a winter day that held a promise of spring. The sky was a deep breath-taking blue and the air chilled, but the sun was warm against our skin. Out of sight, a bird chirped his song of joy. All was right in this world of reality.

Sunny stood in the middle of the parking lot looking up at the sky as if seeing it for the first time and said to me, "Oh, Margie, why is the sun shining when my Rie is dying?" I stepped up beside her. "Honey, God has to send His sunshine to help us through this darkness."

While we waited for the others to park their car, we stood in that cold parking lot, holding each other for support. Sunny pulled away and told me, "Margie, I have one more thing I must do. Will you help me?" Laughingly, I said through tears, "Don't I always?"

"After everyone has greeted Phil, I'm going to ask them to leave the room and give us some time together. I need you to stay and bar the door because," she sighed deeply, "what I have to say to Phil will not be pleasant."

"But, honey…"

"No." she placed a hand on my arm to quiet me. "Please stay in the room with me, I may need you. I don't know how Phil will take what I have to say? I just hope God will forgive me for what I'm about to do."

Dear God, what was she planning? She was so determined to finish what she had started this morning. All this day we had been on a driven mission and now she had one more thing to do.

As we approached the family waiting room, we could see it was over flowing again with friends and family. With all this noise around him, Phil was sound asleep on the couch.

Sunny walked over to Phil and shook him awake so he could greet Woody, Ron and David Lee.

At first I thought he wasn't going to wake up but after Sunny continued shaking him, he finally stirred. Phil opened his heavy eyes, blinked, and mumbled, "I'm too tired to visit right now. Please, just let me sleep."

Shutting his eyes again, he went back to sleep, uncaring. This was not like Phil. He and Woody had always been so close and shared so much. I felt like if anyone could get through to Phil it would be Woody, but Phil refused to acknowledge Woody's presence. I could see the hurt in Woody's face that his Uncle Phil didn't care to talk to him.

Sunny gave up trying to talk Phil into getting up. We sat around the room and visited with the people. Everyone wanted to know the latest up-date on Rie.

Watching Phil as he slept, Sunny quietly sat in a corner becoming more withdrawn. I could tell she was biding her time. Automatically she smiled at the people when they spoke to her, but I don't believe she heard anything they were saying.

After about an hour, the friends began to leave and family members took turns going down to the cafeteria. I gazed out the window watching the sunset slowly fading into pinks and oranges. God was putting on His show of one of the prettiest sunsets I had ever witnessed. I wanted to share this moment with my sister, but then I remembered her words earlier about the sunshine shining when her Rie was dying.

I whispered to myself, "Why God...why do you make this beautiful sunset? Rie was the child that loved your sunsets. I remember the time, she screamed with delight at the display, clapping her hands with sheer joy as if you had put it on just for her benefit alone. Why do you send it now?"

With eyes blinded to the lovely picture outside, Sunny came up behind me and whispered, "It's time."

She turned to the people in the room and politely asked them to go out into the outer waiting room so she could have some time with her husband. Their faces wore stunned expressions as they filed out. Sunny turned to me and said, "Margie, lock the door and don't let anyone in this room."

Silence descended upon the room as I locked the door with a loud click. Standing with my back against it, I held my breath waiting to see what my sister was going to do.

With apprehension, I watched her walk over to Phil. She reached down giving him a hard shake and in an authoritative voice ordered him to get up. He made a moaning noise but didn't wake up.

In frustration, she knelt down in front of him, grabbed him by the collar, and literally yelled into his sleeping face as she barked the command. "Damn you, Phil Eppler, get your lazy butt off that couch and act like a man."

Opening his eyes, Phil gazed into his wife's angry face, now no more than two inches from his own. His eyes were glazed with sleep and he was trying to comprehend why she was screaming at him. He mumbled something unintelligible and made a motion to roll over.

Sunny shook him convulsively and with her hands on his shoulders drew him up to a sitting position on the couch. "Look at me, dammit! You're not going to die...I'm not going to let you...you s.o.b.," She screamed.

I could see Phil's eyes change from sleepy to shock as he watched his wife shouting at him. The cloud of sleep seemed to leave his stunned face as he tried to recognize this person before his eyes. In confusion, he sat up leaning his head against the back of the couch for support.

I stood rooted to my spot against the door. Sunny was essentially a non-violent person that's why I couldn't believe how my little sister was acting now. She suddenly became charged with life and her eyes were blazing at her husband. She sputtered furiously, "You…you can't do this. You're not going to do this to your daughter! She's dying…but not by choice. All this time, she's been so brave. She has never let us down…and you're not," She shook a finger in his face, "I repeat…you're not going to let her down either. Do you hear me?"

I watched the speculative frown knit Phil's brow. She had his attention; suddenly he was fully awake. I don't believe he was even conscious I was in the room. His eyes were glued to his wife's face.

"If you're going to die," Sunny shouted, "you'll just have to do it someplace else. You'll have to leave the hospital because I don't need you here…Rie doesn't need you."

Phil recoiled as if Sunny had actually slapped his face. "Leave?" Rie doesn't need me?" Phil's voice was filled with pain. "Rie doesn't need me…"

"No!" Sunny's voice cut in sharply. "Nobody needs you in the condition you're in."

"Please don't make me leave the hospital," he pleaded.

Sunny's voice became a plea. "Please don't do this to Rie. Don't you see…you're the one letting her down? She loves you. Rie believes you're the bravest daddy in the world. Just because she's in a coma doesn't mean she doesn't need you. She needs you more now then ever before, but she doesn't need you dead or sleeping your life away. One death is all I can face at this time."

Her voice softened. "Phil, you have to be brave for Sunny Marie and me…the way we always thought you to be. Don't you see, if she can face all of this with faith and courage…we must do the same."

Tears began to slide down Phil's white face and he made a movement to brush them away with an unsteady hand. Sunny clutched her husband's hand and placed it to her lips. "Don't you understand how much I need you and love you? I can't go through this without you."

Their gazes held. He slowly reached down encircling her in his strong arms. He buried his face in her hair. A shudder shook his large frame and Sunny kissed his forehead while still embracing him. She looked over at me with an apprehensive glance and quietly said, "We're going down to the chapel for a little while. We have a job to do. Could you take care of everything here until we get back?"

So moved was I that I couldn't answer. I shook my head yes while opening the door so they could leave the room. Then I let the tears flow.

Sunny led Phil away. He was walking on unsteady legs but she was there giving him support. I watched them walk down that long corridor.

Woody asked me, "Where are they going?"

"They have to talk to God for a little while," I answered. An hour later two people walked into the family waiting room looking completely different from the two that had left earlier.

Sunny and Phil stood hand in hand with a glow that actually surrounded them. The strain and exhaustion was absent from Phil's features and he stood tall and erect. Sunny was radiant. I had seen Sunny changing before my eyes but this was the biggest change yet.

Phil hugged Woody, Ron, and David Lee as if seeing them for the first time. Phil walked around the room meeting people and thanking them for coming. For the first time, I heard him talk about Rie's sickness.

Woody took a seat beside his aunt and uncle. "I can't believe the change in both of you. What happened in the chapel?"

Sunny gave a soft serene smile, instinctively reaching for Phil's hand, saying simply, "We were visiting Jesus." The room became quiet as everyone stopped their chatter and listened to Sunny.

Her voice became strong with confidence as she explained. "On the wall of St. Patrick's Chapel, there's a beautiful wooden statue of an ascending Jesus. His arms are reaching out. We knelt before Him. Phil and I talked about how right it was to put our Rie in His arms. I said, 'My Jesus, what beautiful arms you have to hold our Rie with.'"

Phil smiled and said, "We decided to give her back to the Lord and we thanked Him for blessing us by trusting us to raise her for eighteen years."

Excitedly, Sunny said, "God has been so good to us. We trust Him in all things. It was time for us to let go. I told Phil about my visit from the Lord last night and everything I did today. We have now placed the control in God's capable hands…where it should be."

Everyone that came into that room that night was completely shocked at the change in Phil. He took time visiting, talking to everyone while all the time, holding on to his wife's hand. The two had become one, the way God meant it to be.

The nuns would come in and smile and say, "Praise the Lord for His Blessings."

The atmosphere of the room changed. Instead of people giving support to Sunny and Phil, Sunny and Phil gave support to the visitors and clergy. Sunny would give them a picture of Sunny Marie and ask them to keep her in their prayers. A miracle had taken place right before our eyes.

Late the next evening, Sunny asked me to go to the Chapel so she could show me something. We had to travel down a long corridor into an older part of the hospital. Then, we went through double doors outside to a walkway that led to the Chapel. There was a partial covered walkway looking-out over a garden of roses. Along the red brick wall, Sunny showed me the mosaics of the crucifixion of Jesus lining one side. We walked to the last one depicting the Virgin Mary with a spear through her heart.

Sunny lovingly touched it, saying, "When Phil and I came down here, I stopped before this picture and stood observing it for a long time. I really looked at this picture seeing for the first time, not the Virgin Mary, but a mother, she touched her chest, "a mother just like me, a mother that loved her child and had to bear the pain of loss. All at once, I knew her pain and I knew how that spear felt in her heart.

"Margie, Mary had the perfect child and she had to let go. I told Her, in front of Phil, 'Oh, sweet Mary, you know my pain as no one else knows it. You gave up your son and watched the world put him to death on a wooden cross. You stood there and witnessed the horror with tears streaming down your face and the pain piercing your heart, but yet you held strong to your faith. Your son is the reason I can let my child go. I can put Rie in His hands and know she'll always live forever.'"

I reached up and touched the clear, solitary tear inlaid in blue tile and silently thanked this mother for her son. I thanked my sister for showing me this beautiful place and we promised we would both return during the daytime.

We walked back slowly, remembering things that made us laugh. That in its self was a miracle. We had come a long way in a little over a week and now a terrible weight had been lifted from our shoulders. We walked to ICU, stopping outside on a flight of stairs close to our kissing wall. We took a seat on the first step.

Sunny took a shaking breath, "Life is going to be so empty without Rie. You know, Margie, I think the hardest thing to face for me will be not hearing her laughter. It was always so contagious. She knew how to make all of us laugh. Even on days when I thought it was the end of the world, she would do something or tell me something that would have me laughing. Before I knew it, I was feeling happy." Sunny wiped her tears away, "Just like the time I was down because Phil and I had a silly argument. Rie came into the room and caught me crying. She said, 'Mom, what you need is a night out. Get off your buns and let's go for a walk.'

"Margie, to tell you the truth I was so lost in my own misery I didn't want to walk but that didn't deter her one iota. Rie stood with my coat in hand and practically pushed me out the door. When I walked outside complaining, she asked me to take a look at the sky and tell her what I saw. I looked up at the sky. I told her I was still so upset with her daddy that all I could see was the blur from my own tears swimming in my eyes.

"'Okay, Mom,' she said, 'I guess we'll just have to fix that.' And the little rascal proceeded to do just that. She walked me fast; she walked me slow; constantly telling me to take deep breaths. Inhale…exhale. Chin up…chest out. She had me kicking my knees up. She was worse than any drill sergeant was. In between her commands, she would give me advice on how to get rid of tension. Little Miss Know-it-all had me jogging before I realized it. Me! I'm the kid that can't run a half block without collapsing. We must have jogged for several miles when she commanded me to stop and look at the sky. I did.

"She asked, 'Okay, Mom, what do you see now.' I stood in the middle of the street sucking air, but I gazed at the sky for a long time. Then I said, 'I see the face of the moon and she's wearing a cloak of black velvet decorated with thousands of sequins. I see the universe in all its glory.'

"'That's my, Mom,'" Rie replied. Then in a more serious voice, she said, "'Mom, God doesn't want you and Daddy upset with each other.'" "Maybe you're right," I said, "but sometimes married people just say cutting remarks to each other without thinking how it's going to affect the other's heart.

"'How do you feel after your jog.' I told her I felt great. And the truth was, I really did. Rie reached over and ruffled up my hair and giggled. 'I now pronounce you cured of the blues.'

"We jogged back home laughing and giggling like silly little girls. I went back home feeling good. Suddenly it didn't matter what the argument had been about, I really couldn't remember. I walked into the house and marched into the den giving Phil a big kiss.

"'Hey, what's up?' he said. Rie replied, 'Oh, nothings up, Dad. Mom just needed a night out.' You know, Margie, I'm going to miss the way Rie smells." She turned toward me and asked, "Have you ever noticed how she smells?"

I nodded. I did remember all too well the sweet smell of Rie. To me she smelled like springtime.

SUNNY C. EPPLER & MARJORIE M. WOODCOCK 183

Sunny gave a soft chuckle, "I always told her that she smelled like fresh air and sunshine. Rie would laugh and say, 'Oh, Mom, you have me confused with a laundry soap advertisement.'"

"Life is going to be hard for all of us. Rie is everyone's sunshine," I told my sister.

"Have you noticed how Rie's doing it to us again." Sunny grinned. "She's teaching us how to face life head own."

I laughed. It was true; here we were again. Rie was the teacher; we were her students.

Wiping away our tears of laughter intermingled with tears of sadness, we reluctantly stood-up. Silently walking over to the kissing wall, then reverently, we placed our kisses against the wall. A few more lipstick smudges added to the hundreds already there. We whispered our good nights to the sleeping child of the universe just on the other side of the wall. Sunny and I both felt secure in the feeling of knowing that somehow Rie would be aware of our presence.

I started to walk away, but Sunny refused to move. She just stood there gazing at the lipstick marks on the wall. "What's wrong, Sunny?"

"I'm afraid," she confessed brokenly. "I'm afraid what tomorrow will bring. I'm afraid Rie will die and I won't ever see her again. Oh, God, Margie…I'm so frightened."

"I know, honey…me too." I placed my arm around her and began walking back to the waiting room. "But, you know, Sunny, it's all right to be afraid. It's just a journey we haven't walked before. God is embracing us every step of the way. Remember how Rie told us that fear and faith can't abide together."

"You're right." Her lips trembled. "We have to make it, don't we…for Rie? We can't let her down now. We have to have faith."

Sunny smiled but it seemed a bit strained. Too much stress, too much strain, everyday was taking its toll on her. My little sister was tired; her reserve was almost gone.

I held my sister, who is much more than a sister, she's my closest friend and I prayed, "Please, God, protect this sister I love so much. Give her strength."

Arm in arm, we walked back to the waiting room, still talking and remembering our Rie.

WHAT IS LOVE?

Love. What is it?

Love is a small worn stone, smooth from the caresses of gentle waves in the ocean.

Love is an antique brooch not often worn for fear of breaking the fragile clasps.

Love is a rug, often swept clean, but time reveal the pattern of a well-trodden path.

Love is a delicate rosebud. When uncared for slowly dies.

Love is the feeling of silk that covers the wounded heart.

Love is a whispered voice, a hand, a touch that gives comfort.

Love is a kiss that binds the heart as sure as ropes of golden threads.

But love can be many things. To some it's a beginning, to others an ending, and to many it's still indescibable.

CHAPTER 21

Friday morning, rather briskly, Dr. Milan came into the waiting room. There was no, "Hello" or "How are you?" His face wore a grave expression. We had not expected to see him and my heart was in my throat as he knelt down in front of Sunny, taking her hand in his and in a stern, cold voice, he said, "Mrs. Eppler, we have concluded all our tests and Sunny Marie is definitely brain dead. There is nothing more we can do."

Not a word was spoken. Silence filled the room…a dead silence.

Then in a very flat voice, the doctor said, "Sunny Marie is young and we can keep her heart beating on the machines but there's no life left in her brain. Do you understand what I'm saying?"

Sunny met this doctor's professional stare with a worn smile and said, "Yes. Thank you, Doctor. I feel my daughter has been in good hands, but I don't want her to be kept alive by machines."

The doctor cleared his throat and hung his head down for a few moments, almost as if to compose himself.

"I know how you feel, he replied, "but I want you and your husband to discuss this matter more closely and then make your decision. We don't have to make any definite decisions until Monday…if Sunny Marie lives until then."

Taking the doctor by surprise, Sunny reached over and hugged him, thanking him again for all he had done. Then she asked, "Would you like to see what Sunny Marie looked like before her illness? You can also have a copy of some of her poems." He nodded his head, taking the picture and poems. For just a moment the professional mask slipped as he gazed at Rie's photograph. He cleared his throat several times before walking briskly from the room.

My first thought was how cold this doctor acted, but a nun later told me that she had watched him stand at the foot of Rie's bed crying and asking God..."Why?" She heard him say, "It's a damn shame, this beautiful child and I can't do one thing to help her."

On Friday night, Dr. Shamieh asked Phil and Sunny to come to his office so he could explain to them what to expect Monday when the machines were removed. He informed Sunny and Phil that Sunny Marie would be moved to the fifth floor, stressing that a private nurse would need to be hired to be with Rie around the clock until her death. Then he stated, "Sunny Marie's health is fragile, she may not live until Monday."

Sunny asked, "In other words, there is nothing more that can be done?"

His eyes full of compassion held Sunny's. "No," he stated firmly, "nothing."

We felt the full weight of the doctor's words smack us with a force of a ground zero explosion. There would be no miraculous recovery. All hope was null and void. We were absolutely given nothing to hang on to. I think what hit us the hardest was the fact of how little control we have in life. You go through life believing doctors and modern medicine can heal everything. Then you learn the sad truth personally. Everything around you changes...everything but one...and that's God. All we had left was God.

Dedo and the girls arrived from New Orleans. Johnny would arrive Sunday and the family circle was coming together. Hopefully in time to say good-bye to Rie.

Dedo was sitting on the couch with her Aunt Sunny. Sunny reached out taking her hands, she said, "Dedo, can I ask a favor?"

Dedo replied, "I'll do anything I can to help."

"First of all, I want you to take my credit card and buy the boys new clothes. They need dress clothes for the funeral and I know I won't have time to shop." Dedo nodded. "I can do that."

"Honey, this is going to be hard for you, but I know you can do it. I can't trust anyone else to do it, but I want you to go to my house and pack up all of Rie's clothing. I want you to have them." A look of disbelief passed over Dedo's face. She cried out, "Why?"

"I want you to take them home with you."

"But Aunt Sunny…" Placing a hand gently over Dedo's mouth, Sunny pleaded, "Please, don't say anything until I'm completely finished. Rie loves you like a sister and would want you to have all her beautiful things. I could not bear to know a stranger had them."

Dedo was sobbing, "Oh, dear God, Aunt Sunny, please don't ask me to do this. I don't think I can."

Sunny was in complete control, too much so. "Yes, you can," she replied firmly. "I would like you to ask Pawpaw to help you take the bed and everything out of her room." She smiled sadly. "Please, take her clothes and wear them with love. She has so many beautiful things and if Rie could tell you herself, you're the only one she would want to have them."

Sunny looked around the room with unseeing eyes. For just a moment a pained expression crossed her face, but shaking her head as if to dispel it, she seemed to gather her control once more.

Almost, too low to hear, Sunny stated, "I don't think I can go back in my house if Rie's room isn't cleared out."

I was watching my precious daughter hurting. She wanted to help her Aunt Sunny who had been her playmate and friend all her life. I gathered Dedo in my arms as she sobbed, "Mom, I don't know if I can do what Aunt Sunny has asked me do to."

I held her close. "Sweetheart, do what you can and ask God for strength and courage, He'll help you." My heart hurt for this child of mine, she had never been this close to a death of a loved one before.

"Mom, I can't do it while she's alive. It's bad enough when she dies, but not while she's alive."

"The doctor said she would only live two hours or less off the machines."

Doug placed his hand on Dedo's arm when she started to cry, and said, "Please, Dedo, Rie would want you to have her things. Please do this for her. She always thought of you more as a sister than a cousin. I'll go back to Orange with you in case you need help."

Dedo's voice trembled as she said, "Okay...I'll try, but it's going to be tough."

Kissing Dedo, Sunny said, "Don't come back to the hospital without wearing a coat. It's too cold outside."

"Aunt Sunny, I didn't bring one to wear."

"Wear Rie's imitation fur coat, the one the boys gave her for Christmas."

"I couldn't do that right now."

"Please, Rie wouldn't want you to be cold. I'll call the boys and tell them you're coming. They'll help you."

Dedo, her girls, and Doug said their good-byes and traveled back to Sunny's house to take care of the task.

Sunny and I were kneeling on the couch looking out the window at empty space, seeing nothing and saying nothing. Finally, I said, "Honey, I'm so proud of you. You're staying so strong for your daughter."

After what seemed like a very long silence, she spoke quietly, almost in awe, "Where is all this strength coming from. Basically I'm not a strong person, but yet, when I feel myself faltering, this strange strength picks me up and guides me." She grabbed my hand, squeezing it. "Is God preparing me to give up everyone I love?"

"Oh, Sunny, this may be the only tears we ever have to cry on this earth. We never know which one of us will go next." All at once, her tears disappeared. She turned with an impish grin and a glorious light appeared in her eyes. "Wouldn't it be just wonderful if God did work a miracle and Rie would live. They would have to close the hospital down and declare her a saint."

The excitement in her voice was so different, utterly changed from the sadness just seconds before. She reached over and hugged me. "Do you think we could manage a saint in the family?" I hugged her back, laughing, and said, "Why not! I've been working at becoming a martyr…so there should be room for a saint, also."

Sunny actually laughed aloud and it filled the room like music.

"In your dreams," she squealed. "No way! You can't be a martyr…the world isn't ready for that yet…and I'm not either. Margie the martyr." She rolled the words off her tongue. Rearing back she inspected me very closely. She shook her head slowly. "No, Margie," she giggled, "You're definitely not martyr material."

"Geez, thanks for the vote of confidence, burst my bubble, yank the rug from under my feet and et cetera…" I gave a disappointed sigh. "But what a relief." I pretended to wipe my brow. "I don't believe I could have made the grade, so we'll just settle for Saint Sunny Marie instead."

Somehow, we made the night by staying up talking and reading the Bible. We watched the morning light filter though the window as the cold gray day greeted us. Rie was still alive; we had made it though another night.

It was time for another visit with Rie. Sunny and Phil went in first to be with their daughter. As they came out, Pepaw Eppler and I went in for our visit. We stood quietly by her bed. Rie appeared softer and less swollen. Her breathing seemed less labored. She didn't appear at death's door. In fact, she was looking more like our Rie.

I said, "Good morning, little girl. I just want you to know that everything is just like you want it to be. Rie, you would be so proud of your mother. She's so beautiful and strong; taking care of everything just like you wanted her too. She's reading the Bible and trusting the Lord to do what he has to do."

I touched the rosy little cheek with the tip of my finger, loving the feel of this sweet little girl. In spite of all the medicine going into her body, her mother was right, she still smelt like fresh air and sunshine.

"You must not worry about things here, honey," I whispered. "You made it as easy for us as you possibly could. Your faith and courage has rubbed off on all of us. Your daddy is doing better and he's going to be okay now. You should see him visit with everyone. He shows off your graduation photographs and tells them about your poems. He even recites a few by heart.

Your dad and mom are standing together strong just like you always knew they could be. You have wonderful parents." When I finished telling her this, Rie's mouth curved into the most beautiful soft smile. It was such a shock. I cried out, "Oh, baby, thank you for that lovely smile. I'll tell your mother and daddy you sent it to them."

Once again she smiled that slow soft smile, showing the little dimples around her mouth. Her grandfather and I rushed out and told the nurses. They promised to tell the doctors.

We spotted Sunny and Phil walking down the hall. I practically yelled to them the news. Sunny cried, "Oh, thank you for giving me that." We didn't know if it was our Rie's farewell to all of us or if her brain wasn't dead after all. I only knew that both smiles were slow and deliberate as though she was thanking me for telling her that her mom and dad were okay.

On Saturday night, there were so many people that came to visit…more than usual. Because of the crowd of people wanting to see Rie, the ICU nurses were letting more of us in to visit. The doctors had told them time was limited. Nothing was said to us about Rie's ability to smile. It was as if it never happened.

Marilyn, Dave, Sunny, and several other family members were in visiting with Rie. I was standing outside the kissing wall, waiting for my turn when Dave burst through the double doors. His normal bronze complexion was now closer to alabaster white. He didn't see me. He cupped his hands over his mouth and nose, taking deep audible breaths. Between breaths he made jerky mumbling sounds that sounded like praying.

I screamed, "What's wrong!" He didn't answer. His eyes didn't focus. I grabbed him by the shoulders and shook him. Dave! What's wrong?" His lips trembled; his eyes were glazed.

Anxiety and uneasiness touched me like a cold hand of a forbidding stranger causing my heart to plummet to my toes. Words and images churned through my brain that something terrible had happened to Rie and I wasn't there. The hallway started to spin. I closed my eyes for a moment willing away the dizziness. Finally getting my constricted throat to work, I screamed, "Rie's dead! Oh, God, she's dead…isn't she?"

MIRAGE

It feels soft, and comes like death. Peaceful, in a mask of expectancy, I wait, and hear the hesitant footsteps.

The air buzzes with silence and something hears its breath…ah, only myself.

I dare not breathe lest something hear its escape and pounce in my moment of weakness.

My heartbeats pound upward into the blue atmospheric clouds and all below is shadowed by the bird's wings.

Take me to your leader, I must escape my illusion.

CHAPTER 22

Normally Dave is a strong unemotional person that stays cool and calm in any emergency, but this man before my eyes was visibly shaken. Wincing from the pain I was inflecting to his shoulders, he said quietly, "It's all right. Everything is okay?" Dave was pale, shaken, and still having trouble swallowing, but he nodded his head yes.

"Oh, God, everything is okay." I took a deep breath and then another. It helped. Now the walls had stopped quaking before my eyes but my knees still felt watery.

On an indrawn breath, Dave said, "We thought Rie's heart had stopped. We thought she was dead." He passed his hands over his eyes as if to erase the terrible scene he had just witnessed. Clearing his throat of unshed tears, he continued, "Both heart monitors stopped, causing a flat line to form on the machines. Alarms went off. All the nurses in the world came running in, pushing us away while they started to work on her. After close examination, they found Rie was still breathing." His eyes closed for a moment. "It was horrible, both monitor's electrodes had come unplugged." Shuddering he let out a loud sigh while bracing himself against the wall. "I'm telling you, it was rough."

I threw myself against the kissing wall and sobbed openly. "Thank you, God, for letting it be the machines, but please don't let Monday come too fast." The touch of the cool wall against my cheek and the reality that Rie had not died soon restored my calm.

A little later, Dave went back in and brought Sunny out. Her face was paper-white from the shock she had just witnessed. Dave and Phil had to support her on either side as they walked her back to the waiting room.

I took my turn visiting Rie. I heard the nurses talking about the scare with Sunny Marie. They were all in shock themselves because they said this never happened. They said they could understand had it been one or two electrodes coming off but not all of them at once.

I walked back to the waiting room and saw how upset Sunny was. I poked a Valium at her and said, "Take this, you've been though enough tonight."

My sister hates medication and it usually takes an act of congress to get her to take any kind of pill, but this time, without saying a word, she swallowed it. In minutes, she mercifully fell into a deep sleep.

Sunday morning arrived. God willing, my Johnny would be here tonight. My arms of security…my protector…the one who would let me give in to my fears, let me shed held-in tears, and cry with me. I didn't need to be strong with Johnny, because he was my calm strength in an emergency.

Everyone in the waiting room voted to go to Mass in the beautiful St. Patrick's Chapel. The phone on the table rang. "Mom, it's finished." Dedo's voice sounded strained. "We stayed up all night. I packed up all Rie's clothes and personal effects. The furniture has been taken to the little shed in back of the house. The room is so empty…so empty…," she wept as though her heart was breaking.

I held my hand over the mouthpiece to keep Sunny from hearing the sounds. My lips were quivering and I tried hard to keep from crying, too. Dedo continued, "Oh, Mom, that was the hardest thing I've ever done in my whole life. I felt like an intruder. I didn't belong there among all of Rie's beautiful treasures. The tears nearly suffocated me. Mom, are you sure I did the right thing?"

What could I tell her? "Honey, I can't tell you if it's right or wrong. Who knows? It's for your Aunt Sunny to say and right now she believes it's right. She's the one we're worried about and she's the one that's has to face that empty room after Rie's death."

Dedo was silent for so long, finally she said, "Mom, have you heard anymore news from the doctors? Is Rie showing any signs of coming out of the coma?"

I told her how Rie smiled when I talked to her. I omitted the terrible fright we had last night.

Dedo's voice became stronger as she replied, "The happiest day of my life will be when we can put everything back in her room the way it was. God just has to make her well again. Oh, by the way, tell Aunt Sunny, I couldn't find Rie's coat. It wasn't in her closet and the boys didn't know where it was."

I relayed the message to Sunny standing beside me and she asked to speak to Dedo. "Dedo, the coat is there. Look in my closet."

"I did…I've looked in every closet in the house. Doug even checked his car and house but we haven't found it, yet." Looking confused, Sunny handed me the telephone again.

I said, "Don't worry honey, it'll turn up."

In the mist of her tears, Dedo laughed. "The boys and I finished shopping for their clothes. When I told Derek we were going shopping for new clothes, he was so excited. He kept trying on mod stuff and I kept trying to get him into dark slacks and dress shirts. I didn't have the heart to tell him why. Finally, I told him his mother wanted Philip and him to have some new clothes for church. Somehow, Philip knew what the new clothes were for without me telling him. Together, the two of us talked Derek into something suitable to wear."

"Is Philip all right?" I asked. I was still concerned over the way he was behaving.

"Oh, Mom, I worry about Philip. While I was cleaning Rie's room, he kept coming to the door watching me, never saying a word. Three different times he did this. I watched his eyes move around the room at the empty drawers and the boxes that held Rie's clothes. Once, he picked up one of her twirling medals and held it in his hands close to his heart. The fourth time he came, I stopped what I was doing and asked him if he was all right."

Dedo's voice quivered with emotion. He stuck his hands in his pockets and nodded his head yes. I wanted him to talk to me…you know, to open up. I said, 'Philip, I'm so sorry. I'm doing this for your mom. This isn't my idea but your Mom asked me. She can't face coming back and tackling this job. Honey, believe me, I'm not here by choice.'" He looked so lost. He said, 'I know Dedo.'

"Later, Philip came to the door of Rie's room and told me he needed to tell me something. I stopped what I was doing, but he didn't say anything. He helped me carry fifteen plastic garbage bags full of clothes to the shed in the back. Did you know that half of those clothes were made by Aunt Sunny? They had labels in them saying, 'Made by Mom.' When we went shopping he told me again he needed to tell me something, but he never did. I don't know how to talk to him. He's holding something back, but I don't know what it is."

I hurt for Dedo and Sunny's children. I knew it wasn't easy for them to see Rie's room dismantled. "Dedo, give him time. If he has something to say to you, when the time is right, he'll tell you."

Her voice cracked, "But Mom, my heart hurts for him." In a strangled voice, Dedo said, "While I was cleaning out Rie's room, so many memories flooded my brain. I remembered how Rie would ask me to try on her clothes. We always had so much fun when I would spend the night with her. Rie would teach me all the new dances and would dress me in her clothes, fix my hair, and tell me how beautiful I was. So many times she would tell me, 'Now Dedo, if anything ever happens to me you can have my clothes to wear.'"

I could only nod my head at the memory of Rie dressing Dedo up as a teenager when there was nine years difference in their ages. Rie remarked one time that Dedo was her living Barbie Doll.

"Oh, God, Mother, I found a poem predicting her death."

"What? Read it to me."

"Are you sure, it's pretty heavy stuff?"

"I'm not sure I can handle anything right now, but maybe I need to hear it before your Aunt Sunny reads it."

"Rie named it, 'My Death.'" Dedo's voice quivered with emotion as she read: "'The dawn is slow in coming now. The morning has yet to wake the night. I wonder if it would matter anyhow if I were to oppose and continue the fight. My sun has gone down in purple and red, yet royalty I'm not, nor clothed in bloody array. I fear I've been black and white and led throughout the brighter light of day. They limited my guesses and under glass taught propriety, tradition, right and wrong. The perfect child I thrived in class and learned of these, but sang no song. So it is right, I must give in. To fight my death would be a sin.'"

When the poem ended, endless silence filled the telephone receiver. I had no way of knowing when this poem was written but I felt like it had to be recently. Maybe right before she came to the hospital this last time.

"Mom," Dedo said, "Do you think she really knew she was going to die?"

"I think Rie has always been in communication with God. Yes, I believe she knew. She's so much older and wiser than any of us." I didn't mean it to sound profound, but knowing Rie, she lived her faith, something we all fall short at doing.

"What do you want to do with the poem?"

"Just bring it…your Aunt Sunny will need to see it."

"All right, but Mom, tell Aunt Sunny to give me a break, no more. Okay!"

"Sweetheart, you have been a big help to your Aunt Sunny, but I know you would be the first one to volunteer for anything she needed. I love you, my daughter."

Dedo replied, "I love you, too. Oh, by the way, Woody will be picking Dad up at the airport and I'll bring Sylvia. We need to pick up Woody's uniform at the cleaners. We'll hurry as fast as we can."

After I said good-bye, I walked out of that room to sit in the main waiting room. I needed to be alone, if you can be alone in a room completely full of people. For some reason my eyes were drawn to a young black man standing in the doorway. It was as though he was searching for someone. We didn't smile or nod, but just stared at one another.

My first thought was he was very handsome, movie star material. My second thought was he appeared so very sad. But the third thought that crossed my mind was I know this young man. His whole appearance was one of familiarity.

It was a strange feeling. To the best of my knowledge, I'd never seen him before until now. But it was something about the eyes. As we stared at each other, in that instant, it was as though he also recognized me, as if our souls had touched. Neither one of us spoke. The moment passed. He turned away, walking toward ICU and I walked to the waiting room to talk with my sister.

A thought filtered across my mind and I remembered Sunny telling me about a friend of Rie's. Rie was colored blind when it came to people. The color of skin was never discussed when she described them. One of these friends was a black youth named Dale. Rie had never mentioned the color of his skin. Sunny had told me. Dale had been the one to introduce Rie to his best friend, Doug. Dale was in love with Rie himself and had even asked her to go steady with him. Rie told Dale that Doug had just asked her to go steady and she had already accepted. Dale accused Rie of blowing him off because of the color of his skin. It had broken Rie's heart and she cried.

Sunny told me that was the hardest she had ever seen Rie cry. Rie later told her mother that had she been in love with Dale the color of his skin wouldn't have mattered. She loved Doug, but she loved Dale as a friend.

I'd never met Dale before or seen photographs of him, but I told my sister that I was almost sure that the young man I saw in the waiting room had to be Dale.

So I really wasn't surprised when Sunny and I walked into ICU and found this young man by Rie's bedside. He was holding Rie's hand in his. A Rosary was entwined in their fingers and he was talking to her in a soft gentle voice. His cheeks were still wet from his tears but he greeted us with a dazzling smile.

"I talked the nurses into letting me spend some private time with my girl." He swallowed a lump in his throat. "You know, she smiled at me just now."

"She did?" Sunny smiled. "You could always make her smile. I see that you sweet-talked the nurses into letting you break the rules." Then she hugged him and kissed his cheek, "Thanks for coming, Dale. It means a lot to all of us."

He squeezed Sunny hard. "I had to be here." Dale shrugged, trying to regain his composure. Then he looked over at me his smile broadened and said, "You're Aunt Margie, aren't you?"

"How did you know?" I asked.

"It was the eyes. I felt I knew you the minute our eyes met," he said seriously. "Our souls touched for a second."

Funny, those had been my thoughts exactly.

Doug and Dale were always there with us. Sometimes they were friendly, talking…sharing their memories of Rie. Other times they resented each other with jealous looks and sharp remarks.

There were times that Dale would take Doug to his home in Lake Charles, feed him, and give him a place to stay so he could be close to Rie. Through it all, Doug and Dale were there for Rie. Both cried for the same reasons. Their hearts were broken. They loved her. She belonged to both young men and neither one wanted to let her go.

"I LOVE YOU"

When I said, "I love you," I gave to you, from the depths of my heart a love saved and nurtured, innocent and trusting to be yours.

I turned over to you a child's faithful love, a woman's deep and certain love, a girl's carefree and shy love, and the love of maternal caring.

At first, shakily, I stood on my words trusting as a child, loving as a woman, holding shyly back like a girl and caring like a mother, but all the while wary and wondering about this new strange sensation.

So to understand me, understand all of me…the child, the girl, the woman, and someone, above my years who loves you.

CHAPTER 23

Marilyn, Dave, Phil, Sunny, Philip, Derek, Dale, Doug, and I walked down to the chapel for Mass. The nine of us took up two whole pews. The one thing that was utmost in all our minds was Monday...the day our Rie was going to be taken off the life-support machines to die. We were too numb and stricken to be brave. We had to put our faith in God's hands. During the service, we all joined hands to draw strength from each other. God's goodness and love poured forth. We were beyond praying for a miracle. Instead we turned Rie over to God.

The richness of the nuns' voices vibrated from every corner of the chapel setting up an echo. Angelic voices in heaven couldn't have been any prettier.

The beautiful statue of the risen Jesus looked down and stretched his loving arms out to embrace us. We stood waiting...waiting with broken hearts for our fears to subside. Waiting for the Holy Spirit to give comfort, to sustain us. Waiting for God's goodness to give us peace. We reaffirmed and claimed that goodness, and in doing so, we all felt our burdens lifted. And then a beautiful thing occurred.

The sun was shining outside, making the stained glass windows come alive with glorious colors. For some unknown reason, we all turned at the same time, witnessing the sight, For a brief moment of time, a fluttering sparrow pressed itself against the outside of the glass window. We could make out the full silhouette of the tiny bird. We all stood transfixed afraid to break the spell. It was as if God was sending a word of encouragement.

Goose bumps broke over my skin and a passage from the Bible played across my brain. "God knows every sparrow that falls. Fear not, you are of more value than a sparrow." Praise God, if He knows every sparrow that falls than He knows our Sunny Marie and He knows us and hears our prayers? Because of God's message of love, we left the chapel with lighter hearts.

A coincidence…an accident that a sparrow would appear against the glass at that moment…I think not. There had not been a sound to alert us to the tiny bird. Why then, would we all turn at once and witness it? Why would we all have such an over powering surge of God's love at the same time?

Through all of this, I have truly come to realize that there are no accidents in God's great plan. God meant us to see the sparrow. He meant us to feel His love.

Walking back to our waiting room we didn't talk to each other. All of a sudden it was important to be quiet and know the Lord was in control. The doctors had done all they could…now it was in the Great Physician's hands.

I rocked in my corner chanting softly in my head, "People and prayers, prayers and people…beautiful people…prayers from the heart…beautiful prayers. Hurry…Johnny…hurry, please get here before it's finished."

My eyes scanned the room. For an instant, the unwinding reel of time and events seemed to stand still; we were caught in a time pause. I could see Sunny holding tightly to her cross reading the Bible. Phil's face was immobile, staring into space. Marilyn, Dave, Doug, and Dale murmured in a corner. Philip walked the floor never saying a word. His pain was too great and it was far easier to shut everyone else out. I watched him plunged deeper into grief where he wouldn't permit anyone to follow. We were all burdened with grief. Oh, the complexity of human emotions.

Dear red-hair, freckle-faced Derek with the sunshine smile inched closer to me. He whispered, "I've been thinking, Aunt Margie. If Rie dies…" he hesitated looking around to make sure no one was listening to him, "if Rie dies she'll be going to a much more beautiful place to live, won't she?"

I nodded my head yes to his question. It pleased him.

"When she goes to Heaven, I know she'll be happy." He shrugged. "Everyone is happy in heaven." He gave me a very thoughtful look. "But that doesn't mean God can't work a miracle in the mean time. Earth is a good place to live too." His questions called for an answer. Don't let me cry, I begged. Help me to keep this child's enthusiasm high. I looked into the wide honest green eyes of this young boy. Derek had wisdom far beyond his years and faith to move mountains. A tear slipped down my face unheeded.

"God can always work a miracle," I said in an unsteady voice.

"Yep," Derek smiled showing the deep dimples in each cheek. "I believe he can, too," he said with confidence. "No matter what doctors say or other people tell me, I believe in miracles."

"I know you do. Me too," I said while hugging the small shoulders tightly. Oh, God, me too, my brain cried.

"Aunt Margie, why don't doctors believe in miracles?"

"They do and they see miracles everyday, but because they're doctors they have to be honest with everyone. None of us can live forever on this earth. We start dying from the day we're born. God only promised we can live forever in heaven." I was hoping I made sense.

"It's a shame everyone can't have a miracle…isn't it?"

"I think God gives everyone miracles everyday. Some big, some little, but most people refuse to see them as a gift from God. They take them for granted."

"Yeah," his eyes widened, "But if God woke Rie up, right now, we wouldn't take that for granted, would we?"

"Oh, no, definitely not." My face broke into a grin. "We would rejoice, celebrate, dance, and probably go a little crazy with our happiness. I think this whole hospital would go a little crazy."

His smile captivated my heart. His eyes danced as his mind pictured what it would be like. "Uncle Johnny will be here soon," I confided to Derek, "and I just know everything will be better when he gets here."

An hour later, Woody and Johnny arrived. I ran into my Johnny's waiting arms, clutching him close as if my very life depended on him.

I could see the lines engraved into his tired handsome face and tears in his soft hazel eyes. Regardless of the strained look...my Johnny was beautiful. I needed his joking, his eternal optimism, and his love. I needed his courage. Mine was in tatters.

Crying, Sunny hugged Johnny. "Thank you for coming."

Johnny rocked her in his arms. "Oh, baby, I was coming if I had to walk."

Some of the family chose to leave taking Philip and Derek home. Later others decided to go see Rie. It was during this time that Johnny and I were able to visit and catch up. He had a lot of questions that needed answering and I needed his warmth and tender words of love. For a long time we just held each other crying.

Suddenly, Sunny came back to the room with a smile playing across her face. She practically shouted in her excitement, "Rie..." she clapped her hands under her chin, "Rie opened her eyes."

I jumped up and yelled out, "Praise God! How? When did it happen?"

Sunny couldn't wait to tell us. She giggled. "Rie's school friends were all standing around her bed and they asked why was the rose petal pinned to Rie's gown. I told them the story of the wonderful man that gave it to her and when I looked down, Rie was watching me. Can you believe it?" She gave a loud squeal. "It happened just like that. She was watching me." Sunny's face glowed. "It wasn't a vacant stare. Her eyes

were clear and bright with intelligence. She didn't appear to be a vegetable at all. I could've sworn she was listening to the story. Her eyes
were focused and she slowly looked at everyone around the bed. Then
she closed them as if she was tired and needed to sleep for a little while."
Like three children, we jumped up and down with joy.

"Oh, Sunny," I blurted out. "First a smile, then her eyes opening. She's
showing signs of life…our baby isn't a vegetable after all. She can't die
tomorrow. She can't."

Johnny and I went to his mother's that night with the promise to be
back early the next morning. Our hearts were happier; Rie was showing
a change. Surely the doctors would have to change their opinion concerning Rie, now that she was showing signs of coming out of the coma.

Early Monday morning, before daylight, we were back at the hospital. Then came the waiting. We expected the doctor at any moment to
come running in to inform us that Rie had indeed come out of her
coma. We had visions of him coming in red face and apologizing how
he had been wrong about Rie. We continued joking and laughing…just
being silly.

When finally Dr. Milan did come to visit, it wasn't with a red face,
nor was there any words of apology explaining how wrong he had been
about Rie's coma. No, he didn't do any of the silly things we had built up
in our minds.

Instead, the serious face man walked into the room faced Sunny and
said in a business like voice, "We'll be sending Sunny Marie to the fifth
floor in the next hour. As soon as we establish her in the room we'll be
taking off the machines. I don't expect her to live very long after that."

Our hearts plummeted. Oh, God he still believed Rie was going to die.

"No!" Sunny said vehemently. She looked over at me in a panic, then
back at the doctor in disbelief. "But Doctor," she shouted in a frantic
voice, "didn't the nurses tell you? Sunny Marie opened her eyes last
night. She looked at everyone standing beside the bed. Isn't that a sign

that she's coming out of the coma? Surely, she isn't going to die, now," she pleaded emphatically.

The doctor's set expression didn't change, but very precisely, he replied, "Yes, I was informed. I checked Sunny Marie again this morning just to make sure." He scrutinized her thoroughly as if he wanted to make sure she was strong enough to accept his next words. "Mrs. Eppler, I found no change. It was only a reflex action. When Sunny Marie opens her eyes they aren't really seeing anything. It's a vacant stare, nothing more. The situation has not changed. All the tests show that Sunny Marie's brain is dead."

"Well, the tests are wrong," Sunny cried, her voice high and shaky. "It wasn't a vacant stare I saw last..."

He interrupted quickly, "Please don't get upset." The doctor placed a hand on her arm to quiet her. "What you saw last night was a reflex action...no more. The small percent of the brain that's working caused your daughter's eyes to open and close. She sees nothing nor hears nothing."

Sunny started to open her mouth to argue the facts, but again the doctor intervened. "Believe me," he stated firmly, "it was nothing more than what I've told you. If I thought it was more, I would be the first to tell you."

Like a switch being turned off, the light faded from Sunny's face, replaced by an overwhelming visible dread. Misery twisted her features. She struggled to regain her composure. I wanted to scream at the nerve of this man. "Oh please, don't do this to my sister," my heart cried silently. "It's not fair. Don't take her hope away. Leave her that one small glimmer. Can't you see that's all she's got left and now you're leaving her with nothing."

"Have you hired the private nurses yet," he inquired. Sunny's lips quivered slightly; slowly she gave a nod. "I know it's hard on you and your family," Dr. Milan said. Suddenly the harshness in his voice was gone, replaced by compassion and concern, "but I did try to prepare you for her death."

I WISH YOU NOTHING

I could swear you to hell in a breath or curse your life with a few ill-rhyming words, but then I would be as you are and would lower myself to your level.

So, I do not wish your damnation, nor do I hope your life to be filled with misery and sadness. I wish nothing for you my fellow human being, and your name does not enter into my prayers.

I will not agree with any punishing tactics that others offer you, but I will not raise a hand in defending you.

Perhaps I am one that does not count, so it is just as well that I do not count you. It doesn't matter…right?

Thank you. You gave me no reason to feel guilty.

CHAPTER 24

With dread, we all went up to the fifth floor. It wasn't long before they brought Rie, still hooked up to the machines. We watched as they settled her into her new room.

This room, located in the new part of the hospital, was larger than the previous rooms we had occupied before. It had a nice roomy couch flanked by an armchair and a recliner, a desk built against the wall, and big double windows.

From the windows, warm, happy inviting sunshine spilled into the room. How dare the sun shine on a day like today? How dare it intrude into her sorrow?

Evidently the nurses thought so too because they quickly pulled the blinds, shutting out the existence of light. The room was now dark like our spirits. Now it resembled a dying room. All that was absent was the mournful toll of the funeral bells.

Dr. Shamieh came out of the room. His face was filled with compassionate concern. He asked Sunny if it was still her decision to remove all the machines. He patiently explained, "I can leave the machines on Sunny Marie. In cases like this, the machine could keep a her alive for a while longer." The rest of the family was hovered around Rie or talking to the nurses. Sunny and I were the only ones at this time talking to the doctor outside Rie's room. She was holding my hand in a death grip.

"No," Sunny smiled so sadly at the doctor. "It's not my decision to make…it never was. It's Rie's decision. We talked about so many things in our short years together, shared our thoughts and dreams, and were as close as any mother and daughter could be."

Sunny stood up straighter. But I was the only one that was aware of the superhuman effort it cost her. It was my hand she was squeezing the blood out of. There was only a trace of a quiver in her clear voice as she replied, "Rie made me promise that if anything ever happened to her, I would never keep her alive on machines. She promised me, if I died first she would do the same thing. If God wills that she should live, then the machines wouldn't be necessary anyway." Sunny took a deep breath trying to keep from crying and my heart ached for her pain. "Be brave," I whispered more to myself than for her. "Don't break down, little sister…not now."

The doctor drew in a breath and slowly let it out. He was emotional linked with this family and the strain showed on his face.

"Mrs. Eppler," he said, his eyes never leaving Sunny's face. "I don't think you're ready for her to die just yet."

"NO!" Sunny agreed. "No, you're right. I'm not ready for my baby to die, but you forget, this is Rie's choice." Sunny placed a hand against her chest as if she was in pain. "I'm selfish. If it were up to me, I would leave the machines on Rie just to keep her alive, anyway I could. That way, I could walk into that room, touching her, talking to her and keeping her with me for as long as possible." Sunny gave a loud sigh. "Don't you realize? Rie trusted me to understand and carry out her wishes. To be perfectly truthful, I would expect the same thing from her if our roles were reversed."

"I'm worried about you." The doctor's eyes softened. "Are you going to be able to handle her death right now?"

Sunny dropped her head, but only for a moment, then looking the doctor straight in the eyes, she said, "Probably not, but this isn't for me. It's for my Rie. Take the machines off."

The doctor looked at this mother with such a look of respect. He nodded solemnly. Then turning on his heels, he walked to the nurse's station.

When Sunny turned to me, I wasn't prepared for the change in her face. I saw despair and pain...so much pain. It was almost more than I could bear.

After the group of nurses worked over Rie unplugging and moving the machines out, the entire family was left alone with her to say our good-byes. Rie wasn't the only one dying this day. Our world was crumbling and pieces of our heart, future, and memory were dying too.

Now, the awful, unnatural sounds of the machines we had heard all week were silent. Suddenly the silence seemed to scream louder than the machines or louder than our pulsating hearts.

The ever-present IVs still pushed fluid into Rie's veins. A catheter was still attached to the bag under the bed, barely visible. They had left a mouthpiece in the Cupid-bow mouth to assist her breathing. As awful as the prospect of Rie dying was, the room was filled with God's presence. Through our sadness, we all felt it. Rie shined with it. She didn't look like death...in fact she glowed with life. Sunny Marie had put her complete trust in God. We could do no less. I gently tucked my sleeping beauty in one last time; something I was going to miss.

The afternoon wore on. Her vital signs continued to be strong. We talked to her in soft whispered voices, telling her how much we loved her, how much we were going to miss her. Maybe the doctors were wrong and that five percent of brain could hear...maybe, just maybe.

One hour passed...two...then three and four. Her vital signs remained the same...strong.

Once, she went into a spasm of coughing. With the mouthpiece in place it magnified the sound and frightened all of us. We had never witnessed someone dying before and we all jumped thinking this was it. As we hung onto the edge of our seats, she started to breathe normal again.

Everyone took a deep breath, everyone except Woody. Woody ran from the room. I had to run to catch up with him. He was like a blind person running and stumbling down the long corridor, bouncing off the sides of the wall. At the end of the hall, he threw himself against the wall and cried. Terrible sobs racked his body. Something I had never witnessed him doing before.

I grabbed him to me and rocked him the way I used to when he was a small child.

"Honey, it's okay. She just coughed. It was the mouthpiece that made it sound so terrible."

His body became limp against mine and I continued to hold him while he cried. When the tears were spent, he confessed, "Mom, look at me. I'm a policeman, right! I come into contact with death

constantly, but please Mom, I can't go back in that room and watch that baby die." He sobbed, "I just can't."

"It's all right, son. If you want to wait outside, I'm sure your Aunt Sunny will understand." Later, after the nurses removed the mouthpiece, Woody returned to the room taking his turn talking softly to the sleeping beauty.

Sylvia, Woody's wife, and Dedo arrived but wouldn't come into the room. I walked out, greeted them, and repeated what the doctor told us.

Sylvia pulled Dedo aside and whispered, "I can't go in that room."

"You must," Dedo whispered back. "I've been doing a lot of thinking and I feel this is all happening, not so much for Rie, but for all of us. God wants us to be here for a reason. We all have lessons to learn." She gave Sylvia a gentle shake; her voice broke. "My God, Sylvia, she's only eighteen years old. You and I are twenty-six. Rie is so much older and wiser than we are. Maybe it's time for us to grow up." I was so proud of Sylvia. She walked in without any hesitation.

She gave comfort to Sunny and Phil and her husband. She walked up to Rie's bed and took her time speaking words of love.

This was family…the circle of love was united. We all placed our hands on the sleeping child and prayed. Her loving hands were once more in place.

The day wore into night and Rie's vital signs remained strong. Another private nurse was called in at 8 p.m. The gallant, little heart beat strong.

The private nurse stayed busy keeping a log and taking Rie's blood pressure. Sunny asked, "Why are you taking Sunny Marie's vital signs so often?"

The nurse replied, "I'm watching for her blood pressure to drop."

"Is that something that happens before death?"

"That's one of the signs we look for," she said.

"How does it look right now?"

"Actually," the nurse smiled for the first time since she entered the room, "she's holding her own."

"That's good, huh?"

"Oh, yes." The nurse patted Sunny's shoulder. "Let's just say, that's much more than I had hoped for."

Sunny addressed everyone in the room. "Right now while things are good, go home and get a good night sleep. Margie, Phil and I will stay. We'll call if anything changes." She walked up to Johnny and asked, "Do you mind picking up the boys at Mother's house and stay with them at my house. They need a night at their own house for a change. And if Rie dies tonight…" she hesitated, "if she should die, I would rather that you be the one to give them the news. Marilyn and Dave are going to stay with Mother and Daddy just in case."

During the long vigil, we took turns reading the Bible aloud. For those that have never sat by the bed of a loved one waiting for that last breath, all I can say is, it is one of the hardest things in the world to do. You pace your breathing, in haling and exhaling, with the ill person. Waiting…always waiting and wondering if it will be the last breath they'll take.

Somewhere between counting each breath and praying, Sunny and I dozed off sitting up. I don't think either one of us was conscious that we had done so. Maybe that's why we jumped out of our skins when we were awakened by a loud whisper.

"Pssst! Hurry, wake up," the nurse whispered. Both Sunny and I awoke instantly. The nurse placed a finger to her lips. The first thought that went through my mind was this is it…Rie's dead, but why does the nurse want to keep us quiet?

I looked around the room. Sunny had a bewildered expression on her face while she watched her husband.

Phil was pacing, very slowly back and forth, in front of Rie's bed reading the Bible aloud. He stopped and asked, "Am I tiring you?"

I thought the question was asked of Sunny, but to my surprise, Phil wasn't looking at his wife at all. His eyes were focused on Rie. I noticed Sunny's eyes were now watching Rie. I, too, gazed over at Rie and to my amazement Rie was wide-awake. Her eyes were soft gray now but clear and focused.

She was watching her daddy and she actually nodded her head no to his question. This was not a reflex action…it was deliberate.

Bells chimed loudly in my head, my heart, ringing out songs of praise to God. Dear Lord, this child was awake. She's alive.

Suddenly I wanted to shout for joy, but I was afraid I would scare Rie. I'm not sure if I grabbed Sunny's hand or she grabbed mine. All I knew, we were squeezing each other's hand so hard that we lost all feeling in our fingers. This was a small price to pay for such an emotional experience.

Phil read another passage from the Bible. Rie's eyes followed him as he paced from side to side.

The private nurse whispered, "She can see you, Mr. Eppler. I'm almost certain she understands what you're saying."

Phil's voice quivered with emotion. "Honey, do you want me to continue to read the Bible?"

We waited. Our breath, to the point of pain, was held in anticipation of her answer. Never had it seemed more important for us to listen and wait.

Rie continued to stare at her father. Her little head moved slowly up and down in a definite yes. Now there could be no mistake that Rie understood. Oh, yes indeed, our Rie was alive and with us, physically and mentally.

While my soul soared with happiness, my mind was busy thanking God over and over for His blessing. If you could place all the joy of all the Christmases and birthdays and all the wonderful experiences you have ever enjoyed in your entire life in one room then maybe, just maybe, you would be able to feel what we were experiencing that early morning.

We all knew it was still dark outside, 3 a.m. to be exact, but the light that filled that room was brighter than any sunshine we had ever seen. Sunny ran to her daughter, smothering her with kisses. She was sobbing, "Oh, my baby, you've come back to us."

THE ART OF LOVE

You are the artist the tool is love.
Take this sparrow make me a dove.
Mold me as if I was moistened clay.
Fashion me a shape that I should stay.
I want to be Your work of art.
Take out the bad let goodness start.
Write in my eyes the words of stars.
Heal my heart remove the scars.
Undo the flaws smooth out the creases.
Gather together put back the pieces.
Sculpt and trace, love and make me.
Polish and never ever forsake me.
And God, when your work on me is through,
I'll know that I will owe it all to You.

CHAPTER 25

Phil and I danced around the room, hugging each other. Even the private nurse, a stranger only hours before, was now as excited as we were. We all knelt giving thanks to God.

During all of this, Rie stared at us as if we were from another planet. At the blank expression on her face, we realized that maybe she wasn't aware of what she had actually been through.

The nurse pulled Sunny to the side and whispered, "Sometimes after awakening from a coma the patient can have amnesia."

"You mean Rie may not know who we are?" Sunny walked up to her daughter and touched her hand. "Do you know who I am?"

Rie nodded ever so slightly and formed the word mom with her lips. Sunny's voice became excited. "Can you point to your daddy?"

The little hand was shaky, but Rie pointed in the direction of her father. We all applauded. Rie was startled at our reaction. She gazed strangely around the room. Then her eyes came to rest again on her mother. She asked in a labored whisper, "Where am I?"

Keeping her voice low the nurse stated behind Sunny, "She doesn't know why she's at the hospital."

"Honey," Sunny rubbed her arm gently, "you had headaches and the doctor operated on your head. Rie looked perplex. "Do you remember?" Slowly Rie shook her head no. She lifted a hand to her head and rubbed the bandage. "You have been in a coma." Rie's eyes widened in alarm.

"How long?" She mouthed.

"Over a week," Sunny stated. Rie responded with a shocked expression and formed the word, "Wow!"

The nurse advised Sunny not to overload her with too many details. Later would be soon enough. Rie turned toward the nurse and whispered, "Why can't I talk?"

The nurse smiled. "Maybe because you haven't talked to anyone for well over a week. You'll have to start using your voice again."

Rie smiled at all of us. Our joy was tremendous and I guess so was the noise we were making because every floor nurse came running to the room. As early as it was in the morning, they too rejoiced with us. Happiness flowed up and down the long corridors of the fifth floor. I'm sure the patients on the floor thought that bedlam was taking place.

The doctor was called and informed of the changes. A miracle had taken place right under our noses. Sunny Marie was awake.

I called Johnny. "Get up! Rejoice!" I screamed. "Tell Derek and Philip God gave us a miracle after all. Get Rie's room put back together, she's alive."

Poor Johnny, it took him awhile to understand what I was screaming at him for. He thought Rie had died and I had lost my mind. He promised to inform the family of the good news. We expected Rie to be the same person she was before she went into the coma, bubbly, talkative. After all the movies are like that. People wake up from a coma and they act and look exactly the same. But reality is not the movies. Rie was awake, she knew us, but she wouldn't talk and she was far from being the active young girl we knew.

It frightened Sunny. She kept saying, "Talk to me, Rie."

Rie would shake her head no and with a shaking hand to her throat she would mouth the words, "It hurts."

Sunny blamed herself because she had made her talk the minute she came out of the coma, "I've hurt her," she cried.

The nurse explained that the breathing tubes, while Rie was in a coma, might have damaged her throat.

I assured Rie, "It's all right. You talk when you want too. There's other ways to communicate." Rie gazed questioningly at me. "Just blink one time for yes, two times for no."

So by the time the family gathered back at the hospital, we had Rie answering questions by blinking her eyes. Once for yes...twice for no. It didn't matter she was unable to talk; blinking was enough for now. When her throat healed we were sure she would be able to talk.

What a difference. Everyone was full of smiles. The room rocked with laughter. Sunshine poured in. Oh, yes the blinds were now pulled up to their highest point. No more shadows, no more gloom. Rie had returned and she was definitely not a vegetable. Her vital signs were steady, her heart was strong, and every minute showed more improvement.

It was as though, God said, "This child is mine. It is I who will say when it is time for her to die, My time...not man's. For I am in complete control of heaven and earth."

My heart nearly burst from my chest every time my sister met anyone at the door. She would say in greeting, "Isn't this a glorious morning. Rie has returned to us."

We noticed that Rie did not have total use of her arms. The nurse told us she appeared like a person that had a stroke.

During this time, we talked to Rie so much we actually wore her out. So by the time Dr. Shamieh came into the room, he found her sleeping. Rie looked no different than she had in the coma. By the expression on his face, I'm sure he thought all of us were crazy. He was cautious and warned in a very somber voice not to be too optimistic. As far as himself and the other doctor's were concern, Rie was still a vegetable. He told us he would return and check on her later but try not to get our hopes up.

It's funny how all this time we listened to the doctors, believing they knew everything. We decided it didn't matter what the doctors had to say anymore. It was obvious they didn't have the answers. God was in control of our Rie. God made the miracle.

When Rie awakened, I whispered, "This is all so wonderful but I'll be happier when I can see you give that thumbs-up sign." She looked at me and very slowly, her shaking arm moved until she was able to make the thumbs-up sign.

"Oh, baby," I cried. "You can do anything. Praise the Lord!"

An hour later Doctor Shamieh walked back into the room, Rie was propped up on pillows with her eyes wide opened. The doctor gasped, rocked back on his heels and finally said, "Sunny Marie, you are awake!"

I often wondered what went through his mind at this time. By the expression on his face he was completely flabbergasted.

Rie looked at him as if he had just lost his mind like the rest of us. He moved forward into the room and asked hesitantly, "Are you feeling all right?" Without even a pause, she held up her thumb, in her thumbs-up sign, and winked at him.

The doctor stood there with the most astonished expression on his face and responded, "My goodness...oh, my goodness!" He reached over and caught the little hand in his and beamed. Caution gone, he laughed out loud. Just like we were, he was so emotionally involved. The excitement showed on his face and in his voice, but he was just as in awe of the miracle as we were.

Everyone in the room had tears on their cheeks. Dr. Shamieh walked out of Rie's room still saying the words, "Oh, my goodness. This is just wonderful."

The only time now we closed the blinds was while Rie napped. As soon as she would open her eyes I would open the curtains to let the sunshine into the room to match the sunshine in our hearts. On one occasion, as I opened the blinds a white pigeon fluttered against the windowpane. He didn't even touch it, but seemed suspended looking in. Only his wings moved in slow motion.

Another message from God? "Yes, God, we hear you," I said aloud. "The miracle belongs to you."

Sister Margarita stood beside me. I said, "That's the second time we've seen a bird at the window." She smiled and said, "God sends His love on the wings of birds." How true, how true indeed.

Derek and Philip walked around with smiles on their faces. Actually they glowed. They both had Rie constantly blinking, with questions but she seemed not to mind. I heard Derek say to his brother, "Why is everyone so surprised Rie is back, I knew God was going to make a miracle."

Philip's answer was to grab his brother in a headlock wrestling him around the room.

I asked Woody and Sylvia to sing a song for Rie. Woody wrestled with a lump in his throat and shook his head no. He whispered for my ears only, "Mom, don't do this to me. I can't."

"Today you can," I confidently whispered back. "You must." It'll cheer Rie up to have her very own concert. That baby has always lived music."

Woody picked up his guitar, something he had brought along at my request. He cleared his throat a couple of times and with Sylvia's help they started singing, "Walking Piece of Heaven."

It was true; Rie had always loved music. She sang. She played the piano and guitar and even her mother and daddy sing together with their children. Music was as much a part of her as breathing. There wasn't a day that went by that she didn't enjoy some form of music.

Woody and Sylvia's singing was a very emotional experience. Their voices had never sounded better. All their love for this child spilled forth from their hearts and soul. Woody strummed softly on his guitar and the words flowed. "What's that round your head, is it a halo? What's that on your shoulders, is it wings? You must be a walking Piece of heaven. Or is it love that makes us see these things?"

When they started singing, we were watching Rie's reaction. She slowly moved her eyes around the room, from face to face, until she found Woody and Sylvia in the crowded room and gave them a radiant smile.

When they finished, I asked Sunny and Phil to sing. "I can't," Sunny whispered looking doubtfully at me. She drew away.

"Oh, yes you can," I replied softly, placing my arm around her shoulders. "Look at Rie's face. You can do anything…for her."

Sunny relaxed as she glanced at her daughter. "Yes! You're right. We can do anything today."

Their choice was, "Where could I go but to the Lord." It will never be sung as perfect by anyone as it was that day. People gathered outside the room, listening with intense expressions, hanging on to every word. There wasn't a dry eye in that room or on the fifth floor. Nurses and strangers stood lined up in the hall. We weren't sure where they all came from, but they were there sharing with us our miracle.

Rie's reflexes were slow, but her brain was working. She found her mother and father's faces among the crowd of people and gave them a thumbs-up sign. She listened to the music and she could see and recognize her family members. This child wasn't a vegetable. She was Sunny Marie Eppler, child of God.

Word spread throughout the hospital that Rie was alive and awake. The telephone beside the bed rang constantly.

This was not a remission. It was a miracle. Even the doctors had no other way of explaining what was happening to Rie other than using the word "miracle." Everyone seemed to be aware of God working His miracle.

Word spread through our tri-cities, Orange, Port Arthur, and Beaumont (Better known as the Golden Triangle.) Churches were opened in all the cities for prayers for Sunny Marie. Again we seemed inundated with flowers. Rie's room had more flowers than some of the Rose Bowl floats. We kept as many as we could, but again we had to direct some to other patients in the hospital. We let Rie inspect each bouquet, letting her touch and smell the flowers. From the joy on her face at each new bouquet, she didn't seem to mind that they had been picked. The thought crossed my mind that these would have been the same people to send flowers to Rie's funeral had she passed away, but how much better for her now to enjoy the flowers while she lives.

People came, beautiful people with prayers. The room was always full. So many people we didn't know, but it didn't matter. They came for their own reasons and shared our miracle, leaving with joy in their hearts and God's name on their lips. We forgot about the dull gray shadows outside and concentrated on the sunshine inside.

By Thursday, when the doctor came to the door, he admitted, "I don't know what's happening." He appeared disconcerted. "I can't promise you that Sunny Marie will live a day or ten days. We just don't know what the cancer will do."

Sunny smiled over at her daughter and then at the bewildered doctor, she said, "Three days ago you promised us two hours. I don't need promises now…you know, I don't think I'll worry about tomorrow. I'm just going to take each day as it comes. One day at a time will do…minute by minute…step by step. God is taking care of everything now. Please don't make any more predictions. God just wants us to cherish each second we have with her."

This man wasn't prepared for Sunny's answer. To say he was stunned was a mild description. He nodded his head in agreement and hurriedly, walked away.

Later that day, as I walked out into the hall, I heard Sunny and Woody laughing. They saw me coming and quickly elbowed each other quickly becoming silent. The only thing left of their laughter was the gleam in their eyes. Glancing from one to the other, I asked, "What?" Both started to smile. They were obviously pleased about something.

"So, tell me," I demanded. "What's so funny?" I had the feeling that their amusement was directed at me.

Sunny snickered. Woody chuckled and replied, "Mom, we were just discussing who was going to play our parts when they make the movie on Rie's life." He rubbed his hand over his chin and mouth to hide an even wider smile that threatened to spread over his face.

"Well, we have it all figured out."

"And?" I coaxed. He rocked back on his heels. I looked from Sunny to Woody. They both broke into giggles. I waited until they were done laughing. "Well?"

"Well," Woody shrugged and continued, "It's like this. Rie will play herself. Robert Redford will play me. Shirley Jones will play Aunt Sunny and…" They glanced at each other and both broke into uncontrollable laughter.

"Well?" I interjected. "I suppose you have someone picked out for me." That sent them in hysterics again. "Who do you have picked out to play me?"

Woody's eyes danced with merriment. He placed his hands on my shoulder and smiled. "Well, Mom, after much thought we decided we're going to cast you as the oldest, chunkiest nun in the hospital." He put his arms around me drawing me closer and continued to snicker.

"Yeah, right." I slapped at his arm. "Thanks a lot you two. I was thinking more in the line of Elizabeth Taylor." Needless to say, that sent them into peels of louder laughter. I too started to laugh. It felt good…really good. I thanked God silently that we could laugh. It seemed like it had been so long since we could share laughter. I would gladly have welcomed anyone of the beautiful nuns to play me.

At that precise moment, a smiling Father Flynn walked up and said crisply, "Praise the Lord. Laughter is good for the soul."

Like naughty children caught doing something bad, we all jumped to attention. We happily greeted the cheerful priest.

Father Flynn stood with his feet apart, a neat, slender, fatherly figure dressed in black, with an intelligent face that literally beamed with love. "I've heard about Sunny Marie. It's wonderful to see you all laugh." His eyes veered around until they rested for a moment on each of us. "So now tell me, what were the three of you laughing about before I so rudely interrupted?"

At his request, our mouths dropped open. We stood speechless. Finally, we smiled back shyly. "Oh, Father, we have so much to be happy for today," Sunny replied.

"God is good," he said. "I'll be back later to have a prayer with the family." Patting Sunny on her shoulder, he left.

It was true that we had so much to laugh about but we didn't tell Father Flynn why we were laughing at that moment. As the priest walked down the hall, I caught Woody sizing him up. Just from the glint in Woody's eyes, I knew he had already decided what movie star would play Father Flynn's part.

LIFE FORCE

God, you are the sunshine that warms my face in the early morning, waking me up to reality from a shadowed night of life.

THE BEGINNING

I have waited all my life to see You.

I know, in my heart, my soul that You have given me everything I needed on this earth.

And when I die, because of Your promise, Jesus, my life will just begin.

CHAPTER 26

The nuns constantly gave us love and care. We tried thanking them, but they informed us how blessed they felt because the Lord sent Rie to them. They claimed her courage and love for God had reaffirmed their faith. It was amazing how Rie responded to them.

Once, two nuns leaned over Rie's bed and in their soft Gaelic accent whispered, "Ah, Sunny Marie, do you know what we call you?" Rie's eyes widened as she waited to hear. "Saint Sunny Marie," they said in unison. Sunny and I glanced at each other. The words were familiar.

Dr. Milan asked us to start Rie writing with a pencil and pad. He needed to know how her brain was functioning and how well her reflexes were responding.

Rie's unsteady hands worked especially hard trying to form letters of the alphabet and numbers. At first, her work resembled the printing of a child in kindergarten. Three letters would take up a whole page. She used large pencils she could grip in her hand. In striving so hard to master the skill she became frustrated with the end results. She couldn't understand why her arms and brain weren't working like they should. The doctor warned us that because of the trauma to the brain, Rie's memory might be restricted and she could be suffering from short-term memory loss.

It was as if her brain erased the operation from her memory. Every time she would wake-up from a nap, she would demand to know where she was. The reason for being at the hospital always eluded her. Patiently Sunny recited to Rie why she was in the hospital and the reason she couldn't talk above a whisper. It was to become a ritual and varied on how many naps Rie took. During this time, Rie always knew the nurses, nuns, doctors, and her family, but there were times when Rie was unable to recognize her boyfriend.

Every time Sunny finished explaining to Rie why she was in the hospital, Rie would gently pat her mother's hand and whisper, "I'm so sorry you've been through so much pain." It was as if Rie believed we were talking about someone other than herself. We had a hard time keeping it together during these times. This fragile child was more sorry for us than herself. So like our Rie.

The day came when Rie became impatient with writing numbers and alphabets. In no uncertain terms, she told us she had more important things to write to us. We all scrambled for her pencil and paper. Rie was using magic markers because she could pick the colors she liked best. Very diligently she chose green. We looked on with baited breath. With more control than she showed previously, she wrote in large letters her first whole sentence. Sprawling across the entire page, it read. This uneven universe is not as pretty as it was in a place. She lay back on the bed in complete ease. Her message had been given and received. But after reading her words, we were all struck with wonderment.

"Are you saying you visited someplace while you were in a coma?" I asked. She nodded yes. "Were you out in the universe?"

She concentrated, her face deep in thought, then she nodded, no. She waved her hand over her head as if to say farther back. "Beyond the universe?" I questioned.

Her face beamed. Excitedly, she nodded her head yes. "I understand," I replied. "You saw this whole universe because you were beyond it."

Her little face became thoughtful, turning inward. Then she met my eyes. Her lovely eyes became soft and all knowing. Then she nodded her head yes again.

"Oh, baby, I wish we could have joined you." She stared at me for a long time without saying anything, I had the feeling that it wasn't meant to be and she knew it. Already she had revealed too much.

Sometimes she would write the word Toby in bold lettering. Sometimes it would be Sunny Marie and Toby or Sunny plus Toby. To our knowledge, none of the family had ever known anyone with the first or last name Toby. Her mother pointed to the name on the paper and asked, "Who's Toby?"

Rie's eyes softened and a gentle expression passed over her face. "I love Toby," she whispered and pointed to the page.

"But I thought you loved Doug?"

"I love Toby," she answered.

"But where did you meet Toby?" Sunny asked.

"In a place beyond," she confirmed in a louder whisper. "No more questions...okay." She never told us exactly where she met Toby, but we always had the feeling it was beyond this uneven universe.

Her writing reminded me of one of her poems.

> Leaving this plane far behind me, I travel.
> Ethereal of astral substance, I fly as an angel
> seeking the heaven from which I came.
> Mighty God in His glory fashioned the earth below me,
> And I, above the mother spheroid, see its beauty from his view.
> The stars glisten in cosmic dew and the darkness around me
> is untouchable.
> I am immersed in its softness.
> Yet light, too, is visible.
> From God's view there is both, always, together.

One day after a nap Rie expressed her desire to do more writing. With pen in hand, she scribbled. Someone else's friend came to see me today. Her name was Ruth. We were bewildered. Again no one knew anyone named Ruth. Sunny asked who Ruth was. Thinking it was someone from the hospital, Sunny described the nurses, the nuns, and the physical therapists but an annoyed Rie would point down to the sentence and underline the words, someone else's friend.

Finally losing patience with us, Rie replied in a very loud whisper, "You know. Naomi's friend Ruth."

Sunny stared in astonishment at her daughter and replied, "Naomi's friend? Ruth from the Bible?" Rie smiled, pleased that we finally understood. She hurriedly nodded her head yes. Sunny caught her breath. Finally she said, "You amaze me. How wonderful to have such special friends." Of course, how stupid we were, God was still watching over her.

Rie didn't like to use her whispered voice. She made it plain to all of us that she didn't like the way it sounded. By now her writing was improving. Daily, she would write love letters to all of us, starting with Dear Mom or Dear Aunt Margie or whoever was in the room she wanted to communicate with. Most of the time the letters told us how much she loved us and in turn, we wrote letters back to her so she could practice reading.

The doctors were still confused, but one thing they did agree on, Rie was alive and improving. They decided on physical therapy. Like her brain, Rie's body had to be taught lessons.

She was sent down twice a day for therapy. She had to learn to walk. The physical therapist took high top track shoes and constructed metal braces that fit inside to help straighten her feet. During the coma her feet had developed a bad arch making it impossible for her to stand flatfooted. Without the shoes she stood on her toes and would lose her balance.

We worked night and day on those little feet, her mother on one side of the bed and I on the other. We braced her feet against the inside of our elbows, rocking back and forth pressing the foot straighter, making the frozen bones move. It was an exhausting process for all of us, but Rie endured the greater pain. She never complained, determined to walk at any cost. It was so funny to everyone that came to visit, seeing our fragile Rie lying in bed with high-top track shoes and wearing a frilly nightgown. Rie loved her shoes and showed them off to everyone.

On one occasion, Sunny told Rie about a girl who overcame untold obstacles to become an Olympic Gold Medallist. She announced, "Rie, you'll be able to do the same thing. When you get well, we'll send you to the Olympics and you can win a gold medal too."

We all laughed knowing that Sunny was only trying to cheer Rie up.

In a state of aggravation, Rie immediately pointed to her pen and paper. She scrawled hurriedly, Dear Aunt Margie, Please don't let them send Sunny Marie to the Olympics, OK?

I received the message loud and clear and wrote back in large letters. You got it kid. Then I assured her verbally, "I'll fight until death to keep it from happening. From now own, you'll make all the decision concerning your life." She nodded, with a very pleased expression, on her face and agreed that was the best idea.

Everything seemed to be progressing slowly, ever so slowly but surely. We refused to make Rie feel as though she was an invalid. We changed her white hospital sheets to flowered ones from home. Her gowns were changed to brightly colored, oversized tee shirts with happy caption on the front. We placed poster on the walls of beautiful places with biblical quotes. One poster in particular read, Be patient, God isn't finished with me yet. We did everything to make the dull stay at the hospital positive and bearable.

With time, the rigors of Rie's body subsided. She became more like our Rie. One thing that had not changed was the many visitors that came. Even the waiting rooms down the hall were overflowing with visitors waiting their turn to see, touch, and speak to God's little miracle child.

One day, Sunny, Phil, and I were walking to the hospital from the parking lot when we heard someone shout. We stopped and looked around. Running toward us, a suited man was literally pulling a well-dressed woman by her arm. No sooner than they came to a stop in front of us, the man quickly introduced himself as one of the team of doctors who was working on Sunny Marie. In a breathless voice, he said, "Mr. and Mrs. Eppler, I hope you don't mind but I wanted my wife to meet the parents of our miracle girl." The woman grabbed my sister's hand and replied, "Oh, I've heard so much about you and your lovely daughter. It's a pleasure to meet you."

We thanked the couple and assured them that it was indeed our pleasure to meet both of them. As we continued walking to the hospital, Sunny said under her breath, "Sunny Marie is making celebrities out of all of us."

I assured her we could handle it. Little did I realize that this was to become a common occurrence? Sometimes in the elevator, cafeteria, and in the hallways of the hospital strangers would recognize us and ask about Rie. We had people visiting because their neighbor was Sunny Marie's nurse or they had friends or relatives in the hospital that told them about Rie. A lot of people heard about Rie through their church. Sometimes whole adult Sunday school classes would come. Kids from school, friends, and family were an everyday occurrence, but the strangers that came daily were mind-boggling.

We had a real American Indian that came with Bible and a bottle of oil in hand to anoint Rie. A Moslem placed his Koran under her pillow. Jewish, Catholic, Protestant, and people that had never accepted any religion, but wanted to experience God's miracle, flocked to Rie's bedside. There were some that literally couldn't walk through the door as if they were kept out by some unseen force. God's love was working. You could see it, feel it, and most of all, be part of it.

Rie seemed to enjoy everyone, but it was hard on the rest of us. People wanted to hear Rie's story. We were constantly telling it until our throats were raw and our nerves were ragged. It wasn't unusual for us to literally lose our voice. If Sunny was telling the story, Phil would then take over, when he could no longer repeat Rie's story, I would tell it. There were always new faces needing to hear. At one point, we had to place a sign on the door to limit the number of visitors. When that failed, we placed a sign for family members only. Needless to say, that also failed. People were determined to visit. Rie loved seeing the people. Finally, we just accepted it.

As Rie became more aware of everything around her, she decided that she had enough of the IV and catheter, and proceeded to remove them, herself. When the nurses wanted to replace them, Rie refused. We made her promise to eat or the IV would be put back in her arm.

We had to battle food down her constantly, but at last she started eating. She now weighed around 60 pounds.

The doctors decided since Rie appeared to be improving, they would start cobalt radiation treatments. They were still working in the dark concerning her condition and didn't really know what effect this was going to have on the cancer in her brain. Oh, yes. The cancer was still there. The operation had not been a cure. They told us because of the extreme dosage of radiation Rie's hair would never grow back again. Everyday for six weeks Rie had a cobalt treatment. The thought of radiation going into that little brain was frightening. It's funny how experts come out of the woodwork. I watched family members and close friends advise Sunny and Phil not to put Rie through such an ordeal. Sunny would listen patiently to them. Quietly she would say, "We've come this far with God, we'll continue on until he tells us differently." The people would look over at me as if I could do something to change my sister's mind, but when I just smiled at them they became quiet. Again we put our faith in the Lord.

When the doctors told us Rie's hair would never grow back, Johnny took Sunny shopping. A few hours later, they came back with a beautiful, long red wig. It looked exactly like Rie's hair. Johnny and Sunny had also come back with a bag of toys. Children's blocks, dart guns, and coloring books, everything for Rie to keep her from getting bored.

When it was time for Johnny to return to Indonesia, Rie became depressed. Neither Rie nor I were ready to see him go.

When Johnny said his last good-bye, he kept crying and couldn't tell her what was in his heart. He lovingly took her pen and paper. He wrote, "Dear Little Rie. Uncle Johnny has to leave tomorrow, but my prayers and thoughts will be with you all the time. I want you to know that we all love you very much. Please say a special prayer for me because when I first got here I asked the Lord for a favor. I told him that I would try to be a better man if he would make you better and he has. Now I need all the help I can get. Love you, Uncle Johnny.

She wrote back, "Dear Uncle Johnny. "You are a good man. I love you." Johnny folded her letter and put it into his shirt pocket over his heart.

We all cried as they hugged and kissed. Johnny wanted to stay but once more he would have to rely on the phone calls and letters to keep him informed.

With the catheter out, Sunny and I had to sit Rie on the bedpan. All Rie had to do was raise one finger and we would usher everyone out and place her on the gold-colored pan. It was a simple task; anyone could do it…right. WRONG! Because of Rie's drastic weight loss she fell into the pan becoming wedged. She was stuck…literally.

Not only was she stuck, but also at the same time, she began to slide off the bed. Muttering under her breath, Sunny climbed onto the bed with Rie and placed her hands under Rie's armpits trying to pull her out. When that didn't work, Sunny shouted, "Do something? Pull, Margie!"

I was leaning over Rie trying to pull her hips loose. I yelled back, "I'm pulling, I'm pulling. Now you lift her higher and push. PUSH!"

"Push what?" Sunny cried.

"I don't know, just push." Before long we were shouting at each other. "Push! Pull!" Rie patiently let us slide her one way, then the other. We were working so hard that perspiration beads were forming over our lips and on our forehead.

While we were pushing and pulling the sheet were slowly sliding off the side of the bed. The situation became so ludicrous; we became hysterical with laughter.

We made so much noise that the head nurse came running in shouting, "What in heaven's name is happening in here?" There we were caught. Sunny was standing in the middle of the bed bending over Rie, who was now sprawled halfway off the bed, straddling me. I was lying on the floor under the entire bed clothing. Only my face was visible. Rie was still stuck in the bedpan.

The poor nurse just stood there in total shock. By the stunned expression on her face, we weren't sure if she wanted to laugh or cry. We were doing both. To our humiliation, several other nurses and nuns came running in. They just stood in the doorway watching us with concerned expressions on their faces. Sunny and I had nowhere to run or any hole to hide in. All at once, we heard a strange sound. All our gazes turned toward Rie. Wonders of wonders, Rie was laughing out loud. It was the first time since the operation that we heard her beautiful laugh. We all joined in.

The head nurse found us a smaller bedpan used for children and made us promise to use powder on the surface before we sat Rie on it. The nurses already knew our reputation as spastic nurses. They decided our motto should be, we either cure or kill.

Rie never once had a bed-sore. My job was to lather her down with lotion three times a day and massage her back and hips. I refused to let that little body get one pressure sore. But medicine was another thing entirely. The medication given to her to control the seizures caused her skin to break out in terrible hives. We fought that daily with plain cornstarch thought of by one of the nurses that worked in pediatrics. We went through a case of the stuff.

All the nuns of the hospital would take turns visiting. We knew all their names and loved each one. But one day a nun came by to visit that we had not seen before. She only stood just outside the door peeking around the corner. Most of the nuns were friendly and would come in and talk. But this particular one only looked in briefly. When we invited her in she hurriedly left without saying a word. We couldn't understand what her problem was. One day I was placing Rie in the wheelchair to take her down to therapy and the feet supports weren't adjusted in the right position. When I released them, they fell off with a loud clang. Before I could pick them up a gruff voice said, "Now you've done it. You've broken the chair." Startled, I looked up. A very stern expression greeted me from the aging face of this illusive nun. I apologized profusely, completely intimidated by this lady. She took off down the hallway. I had the feeling she was going to tell someone in authority and have me kicked out of the hospital.

A few hours later I was to eat my words. The same little nun came back bringing a little basket of silk violets. She came to the door and asked, "If you're through breaking the machines, I would like to see my baby, now?"

At first I wasn't sure who she meant but I was positive the flowers weren't meant for me. She was looking past me to Rie. She walked over to Rie and engulfed her in a hug and crooned over her. She turned to me with tears sliding down her aging cheeks and informed me that this was her baby.

Later we found out that she was the oldest nun at the hospital. She would soon leave her duties at the hospital for retirement to the Mother House. She visited everyday. We loved her as dearly as the rest of the lovely nuns there. That's the way it was at St. Patrick's hospital. Everyone that came into contact with Rie became a part of our inner circle of love. Our family grew and our love expanded.

There were days when Sunny would go shopping and come back with armloads of packages (we were constantly in need of something from the outside world). She would automatically dump the bags on the nearest open spot.

On this particular day it just happened to be on the desk. Now that wouldn't have been so bad except for the fact that the desk now belonged to Rie. We told her it was hers and she used it to display all her religious gifts. There were crosses of all kinds, Holy Water Bottles,

Bibles, and pictures of Jesus. When she saw that her mother had unloaded the packages on her desk she became very agitated and hastily scribbled a letter. Dear Mom, "Please do not mess up my Jesus corner again." Sunny murmured a fast, "I'm sorry." Then Sunny and I proceeded stacking the packages in a corner. After the area was cleared, Rie smiled sweetly and whispered, "Now, that's better."

Rie was getting better. For the first time she was conscious of her environment. It was another step to normalcy.

Sunny and I stayed every night with Rie. I slept on a sofa that made into a bed while Sunny slept with Rie cuddled in her arms on the hospital bed.

Outside the days changed from dreary to sunny. Spring was just right around the corner. Rie seemed to be free of headaches and time seemed to be working to her benefit. As she grew stronger, we became more confident of our future.

Dave and Marilyn were visiting one day while Sunny was making up the bed. She was having a hard time moving Rie from side to side. Rie was still bedridden.

Dave was standing watching and listening to the grunts and groans of Sunny as she moved her daughter. Without a word, Dave scooped Rie up into his arms. He sat holding her while her mother finished the job. Rie's eyes became enlarged and she reached over squeezing his arm. "Uncle Dave, I'm impressed," she whispered. Uncle Dave kissed her cheek and laughed. "Me too."

That same day we took our Rie down to the hospital cafeteria for the first time. Dave pushed Rie's wheelchair to the table and asked her what she wanted to eat. Rie concentrated very hard and then whispered, "I want a fudge ice cream bar."

"You have fudge bars every day," Sunny declared.

"I know." Rie smiled. "I want another one now before I starve."

Sunny explained to Rie that the hospital cafeteria was noted for their good Cajun cuisine and if she didn't like that she could have a number of other things she liked.

With elbows on the table, Rie placed her long fingers under her chin, listening to her mother rattle off all the food that was displayed. Rie tapped her fingers against her chin as if she was in deep concentration. "Do they have hamburgers?"

"Yes," Sunny replied, "and hot dogs."

"Wonderful," she licked her lips. Then she said, "I'll have…" she hesitated and looked over at me and grinned. "I'll have a fudge ice cream bar." She was back to her teasing self. I threw up my arms and cried; "Now why didn't I think of that. Dave, please get Miss Rie a fudge ice cream bar before she starves."

Before we were finished with our meal, Rie had finished several ice cream bars. As we were eating, people passed our table calling to Rie by name and saying hello to her. She would smile, waving her hand at them. Finally, Rie glanced over at her mother and asked softly, "Do I know these people?"

Sunny laughed. "No, Rie, but they know you."

Several days later, Ron, Marilyn's youngest son, came to the hospital to visit Rie. He had one of his college friends, Moose, with him. Both young men were tall and well built. They sat around Rie's bed telling her about college and the beautiful weather outside. Moose asked Sunny if she noticed the Azaleas blooming outside the hospital. Sunny said she hadn't been out for a while.

Moose asked, "Could we carry Rie outside and show her the

blooming flowers?" Sunny hesitated. Rie hadn't been out of the hospital since before her coma. Sunny asked Rie, "Do you want to go outside and see the flowers?"

Rie clapped her hands. Her face beamed. It was settled. Placing Rie in a wheelchair, Ron and Moose took Rie around the outside of the hospital showing her the beautiful sights of flowers, butterflies and birds. Rie's face was glowing. Ron managed to pick a whole bouquet of different colored Azaleas without anyone seeing him do it. I'm not sure the hospital would have approved of their flowers being picked, to our surprise Rie didn't either. Rie's little arms were full and she appeared happy. Ron and Moose took turns waltzing her and the wheelchair around the parking lot. She beamed her pleasure at their antics. People stopped what they were doing and stared.

Wearing pink blooms behind their ears, Moose and Ron rolled Rie back through the halls of the hospital. Nurses and nuns asked Rie where she managed to get so many flowers. She just smiled lovingly up at Ron and Moose and pointed her finger at them. The young men managed to wear the most innocent expression on their faces.

Before leaving, Moose asked, "Will Rie get better?"

"She's showing improvement everyday," I said. After giving Rie a kiss good-bye, big Moose wiped hurriedly at his eyes.

The day finally came to bring Rie home. It was the end of March and the time of year for Miracles. Spring was everywhere one looked; flowers, butterflies, and chirping birds. It was God's promise of new life.

The day we were to leave the hospital, Rie wrote on her pad. I know a spirit named Whitney Boak. Sunny looked at the writing not sure what Rie was saying and asked, "Who is Whitney Boak?" Rie underlined the word spirit. Then she wrote the name Toby and Whitney Boak together. Sunny asked, "Are these people...I mean spirits from the other side?" Rie's face broke out in a soft smile and she wrote on one page in large letters the word, YES.

I hugged her in my arms and said, "Oh, Rie, you're so lucky. You know people on both sides." The smile she gave me was so knowing...so sincere. I truly believed that she really did have friends on both sides. I do know that when she had trouble remembering other people she always remembered who Toby and Whitney Boak were. They were beloved entities that were always with her.

Moments before we left the hospital, we received a phone call from our local newspaper in Orange asking Sunny if it would be all right if they took pictures of her house and could she tell them about the signs on the highway. Sunny looked at me questioningly and asked, "Do you know about signs on the highway?" I confirmed it was the first I had heard of it. She then proceeded to tell the reporter she didn't know what he was talking about. He laughed and said, "If you really don't know then I'm not going to be the one to tell you. But I will tell you this Mrs. Eppler, you're in for a big surprise."

Thanks to Rie's many friends…we were indeed. The day we left the hospital was a shimmering sunshiny day. Wild flowers were blooming on the sides of the road. It was a beautiful day to go home.

Our surprise started at the bridge leading out of Lake Charles. For forty miles, colorful large poster signs were stuck in the ground every mile welcoming Rie back home. Signs that read: Glad to have you back. We love you and miss you. Follow the yellow brick road…to home. Welcome from all of us who love you.

Even at the state line, taped to the giant granite outline of Texas was a sign that read; Welcome to Texas…Home of Sunny Marie Eppler. Phil pulled up in front of the sign and showed Rie. We all applauded loudly at the nerve of the kid that thought of covering the state of Texas.

As we turned into our street, traffic was stacked up. We proceeded slowly down the street wondering why traffic was so slow. Then we saw the reason.

People were looking at Rie's house. The house, yard, and trees were completely decorated with long tailing lengths of white toilet paper gracefully blowing in the spring breeze. Large hand-painted poster signs stood over the yard proclaiming this the home of Sunny Marie. Bright, yellow ribbon bows adorned the trees like blooming flowers. Thousands of yellow bows were tied on every limb of the trees all the way to the top, a feat that impressed us all. We stood in silence, completely in awe at our surroundings.

A man yelled from his passing car, "Hey, what's going on?" I shouted back, "A miracle!"

He honked his horn and shouted, "Praise the Lord!" Bouquets of flowers lined both sides of the porch and hundred of cards were stuck in the door, an overload from the full mailbox. Inside there was food to feed an army.

Rie kept wanting to know why anyone would decorate her house. I told her, "All that you see was done with love. It's for you."

"For me?" she mouthed the words. "Yeah." I poked Rie in her chest and replied, "Just for you." That seemed to please her.

Picking Rie up in his strong arms, Phil carried her around the yard. Her face was flushed from the sun and she waved a yellow ribbon in her fingers whispering loudly, "Just for me." Actually Rie's miracle was not just for us, but also, for all of the beautiful people that came in contact with her. God knows that we all need a miracle from time to time. Thanks to Mother, Daddy, Johnny, Dedo, Derek, and Philip, Rie's room was assembled once again. They worked from photographs so posters on the wall, belongings on her dresser and desk would be in their original place. The only thing different was the wall color, curtains, bedspread, and sheets.

Mother and Daddy were afraid Rie would have bad memories of her illness if things weren't changed a little. They painted the room an off white and hung soft blue curtains. The canopy was discarded, the tall posters taken down. Now light could filter into the room from the double windows. A blue-flowered bedspread and sheets with a nature scene covered the bed. The whole effect gave the illusion of springtime.

Philip was the one responsible for hanging Rie's clothes in her two closets. He remembered which closet held which clothes. All were there except her fake fur coat. That had never been found.

Rie had no knowledge that her room had been dismantled or how long she had been away…time meant nothing in that complex little brain of hers. When Rie entered her room she immediately noticed the color of her walls had been changed and asked softly, "Who painted my room?"

Mother hurriedly explained she was the one to make the changes. Daddy explained he was the one to take down her tall posts and canopy.

Rie gave a slow nod of her head. She walked slowly around her room touching her things. She touched the curtains and looked out the window. Very gently she ran her fingers over the bedspread and then over the sheets. For a moment her fingers followed the design of the yellow rose on the silk pillows. Then she held them up to her nose.

"Hmmm. Everything smells new," she whispered.

Mother and Daddy hovered just inside the door. They appeared nervous as they waited for Rie's approval. It was a small thing they did for Rie, but I knew it had been a labor of love.

Rie stood in the middle of her room and took her time contemplating the changes. Finally she said, "I like blue. It looks soft and comfortable. It's beautiful." She smiled brightly. "Thanks Mawmaw and Pawpaw, you did good."

Their faces beamed with her praise. It had been one and a half months since the day Rie left her home to go to the hospital, but to us it had been a lifetime. We had grown so much older.

NO TRESPASSING!

The Jack-in-the-box shivers under the lid.
Toy tin solders are cleverly hid.
All small trinkets are high on the self.
Bright-eyed piggy banks conceal their wealth.
The bed is made, the pillows are fluffed.
The little red donkey is newly restuffed.
The bouncing balls are put in a box,
And into drawers have gone hankies and socks.
The floor is swept, the books are straight.
The mother is finished, but dinner is late.
The child runs in and shakes his head.
He throws around his toys and unmakes the bed.

This uneven universe
is not as pretty as
it was in a place

(Rie's first writing
after coming out of coma)

Pawpaw   Rie   Mawmaw

First Day Home From Hospital

CHAPTER 27

It was a time for rejoicing. That night we had a special gathering of all the family members, which seemed to please Rie. We joined hands in a circle of love and said the Lord's Prayer. The voice that rose above all the rest was unbelievable. It was Rie's. That was the only time since the surgery we heard her speak aloud and the last time.

What made this meeting so unique was the fact that we had never prayed aloud in unison as a family…it felt good. We were in God's company.

A few days later, Sunny had to go to the store and I was baby setting Rie when a long black Limousine pulled up in the drive. I went to the door and young African-American man dressed in a black tuxedo met me at the door. He introduced himself, as Joe Brown, a friend of Rie's from school. She recognized him immediately.

"Rie, I didn't know you were ill until just a few hours ago when I was talking with one of our school mates," he said hugging her tightly. "I'm on my way to the airport to fly to Hollywood." His young face beamed with pride. "I'm an actor now." Rie's eyes widened with surprise.

"Oh, that's wonderful," She whispered.

"I've signed a contract with a studio." His face took on a serious expression. "But that's not the reason I'm here." He shook his head and smiled into her eyes. "I wanted to see you before I left and wish you a speedy recovery."

"Thank you," she mouthed. He hugged her to him and she squeezed him just as tightly back. His voice became thick with emotion. "I'll keep in touch." He took her out stretched hand in his and she whispered, "Thank you for coming and good luck to you in Hollywood."

"You bet," he replied. He turned to me and said, "I couldn't leave town without seeing Sunny Marie. Of all the people I know I can't believe this has happened to her. Tell Mrs. Eppler I'll call." And he did throughout Rie's illness.

The next day a local television station called and wanted to do a feature on Orange's very own miracle. We didn't want to expose Rie unless she approved. We told her about the station wanting to do the interview. She sat as though deep in thought for along time and then she gave her approval. We placed the wig on her head. She took it off. "Don't want it," she replied. "I want to be me." And she was. She appeared before the camera without it, in the wheelchair and smiling sweetly in spite of her little mouth covered with cold sores. She waved at the camera and whispered, "I love everyone watching."

After the story ran, there wasn't anywhere we could go that people didn't stop us to say that they had seen Rie on television. We were told how her appearance on TV affected their lives.

Our days passed with us visiting Mother and Daddy twice a day. We entertained friends coming to visit. At night Rie, Sunny, Philip, Derek, and I would sit around watching television. On one such night, Rie decided she wanted to go to bed early. Because of Phil working shift work, Rie was sleeping with her mother in the king-size bed.

We tucked Rie under the covers and Sunny and I lay across the bed talking girl talk. Rie listened quietly. Sunny asked me, "Have I ever showed you the nightgown Phil bought me last year?" Phil was always buying Sunny pretty things, but I couldn't remember Sunny showing me a nightgown. "No," I said. I glanced over at Rie and asked, "Have you seen it?" Rie shook her head no.

"Sunny, why haven't you showed it to Rie?" Sunny's eyes began to crinkle at the corners and her lips twitched, "It's not that kind of nightgown."

Rie and I looked at each other and I saw Rie's eyebrow rise up.

Sunny was busy rummaging through her dresser drawer. She turned quickly holding something behind her. She reminded me of a child about to burst with a secret.

"Well? Are you going to show it to us?"

Sunny's face became serious. "First you have to promise, cross your heart and never tell anyone," her voice became low and secretive and she placed her finger to her lips, "and never let Phil know I showed you."

Her eyes looked first at me and keeping with the game we were playing, I made a cross over my heart. Then she looked at Rie and very seriously, Rie made a cross over her heart. Then Rie broke us up by making a motion with her fingers of zipping her lips together. Her lips were sealed. We were three naughty children again.

Sunny quickly disappeared into the bathroom behind a locked door. Again I gazed over at Rie and this time Rie wiggled her eyebrows at me.

I'm not sure what possessed Sunny. I'm not even sure that I want to know what possessed my sister to cause her to act the way she did. It was just one of those crazy things. She's like that. One moment she can be very serious and mature and the next she can do something totally out of character.

Before Rie and I knew what was happening, Sunny ran out of the bathroom, jumped on the end of the bed feet first. There she stood dressed in a see-through, red lace, full-length nightgown with tiny panties underneath. Tiny black ribbons that went down the sides tied the front and back of the garment together. The gown and panties were shocking enough, but what made it more so, was the fact that it was worn over Sunny's yellow sweat shirt, blue faded jeans, and dirty jogging shoes with bright pink socks. It was an absolutely hilarious exhibition. "Well?" Sunny eyed both of us. The full effect was staggering.

"What do you think?" Rie and I were still in shock. Speechless to be exact. I cleared my throat. "Phil bought you that?"

It came out in a mumble. "Yep, for my birthday."

I started to giggle. "I can't believe Phil bought you that."

"Daddy did?" Rie questioned in disbelief. "Oh, no!"

"Believe me, when I opened the box, I couldn't believe it. I've always worn pajamas since the kids were big enough to notice what I wore to bed. Until this very moment, I've never had the nerve to show it to anyone." She made a sudden turn, flipping the back panel up, she turned upside down mooning us, but to our relief all we saw was the back end of her faded jeans. She straightened up and smiled. "You two are the first."

"Thank God for small favors," I replied.

As if on cue, one of the boys began playing his stereo in another room. A loud thumping drumbeat filled the air. Sunny began rotating her hips and rolling her head around and fluffing up her long hair in a bad impression of a striptease artist. One by one, seductively she untied the tiny ribbons, Rie backed up as far as she could giving her mother all the room she needed to make a fool out of herself. We watched in complete horror.

"Oh, my goodness, I didn't know you had it in you," I drawled.

Rie clapped her hands with the music and whispered, "Go Mom, go!"

When Sunny stomped around the bed dancing, Rie and I rolled with laughter until we were actually crying. Our loud commotion brought both boys to the door. Philip and Derek stood silently watching; their mouths had dropped open. Both little faces were perplexed.

"Mom? What are you doing?" Philip demanded.

Sunny came to a complete halt and looked over her shoulder and said, "What does it look like I'm doing?" He shrugged. It was clear that from the expression on his young face, he hadn't a clue. "Well, I'm dancing." She said it as if it was the most natural thing in the world for her to be standing in the middle of the bed dressed in a red lace nightgown over her jeans. That sent Rie and I into harder peals of laughter.

"But, Mom," Derek said, "Why?"

I had the feeling both boys thought their mother had completely lost it. I was wondering myself, but one look at Rie's face I knew everything Sunny was doing was for her. Rie was staring up at her mother with tears of laughter pouring down her radiant face. She had the most adoring expression.

Sunny smiled at the boys and announced, "Either sit down and enjoy the show or leave." Both boys hurriedly left. It was more than they could take. The show continued until we couldn't laugh any longer.

Much later, when we lay on both sides of Rie while she slept, Sunny squeezed my hand and said, "It was good to hear Rie laugh, wasn't it?"

"Very good," I murmured squeezing her hand back. "I think the picture of her laughing at you dancing will remain in my heart forever."

Just the memory of Sunny dancing brought laughter bubbling up until it spilled out. "All kidding aside, did Phil really buy that gown for you?"

Sunny playfully slapped my hand away. "You doubt my husband is romantic?"

"No," I giggled. "I just assumed he had better taste than that."

"Normally he does, but the girls at my work talked him into buying it for me as a joke."

"Oh, thank God," I said laughingly. "I was beginning to wonder about Phil." We laughed and talked late into the night. It was good to hear my sister laugh. It was a precious time God let us share.

Days passed without us really knowing or caring what day it was. Doug came less and less to see Rie. Word was filtering back through Rie's friends that Doug was seeing another girl. Rie didn't seem to be upset by this but showed a sort of relief that maybe Doug could find comfort somewhere else.

"That's good," she said, "Mom, I need to free him. He's not strong enough to walk this walk with me. I have so much to do and not enough time to do it."

She took off her beautiful promise ring and handed it to her mother and replied, "Give it to Doug." What could we say…what could we do? This was her choice.

Sunny stared at the ring in her hand and then at her daughter. She asked, "Are you sure this is what you want?" Rie met her mother's eyes. They weren't sad eyes just very direct and determined.

"Yes, it's what I want. When you give him the ring, tell him I love him and will always love him." She turned over and fell asleep.

Sunny called Doug and asked him to come over. When he came over I stayed in Rie's room while she slept. I could hear Sunny repeating Sunny Marie's words to Doug. I could hear the tears in her voice and the angry slam of the front door. It was the last time Doug came by or called.

Sunny broke down in tears after Doug left. I put my arms around her while she cried. "Margie, that was so hard," she sobbed softly. "He didn't understand. How could I explain Rie's thoughts…when we don't fully understand them ourselves?"

"Honey, you had to do what Rie wanted."

"They talked about marriage for so long. I watched his dreams crumble with every word I said."

"They were Rie's dreams too, but now there has to be room for different dreams. Rie told us she has work to do."

"Work? What is she talking about?"

"Only she knows what she has to do." I shrugged. "Whatever the reason, she needs to be free. We have to respect her wishes." Things would become clearer as days progressed. Rie continued talking to us in whispers. Her writing became more intelligible, sometimes she would write whole pages. We were amazed at some of the things she would write us.

One time, she wrote, "Are you happy to have me back?" We assured her over and over that we were indeed happy to have her back. She wrote, "I tried everything I knew to get back but you have to take me the way that I am."

Little did she know we would have taken her on any terms? One day, I asked her if she was going to go back to school. She replied no. When I question her about her answer, she wrote, "I wouldn't fit in any longer. I'm much too old to go back to school now." In my heart I agreed with her. She was old beyond her years. Rie was like a Barbie doll to dress. Her mother made sure she was dressed each day in the latest fashion so she could greet her friends from school. When she wasn't wearing the wig, I would tie a matching scarf around her head. We placed sassy little hats on her head with matching earrings. She was beginning to look like the old Rie.

One day after dressing her in stonewashed jeans and plaid shirt and vest, Sunny rolled Rie in her wheelchair in front of the TV to watch her favorite show. We walked into the kitchen to pour a cup of coffee. When we walked back into the living room, Rie was out of the wheelchair and standing in front of the television set turning channels.

Shocked and not realizing what she was saying, Sunny screamed out, "Rie, what are you doing. You can't walk!"

Rie turned a startled face to her mother. Her long thin legs buckled underneath her and with a loud plop, she sat down immediately on the floor and said, "Oh, I forgot." Then we all sat in the middle of the floor rocking with laughter and rejoicing because this was the first time Rie had walked by herself.

Laughter filled the house. That was a turning point for Rie. She began walking unaided.

At the beginning of May, a cat scan was taken and the doctors claimed they didn't see any sign of the tumor. Again rejoicing was in order. Sunny's church gave Rie a night for blessings. It was full. We were at our happiest. No more worries. Now we would look forward to the day Rie would be totally well.

Rie was asked by her good friend, John Ennis (the same boy who had split his pants dancing with her) to go to the senior prom. Rie said she would go, but only if her mother and father went with them. Sunny went shopping that same day for a beautiful dress for Rie to wear. Dressed in her long dress and wearing her long red wig, Rie appeared like the Sunny Marie her peers all knew and loved. When Rie and her date arrived at the prom, there were banners with Aloha Sunny Marie, hanging over the walls.

When Sunny and Rie were in the restroom, they overheard two girls talking, "Have you seen Sunny Marie?" One girl asked. The other one replied, "Gosh! She looks great after being in the hospital so long. I thought someone said she lost her hair."

"Evidently it's grown back. It looks the same to me…gorgeous like always."

What the girls didn't know at that precise moment, Sunny and Rie were in the stall next to the mirror. Rie was in the process of pulling off her wig and scratching her bald-head. Sunny told me that later they both had a good laugh after the girls left the restroom because Rie threatened to flush her hair down the toilet.

The fun times were good but then again how would we know about the good times without the bad? There were times when bad seemed to rain down in buckets.

Graduation was only a few days away. Sunny was concerned for Rie to try to walk across the uneven football field. She called the school to ask if it would be all right to have Rie receive her diploma in a wheel-chair. Sunny talked to the school counselor about the possibility of Rie being pushed across the field by Phil. Then she would be able to walk across the outdoor stage and receive her diploma. The counselor said she didn't see a problem with that. She promised to talk to the principal and call right back. The call came several hours later. The counselor told Sunny that the principal didn't want Phil to push Rie onto the field; the young person next in line could do it.

Sunny asked, "Is the person next in line strong?"

"No," the woman said, "It's a girl the size of Rie."

"There's no way a small-sized girl can push that wheelchair in soft grass, besides," Sunny replied, "parents of that child aren't going to enjoy taking pictures of their child pushing a wheelchair. It would be better if her father could push Rie."

"Good point," the lady said. "Let me talk to the principal one more time and I'll call you back."

The call came back immediately. "The principal is not in agreement with that."

I watched Sunny's face turn a beet red. She had to take a breath before she could talk. Finally, she replied, "You just tell your principal that Rie doesn't need her diploma."

Mrs. Eppler," the counselor cried, "please don't take it like this. It really isn't my fault."

"Then whose fault is it?" I could hear the tears in my sister's voice as she explained. "You know after twelve years of having a child that has done everything right in school; an Honor Student, head twirler, member of student government, numerous awards winner for the school, and you tell me that she can't participate in her own graduation because of a wheelchair?

At this point in the conversation, Rie stood up from the rocking chair and walked over to her mother. Taking the phone out of her mother's hand, she hung it up without one word of goodbye. She pulled her mother in her arms and patted her lovingly. "It's all right, Mom," she crooned, "it's only a piece of paper. I don't need it."

Knowing Rie, her school days were important, her learning a joy. At least, they couldn't take what she had been taught away. I wanted to cry out my rage of these unfeeling people. This little family had been through so much and yet they were being dished out more heartache.

The graduation went on without Rie and her family. Somehow the graduating seniors heard about Rie not being able to attend the graduation. They left an empty chair for her and had a special prayer when her name was called to come forward. I'm sure even this didn't set right with the principal. It probably slowed up HIS ceremony.

Nothing more was ever said about Rie's diploma. Sunny never told anyone about the conflict that had occurred, but she never felt the same about the school system again. Rie's diploma was never sent. It was conveniently forgotten.

John Ennis came back to visit but this time it was with bad news. One of Rie's really good friends, J. R., was killed in a car wreck. This was the only boy she had ever dated while she and Doug went together. The occasion was Sadie Hawkin's day and at the last minute Doug was unable to come home from college. Rie called Doug asking him if she could take J. R. in his place. Doug gave her his permission knowing the two were just good friends. Now as Rie was being told of her friend's death, she took the news very calmly.

After John left, Sunny asked Rie, "Honey, are you all right?"

Rie gazed at her mother for a long time and said, "Yes."

"I know you're going to miss, J.R."

"I'll be seeing him soon," Rie replied.

Sunny thought Rie hadn't understood what had happened to her friend and said, "But, honey, you can't, J. R. is dead."

"I know," Rie patted her mother's shoulder. "I'm going to bed for a little while."

"But, Rie, what are you talking about," Sunny cried. When Rie continued to her room without answering her mother turned to me in frustration. "What does she mean, Margie? Rie isn't going to die now. The last test showed that she didn't have a brain tumor anymore. I watched my sister give a great shudder. Then she whispered, "I don't want Rie to ever have to go to the hospital again. I just want all this illness behind us so we can be normal like we use to be."

I couldn't wave a magic wand and make life better for my sister and her family. I couldn't promise all would be better in the coming days. All I could do was comfort my sister and be there for her.

Pawpaw and Phil decided to make life better. They made the decision to tear out the living room wall replacing it with a large patio window so Rie could have a window to the outside world of sunshine and the small hidden garden beyond. She could see the rose bed, butterflies, and watch the birds feed, something she would do for hours.

Sunny, believing Rie was drifting into depression, decided it was time for Rie to start playing the piano again. Rie sat in front of her piano's keyboard, placing her fingers in the right position. She ran her fingers up and down the scale, but no sooner than the notes died, she closed the cover with a loud bang refusing to play another note. Even with all our encouragement, Rie refused to attempt to play her beloved piano again. Sunny knelt beside her daughter. "What's the matter, Rie? Don't you want to play?"

Rie had a sad expression on her face, as she answered, "No Mom, I don't want to play anymore."

"Never?" Sunny questioned. I could hear the distress in her voice.

Rie smiled sadly at her mother. Almost as if apologizing, she touched her mother's face. "I don't have time," she whispered.

Her mother started to say something, but I touched her hand to get her attention. "Sunny, remember the time in the hospital when you told Rie about the girl that became an Olympian and Rie wrote me the letter asking you not to send Sunny Marie to the Olympics. I promised her no one would make her do anything she didn't want to do. I gave Rie my word that her life would be hers to decide."

"I know," Sunny murmured, "but I'm going to miss her playing." Sunny bit down hard on her trembling lip. We all would but it was for Rie to make that decision. Just like Doug, the piano was another closed chapter in Rie's life.

We were kept busy daily as young people came to visit Rie. She would hold court sitting at the dining table writing to her friends. Rie was embarrassed about her voice and asked her mother to please inform her visitors why she was unable to speak in a normal voice. Sunny carried out her wish. It was nothing to see three or four visitors at the table with pens in their hands communicating with Rie by writing. Even though it was silent there was still a lot of laughter and silliness.

On one occasion, Rie's friend, Paul Gautier, came to visit. He found Rie in bed eating her evening meal. Paul was a handsome boy, medium height, dark hair, dancing eyes, and friendly. Not a shy bone in his body. Paul had been in drama with Rie and he had that certain flair. Rie often referred to him as debonair. It wasn't unusual to see Paul walking around the local shopping center wearing a top hat and swinging a cane. Paul made himself comfortable. He climbed up on the end of the bed sitting Indian style and proceeded to tell Rie about their friends at school. He informed Rie he would be going to New York with the Drama department.

Rie took out pen and paper and wrote to Paul, "Dear Paul: From the first moment I met you I knew you would go far. You're the best actor our school has ever seen. I'm proud to call you my friend.

Paul wrote her back. "My Dearest Sunny: I wish that you could know how much I'm going to miss you when I go to New York. I'll be away but you know that I'll really be here with you too. I will be wining and dining with big Broadway stars like John Hancock, he's real good. I must go pack and then fly away to another place but I'll only be gone a short while and then we'll be together again. I know you'll hate to see me go but try to hold back the tears and don't stop eating or hold your breath just because I will be somewhere else. Have a good laugh and a good strong voice when I get back. We'll go out on the town and disco. (Hey, we could ask John Ennis to come. I hear he can really get down.) Love you Elephantly. (That was the biggest thing I could think of) P.S. I'll sneak you the Statue of Liberty back in my luggage."

After Rie read Paul's letter, she laughed. Then Paul said, "I mean it, Sunny Marie. When I get back I want to take you out to a fancy restaurant. What kind of food do you like?" Rie's little face puckered for a moment. You could really tell she was concentrating. Finally her face lit up and she replied by writing, "Why don't we eat here? Can you cook?" Paul responded by standing up in the middle of Rie's bed and giving her a large theatrical bow. "I'm Paul Gautier, the famous Chef of French cuisine. I'll cook you anything your heart desires."

"Rie's face became serious as she studied the young man before her. "Anything?" she replied in a whisper.

"For you Mademoiselle, I'll fix anything you can eat."

Rie tilted her head one way then another while she concentrated. Finally she scrawled across her paper. "Can you fix Campbell's Soup?"

Paul didn't blink an eye, but replied, "But of course. It's my favorite dish. What flavor would you be wanting?"

Rie met his eyes. "How about Vegetable?"

"Wonderful choice, my lady. Vegetable it is as soon as I return from the Big City."

Sunny and I couldn't hold back the laughter any longer. Much later, Paul said his good-bye to Rie. He hugged and kissed her, promising to keep in touch. I watched Paul leave. For all his carefree humor and easy laughter, he was crying.

I was amazed at the closeness Rie had with her friends. I never met one of the young people that came to the house that I didn't like. They were good kids, well mannered, and very intelligent. They were caring and loving but most of all they loved Rie.

Others loved Rie too. Just like Bill, the little forty-five year-old retarded man that came everyday with a rose for Rie. He lived with his mother and he knew Rie from Church. Most people didn't have time for Bill but Rie did and I guess that's why he loved her.

Like clockwork, Bill would come around two in the afternoon. He would walk into Rie's room and hand her a beautiful bloom. (His mother told Sunny that he wouldn't leave the house until he had picked the prettiest bloom from their Rose garden.) Rie never let Bill know that she didn't approve of picking roses. She accepted it with a hug, thanking him for his thoughtfulness and telling him it was the prettiest she had ever seen. For him she talked in her whispered voice because

she knew he would have trouble reading. If he was aware that she talked any differently, he never showed it. Everyday he stood at the end of Rie's bed crying and in his singsong speech he would say. "Sunny Rie, you get well, now. I pray to God for you and He's gonna make you well again. You know, I pray every night. I tell God, you're my girl and He has to make you well." The words were always the same but they came from Bill's heart.

This went on for a couple of weeks. Suddenly Bill stopped coming. Rie became worried and asked her mother to called and find out why Bill had stopped coming to visit. Bill's mother informed Sunny that Bill was ill. She said Bill couldn't handle emotions very well and he was getting far too emotional where Rie was concerned. Sunny told her to give Bill our love and we would keep him in our prayers.

Bill was special. We all missed Bill and his roses. Blessed are the pure in heart: for they shall see God.

HUMOR ME

I don't expect your compliments.
I don't want sympathy.
I really don't want to be pitied
Or any big fuss made over me.
Even though you are my best friend
Who understands when I frown.
I really do enjoy it…
The attention when I'm down.

Dad and Rie on way to Cobalt treatments

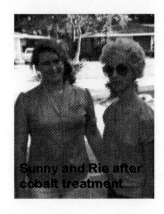

Sunny and Rie after cobalt treatment

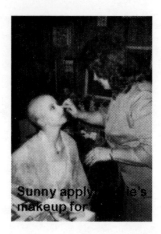

Sunny apply___ ___e's makeup for ___

Dressed for Prom

Sign at room

Rie in her short wig

CHAPTER 28

By July, Rie seemed to be improving. Having accepted the sound of her whispered voice, she was talking more. Her humor and speech was back to her old self. The only thing out of sync was her walking. She walked but wobbly, having the stride of someone that has had a stroke. One leg would raise higher than the other. Doctors weren't sure she would ever overcome this.

To Sunny's horror, Rie was becoming independent. She wouldn't allow her mother to be with her when she went to the bathroom or took her bath. Rie even locked the door behind her. Sunny fixed that by taping the bolt so Rie could turn the knob in lock position but the bolt would not shoot into place.

Rie was adamant about sleeping in her own room. Sunny would only allowed it if she could sleep with Rie. Sunny was afraid Rie was too unsteady to get up at night to go to the bathroom by herself. Sunny advised a way to pin a ribbon or tether from her pajamas to Rie's gown so if Rie did get up in the middle of the night to go to the bathroom she would wake Sunny up.

One morning I walked over to Sunny's at seven to have our normal morning cup of coffee. I found her crying in the living room. "Honey, what's wrong?"

"Its Rie," she whimpered. "She fell against the cabinet door in the bathroom early this morning. At first I didn't believe it was that bad of a fall until I noticed Rie began to act slow. She doesn't want to get out of bed or talk to me. It's as if she's closed down. I have a call into the doctor now."

"She went to the bathroom by herself?" Sunny nodded. "You know how she is."

"But I thought you had that taken care of with the ribbon."

"I did," she cried, "but Rie unfastened it from her gown. I didn't wake up until I heard a loud noise. I found her lying on the floor holding her head."

"Oh my, God!" I stifled the urge to cry.

When the doctor called back, he advised us to bring Rie to the hospital immediately. Rie had another operation on her head to rearrange the stunts. The fall had dislodged them. It was at this time we learned that the tumor had returned with a vengeance. I can't minimize the overwhelming effect this had on all of us. Depression, frustration, and disappointment set in. I watched Sunny and Phil walk around in a deep gloom. Rie was holding her own but for how long.

We fought against the word defeat by reading the Bible. We didn't want to accept the negative power that overwhelmed us. It was hard to entertain visitors and family. But we knew if we gave in, Satan would claim the victory and all that Rie had fought against would mean nothing. Prayers became as voluntary as breathing.

After a week we brought Rie back from St. Patrick hospital. We had been home just under a week when Rie became sick with sore throat and breathing trouble. She refused to eat. This time we put her under Dr. Jones care at the Orange hospital. In Rie's weakened condition, the doctor started intravenous feeding so she wouldn't dehydrate.

Benny, my son, arrived. This was his first time to see his cousin since she became ill. He had kept up with her progress over the telephone.

When Benny, Sunny, and I walked back to Rie's room. We were immediately confronted with a situation. One tall head nurse and two of her aids were huddled in a corner with obvious fear on their faces. When they saw Sunny, they rushed up to her and all started speaking at once.

The head nurse finally took charge of the situation. "Mrs. Eppler," she said in her most professional voice, "Your daughter has tried to karate chop all of us."

"What did you do to my daughter?" Sunny replied calmly.

All this time, Rie looked the picture of innocence. To think this small girl could hold three large women at bay was hilarious. The smallest was at least 175 pounds.

They explained they were trying to give her a bath. "But did you tell her that's what you planned or did you just start taking her clothes off?" Sunny questioned the three.

"When I pulled her gown over her head, she kicked me all the way to the wall and karate chopped the others," the larger aid complained loudly. Her big breast heaved. She reminded me of a German officer addressing her men. I was expecting her to click her heels together.

I noticed Benny having a hard time keeping a straight face.

He whispered to me, "If they only knew just how skilled Rie was in karate, they would have known that she had been merely warning them to stay away."

Benny walked to her bedside and took a seat. When Rie saw him she grabbed him around his neck, hugging him. "You finally came," she whispered.

"I had to see you, little girl," Benny whispered. He was visibly shaken and held onto his cousin as if she was going to disappear. "Did you karate the nurses," Benny asked in a conspiratorial whisper. Rie gave him a mischievous little smile. She nodded her head, yes, and had a very pleased expression on her face.

"Well, good for you," he said, smiling back. "With everything happening to you, I guess just this once you had to lash out." Bright eyed, Rie agreed.

Sunny asked the nurses flatly, "Why didn't you explain what you planned on doing to her and let her be a part of it?"

"You must understand, Mrs. Eppler, we have a job to do," the head nurse said. "We have a lot of patients and not enough time."

"I understand that," Sunny said just as firmly, "but try to have a little compassion for the people you're taking care of." She gave a deep sigh. "From now own, you won't have to bathe my daughter. My sister and I will give Rie her baths." The head nurse and her aids were extremely happy. They instantly agreed and hurriedly left.

Rie and Benny were in deep conversation. He was telling her that he was going to marry, Dana. Rie's little face became sad. "You're going to leave," she asked. "I'll be back soon," he said.

"Please don't go," she begged. "I haven't seen you enough." None of us had seen Benny enough but he was on a tight schedule. He was my prodigal son. Rie touched his face lovingly and whispered more for him than for us. "Benny, you be good. You have a long road to walk."

Benny nodded his head and replied, "You just be home when I return. Will you pray with me before I go." Rie agreed and we all bowed our head while Benny prayed. He then quickly hugged his cousin good-bye before he went out into the hall.

It was there that I found him crying. I placed my arms around him. "Mom, I don't want to leave but I have to," he said in between sobs. "I love that little girl in there and I don't know when I'll get to see her again. God just has to keep her well until I return."

It was hard saying goodbye to my son and seeing him leave in tears.

One morning around two, I was by myself with Rie when she became extremely ill. Her fever soared. Her coughing became worse. Her whole body convulsed every time she coughed and she would grasp for air. I had never seen her in such a condition. The nurses came in and out. I asked one of the nurses, "Please do something to help her."

"Her fever is very high," the nurse affirmed while reading Rie's chart. "I don't see any instructions by the doctor."

"Isn't there something you can give her?" She looked at me apologetically. "Not without the doctor's permission."

Just as firmly as I could, I said, "So call him."

"I can't but I'll send the head nurse in." When the head nurse came in, she checked Rie, looked at her chart and said, "I'll call the doctor at first light." Rie's faced turned purple, wheezing so hard to get her breath. I blew my stack…a mild word, really. I went a little wild, but I was determined to get help for my baby. Here we were in the hospital where they were supposed to help the sick and they were all afraid to call the doctor.

"Why can't you just call the doctor now," I fumed.

"It's not our policy unless it's an extreme emergency." I was under stress, maybe even "battle fatigue. I felt as though I was doing battle with Satan, himself. I took a deep breath counting to ten. I let it out slowly and prayed a silent prayer, afraid of what I wanted to do with the head nurse. Even a soldier goes to battle for his belief. I was fighting for this child's life.

"I've had it!" I said on an indrawn breath. "I'm tired of demanding that you call the doctor. I'm weary of your excuses. This child is extremely ill with no medication on her chart to help her. Either you call the doctor immediately or I will embarrass the whole lot of you by taking Rie down to the emergency room on the first floor for help."

She immediately turned on her heels and departed from the room. Instantly I called Sunny. We decided if this hospital couldn't help, then we would take her back to St. Patrick. Needless to say, before I got off the phone with Sunny, the doctor came walking into the room. He had been at the hospital already with another patient so he was able to come immediately. When Dr. Jones walked in the door, I wanted to hug his neck and whoop with joy. He took one look at my pale face and said, "Hi, Aunt Margie, you baby setting tonight." All I could do was nod my head while tears flowed down my cheeks.

"I hear you girls are having a little problem." He patted my shoulder. "All of you have been so strong, don't give up now. Everything will be all right."

My knees were so weak I slipped down in the nearest chair. When he examined Rie, he found she had pneumonia. I never asked what he told the nurses but after that night, the nurses were told to call him, no matter what the time. The nurses all walked a mile around me.

In the days that followed, Rie fought bravely against the pneumonia. She was constantly on breathing machines and heavy medication. It was during this time that I saw my sister completely lose it.

The blood lab was constantly drawing blood from Rie. Her veins had all but collapsed. Which meant they would have to poke her several times before they could find a vein. One nurse came in and tried three times to draw blood. Rie cried out in pain. She had never done this before. Still the nurse tried yet again. I heard a muffled sobbing and thought it was Rie but it came from the corner. Sunny had slipped down in the corner of the room with her fingers shoved in her mouth to keep from yelling. Her whole body shook from convulsions.

We had seen blood taken many times at the other hospital and after three times if the nurse couldn't find the vein they went for help. I placed my hand on the woman's shoulder and the fury in my eyes and voice must have registered, "If you can't do it, call someone who can. Rie can't take much more of this." I pointed a finger in my sister's direction. "That little mother has been so brave watching her daughter be brave. Do you think you could watch while you're daughter was being tortured?"

The woman stared at me for a long time. Neither of us spoke. Then she said, "I promise, Mrs. Woodcock, if I can't find the vein this time, I'll get help."

Maybe it was determination on her part or maybe she was afraid of who I would tell, but on the next try she secured a vein and drew blood.

On another occasion an older unsmiling nurse came in and started to give Rie her medication. It was a red liquid in a tiny white cup. As the nurse reached for it, she accidentally spilled it on the tray holding the medication. She hurriedly picked it up but not before most of it had soaked the napkin on the tray. She held the cup out to Rie. I placed my hand on her shoulder and asked nicely, "What are you giving her?"

Rie's big eyes widened and looked over at me. The nurse stopped and turned toward me with a raised eyebrow. "This medication is for her seizures."

"How much does she usually take?"

An angry expression crossed her face and melted into perplexity. Maybe the woman wasn't used to answering questions, but she honestly appeared shocked. I thought she was going to ignore the question altogether but at last she answered, "She takes a cup full," pointing toward the almost empty cup. There was only enough red liquid to coat the bottom.

"But the cup isn't full…is it?" I stated. Rie looked in the cup, then at me. Her little face wore a frown.

"It's enough for what she needs," the nurse stated boldly.

"Are you a doctor?"

"No, but…" I didn't let her finish. I was having a very hard time being civil to this older woman. I prayed silently to God to forgive me. I'm sure the nurse was worried about me telling her superiors that she spilled the medication but I was worried about Rie.

I tried again. This time I smiled sweetly but didn't mince words.

"I think you need to get a full cup…don't you?"

"I'll be back," she fumed. The lady exited the room in a rush. As I was counting to ten, I felt a little pat on my hand. I looked into Rie's eyes and saw her smile. She whispered, "You did good, Aunt Margie."

"You and me, kid. All the way."

She turned her little thumb up and whispered softly, "Yeah, you and me, all the way." She smiled sadly. "I'm sorry for you and Mom. My illness has been hard on both of you."

"You have been so brave; you keep all of us going," I managed to say over the lump that refused to move from my throat. "You're a class act, kid."

"Thanks, Aunt Margie." She smiled showing all her dimples. "I love you. Mom and I couldn't have made it without you." I was on the verge of tears as I hugged her. Several minutes later, a new nurse returned with Rie's medication. Nothing more was said.

Despite poor nursing, overdosing, and the evil that sometimes surrounded us, Rie lived though these times with God's help.

I don't remember when it actually started, only that it did. Sometimes, Rie would be talking to me or listening to my conversation but her eyes would be turned toward the corner of the room. Once, I asked, "Do you see something in that corner?"

"Yes," she answered.

"Is it good?"

"No! "

"Do you want to talk about it?"

"No!" she said flatly. And that would end the conversation. At that time she wasn't ready to tell us or maybe she thought we weren't prepared for the answer. Whatever or whomever it was remained her secret. On other occasions, Rie's face would light up and she would talk softly to someone standing by her bed.

When I asked whom she was talking to, she said, "Michael was here." Another time, she told me she was talking to Daniel. Finally I had to know. I said, "Are you talking to Angels?" For a moment she didn't speak. Then as if making up her mind about something, she replied, "I've always talked with angels for as long as I can remember." Her little face beamed with a radiance that literally made her eyes sparkled with tiny lights. "Angels are with all of us. You know God sends his angels to protect us. In the darkest hours God says to his children, 'Fear not; for I am with thee.'" She smiled.

I smiled back feeling strangely comforted. In that moment, I had visions of kneeling Guardian angels with flashing swords surrounding her bed, protecting her from demonic assaults. I, too, always believed the Lord sends us Guardian angels to protect, but I think that in Rie's case she had dozens. There was always a spiritual current around her that one could actually feel.

On a day that Rie had been taken to X-ray, I was sitting in her room waiting for her return. A young man came to the door and peeped in. He was dressed in pajamas and bathrobe and appeared to be in his early thirties. He was a handsome young man, big with an outdoors look. He smiled and said, "Hello." I smiled back and asked if I could help him with something.

His eyes searched the room. Then he said, "Where's that girl?"

"Oh, do you know, Sunny Marie?"

"No," his eyes focused back on me, "but I'd like too. I've seen her as I pass the room. She always smiles at me and waves."

Rie always smiled at everyone, but I didn't tell him this. Something had drawn him here. I invited him to sit down to wait for her return. He held his hand out and said, "My name is Thomas. I have a room down the hall. Are you her mother?"

"No," I said. "I'm her Aunt Margie. Her mother and I take shifts sitting with her so she's never by herself."

His face became serious. "Your niece is very sick isn't she?"

"Yes...very." "Terminal?" I nodded. I never could get used to that word. It always sounded so final.

"Oh, man!" He caught his breath. "It's not fair for someone that young to be seriously ill...is it?"

"No," I agreed, "Sunny Marie's special. She's very brave and probably has more courage in her little finger than we have in our whole body."

He took a seat opposite me. "I know that I'm a stranger but could you please tell me something about her? I mean," he appeared to be embarrassed, "if it wouldn't be intruding."

Here I was singing my baby's praises yet again. He listened, not once did he interrupt. An hour later, when Rie was wheeled back to the room, he was still there. "Sunny Marie meet Thomas," I said, "He's been wanting to meet you."

"Really?" Rie eyed the tall stranger. Their eyes held for a long moment and during that time the fine line was crossed and a stranger was turned into a friend. She held out her hand and replied in her husky whisper, "Hello, Thomas. I've seen you before."

Thomas interlaced her slender fingers with his own. "Hello, Sunny Marie." He smiled broadly. "You're name is as pretty as you are." She thanked him shyly.

"Will it hurt your throat to talk to me?"

"No," Rie grinned, "but it might bother your ears to listen."

He threw back his head and laughed. "I've never had a girl whispering to me before. I might get to like it."

Rie stared at him in amazement. Thomas sat by her bed holding Rie's hand and talking softly to her for hours. He came every morning and stayed until the nurses would call him back to his room. As far as we knew he never had any visitors. During late hours at night while Rie slept, he would talk to me about Rie. Sometimes he was content just to watch Rie sleep.

This man was nice and likable but hard to get to know. He never answered questions about himself or why he was in the hospital. He only wanted to talk to Rie or about Rie. And the odd thing was Rie never questioned him, but took him at face value. Rie had a way of reading people. It wasn't something that came with the illness it had always been there. She could gaze into a person's soul and know them.

One time while Thomas was visiting and they were laughing together, he asked, "Sunny Marie, when you get out of the hospital, will you go dancing with me?"

Her gaze studied the inner man. Her face broke out in a mischievous grin. "I haven't been dancing in a long time."

"Me neither," he replied. He closed his fingers over hers. "I'll take you to a fancy place where we can eat a big steak and drink a bottle of champagne."

"Make it ice tea and we'll call it a date." Her eyes danced with merriment. "But you'll get out of the hospital long before I will." Then a shadow crossed her face. She covered their held hands with her other hand. "When you leave, remember me."

He gave a throaty laughed and replied, "Little girl, you're not one to forget."

She laughed with him, but as if a veil fell across her eyes, her face suddenly became serious again. "No," she murmured, "not little girl. The little girl in me grew up a long time ago."

"Eighteen years old isn't very old compared to my thirty-two." He smiled. "But you're right, you don't act like a teenager," he replied. His knuckles stroked the soft curve of her cheekbone. "You're an intelligent young woman, old beyond your years." He exhaled a loud breath. "Why didn't I meet you along time ago."

"Maybe because it wasn't meant to be," she countered.

He met her eyes with a melancholy smile, "But maybe my life would have been different if I had."

"Thomas, God gave you the ability to make your life anything you want it to be," she stated firmly. "It's for you to decide in what direction you need to go."

Thomas was silent for a long moment. "You don't think it's too late for me?"

Eyeing him thoughtfully, she quietly replied, "If you do it for God, it's never too late."

His eyes watered with tears. "Thank you," he replied in a whisper. "I guess I needed someone to tell me that."

Sunny and I was never sure what that conversation was about. We asked Rie but all she would say was, "Thomas needs to find God in his own way."

On one occasion, Thomas confided, "I haven't been in church since I was a little boy, but because of Sunny Marie I'm going back as soon as I get out of the hospital. There is a lot of things I need to get right in my life. I want God to know me when I pray for Sunny Marie."

"He knows you, Thomas," I said.

"Yeah, but we need to get better acquainted." For some reason this young man needed Rie, her strength, her love, and her knowledge of God. The day he left the hospital he came by Rie's room. He hugged and kissed her good-bye. He held her so long, it made Sunny and I nervous. Rie whispered, "Go with God, Thomas."

"Yeah, I'll have to do that now," his voice quivered. As he said good-bye, I had the feeling that this man was going to do a lot of soul searching in the days to come. People like this we didn't say goodbye to, only that we'll see you later.

TRANQUILLITY

There is serenity in knowing, yet there is the puzzlement over the mystery of why one knows the thing one does.

It is not the quantity or the quality. There is a distinction as to the type and density of knowledge.

I just know that I love you, yet even though I know not why. I am sooth inside…peaceful.

CHAPTER 29

Rie once again came home from the hospital. Despite the brain tumor, Rie seemed to be on the way to recovery yet again. It was time to go back to my blue and green jungle and to my Johnny. As I said my good-byes, I understood the expression in Sunny's eyes as I started to leave. It was the look of dread, of what tomorrow would bring. We all lived from day to day, but sometimes the uncertainty of tomorrow would creep in without warning.

"Keep the faith," I said squeezing her, praying I wouldn't cry. "You know, it's going to be hard making each day without you."

"Naw!" I laughed. "You and Rie are seasoned troopers."

"But you're breaking up the team of the three Musketeers."

"The best team," I joked. I looked over at Rie. I just stood quietly absorbing her loveliness, Little Miss Radiance. I was going to miss this miracle kid. I planted a kiss on her cheek and whispered in her ear, "Take care of your mother." She whispered back, "I always do."

I can't begin to count how many times we all said we loved each other. We had all shared so much in these troubled times (Sunny called them, the Good, the Bad and the Ugly times.) Leaving was tearing my heart out, but Johnny needed me, too.

After my good-byes to Mother and Daddy, Marilyn took me to the airport. I knew our good-byes would be less emotional. Boy, was I wrong! As the plane took off, I saw my sister hanging onto the fence sobbing for all the world to see. By the time the jet roared on take off I was near hysterics. Waving to my unseeing sister, I swallowed back the tears that threatened to choke me.

After awhile the plane leveled off, I finished wiping the tears from my eyes. While unbuckling the seat belt, I became aware of the pretty young woman sitting next to me. I smiled. She smiled back. We introduced ourselves between Beaumont and Houston, which is only a short flight.

I told her I was going to Indonesia. I really didn't say exactly where in Indonesia because it is so large a territory. It consists of Sumatra, Java, Celebes, the south part of Borneo, and about 3000 small islands. My location would be unimportant for someone unfamiliar with the area. We enjoyed each other's company and by the time we arrived at the Houston airport, we felt as though we were old friends. She quickly tore off her name and address from a printed check and said, "Please write." We hugged. I didn't even take the time to give her my address because I knew in my heart I would probably never see her again, but I placed her name and address in my billfold. But God had plans for this seemingly, unimportant encounter.

After my return to the jungle, Sunny's first letter informed us of Rie's improvement. I was so elated, that I stood on my pouch and shouted it to everyone in camp so they could rejoice with me.

In one letter Sunny informed me that Rie was receiving so many visitors that they needed to get away. Woody talked her into coming to his apartment in Houston for a couple of weeks. As Sunny wrote, "It's our oasis in a cement world of glass and tall buildings." Woody's apartment had a swimming pool where Rie exercised daily. It was during one of these times they made a cassette tape. Woody had recording equipment and Sunny, Phil, Sylvia and Woody sang all the songs that were our favorite. We played it for all our friends.

Later as the letters arrived, Rie's health went up and down. One day she was well and happy and the next she slept all day. But one thing remained constant Rie refused to eat. Sunny's letters talked about the pain of each and every meal, one cracker, one teaspoon of soup. Sunny claimed she could literally see the weight disappear from Rie's bones. Sunny's words were, "I beg. I plead for just one bite. Rie pats me lovingly on the shoulder and tells me she's not hungry. Her words are, 'I'm receiving all the nourishment I need each and every minute of the day.' Oh, Margie, she's starving herself. I'm angry with God. Why is God letting this happen to my baby?"

My heart ached. This was the girl that loved to cook the mother that would have homemade cookies after school for her children. I knew if it were possible, she would have cooked anything for her child. But I knew in my heart that the nourishment Rie was talking about came not from food but from God.

The next letter told us, Rie had gone to the hospital for a stomach tube. Sunny was so happy because the doctor told her to feed Rie anything that could be poured through the tube. As one of her letters stated, "I refuse to let her starve without a fight. You would not believe the healthy concoctions I mix in the blender to pour into that tiny tube. Rie seems to be gaining weight slowly but surely."

In yet another letter, Sunny told us of another operations on Rie's head to position the shunts. "Rie looks good after this third shunt operation," Sunny wrote. "She came through with flying colors and seems to be more talkative and active. Looks like things are turning around for us."

It was only days after I received that letter, Sunny called, "Margie, Rie and I need you. The cancer is winning. There is nothing more the doctors can do." I knew without her saying anymore that she was telling me the end was near. To this day, I'm not sure what I said other than I would be there as soon as possible. The company said they could get me on a plane that day. So I hurriedly packed for my trip. I needed a couple of small toilet items so Johnny drove over to a small Indonesian store in our camp that had recently opened. Believe me when I tell you—it was a small native store with a very limited supply of goods.

On Johnny's return, he held out a sack and said, "Take this to my Rie."

I couldn't imagine what he had found in that tiny store to send to Rie. In the package I found a cassette tape. On the cover was a picture of a blonde girl named Evie. I said, "Honey, what kind of tape is it?"

Johnny looked at me with wonderment on his face and replied, "I walked into the store and heard this tape playing. I just stood there listening. Marjorie, I couldn't stop listening until I heard the whole tape. That's why I took so long in returning. You don't have time to hear it before your plane leaves. Every song belongs to Rie."

We were in Indonesia where the majority of the people are Muslim. I noticed that this tape was in English containing Christian music. I was anxious to hear the tape that had made such an impression on Johnny. When I arrived back at the hospital, I went directly to Rie's room knowing I would not leave my sister's side again until Rie either walked out of that hospital room well, or until she went to live with Jesus.

I walked into a dark, quiet room and found Rie sleeping. Just the tape recorder was playing. Sunny was standing by the bed holding on to the sidebars. Marilyn and Dave were sitting near by. A Bible tape was speaking softly in the back ground, telling the stories of Jesus.

Marilyn and Sunny saw me. We walked out into the hallway for our greeting. When Sunny hugged me, she didn't let go but held me and whispered in my ear, "You made it in time."

"Did you doubt God?" I said, squeezing her back. "He made sure we were together in the beginning and He's making sure we're together at the end. He never does anything halfway." I dried her tears. "What do the doctors say?"

"They say," she took a deep breath, "there is no more time left. Everything in her body is failing. It's only a matter of days, maybe hours. The pain in her head is worse, that's why we keep the room dark."

"Does she know?"

"You know Rie, she doesn't want anyone talking behind her back."

I took a deep breath. "Another death sentence." I gazed at my sister. She looked tired. "How do you feel about it?"

"I feel like the end is near," she said softly. "Remember the story from the Bible about Jesus raising Jairus' little girl from the dead. That passage was important to us. We could relate to it. Jairus' young daughter had died and when Jesus was told, he said, 'Don't be afraid! Just trust me, and she'll be all right.' Then Jesus took the little girl by the hand and called, 'Get up, little girl!' And at that moment her life returned and she jumped up.

"Margie, it didn't say in the Bible how long the little girl lived after she arose from the dead. That part wasn't important. The important thing was that Jesus gave her parents a miracle. Jesus only promises forever through him." She sighed. "God gave us the same miracle as he gave Jairus. He gave us Rie back from the dead. Now we have to give her back to God."

Sunny was a fighter, but one look at her face and I knew she was spent. What she said was true. I walked back into the room. The child that lay there was just as beautiful as I remembered. The little face was still round and the skin was still soft but she was down to about fifty pounds. The little bald head was growing fine hair that looked like baby down, hair the doctors told us would never grow back. I stood quietly. Rie opened her eyes and smiled at me. Her voice was weak but she managed to whisper, "Hi, Aunt Margie."

"Hi, Kid. It looks like you've got your spastic nurses again. Can you handle it?"

She chuckled softly. She touched my hand and the little face lit up in a brilliant smile, "Yeah, everything will be all right now."

What will be all right now, I wanted to ask but I wasn't sure if I wanted to know. "Hey, sweetheart, Uncle Johnny sent you a tape filled with wonderful songs."

Her eyes widened. "Oh, great! Play it now?"

Sunny stopped the tape of the Bible. She replied, "Marilyn and Dave bought her the taped collection of the Living Bible and Rie's been listening to the tapes constantly. Rie claims it helps her head."

I put Johnny's tape on. The upbeat music filled the room with Evie's beautiful voice. It drew people in like a magnet. I understood why Johnny was so moved. Especially the song, "I'd like to be remembered as the girl who sang her songs for Jesus Christ." That was what Rie had done this whole year. Giving Jesus all the praise and glory. We all watched Rie's little foot keep time with the music.

She insisted that we play the music for the sisters, nurses, and doctors that came into the room. Everyone was singing the songs. Rie listened to that tape everyday and loved it. Our days were spent in music and the long nights were filled with the Bible tapes.

Rie was still having a lot of company from school. Her friends were now in college and it amazed me how they found time between classes and their studies to visit. Dale came as often as possible bringing his guitar, serenading Rie with soft music and singing. I noticed too, that two young men I hadn't seen before came nightly. One was of medium height, dark hair and handsome, named Jeff Smith and the other one was John Kuhn, a good-looking kid, tall and blond. John and Jeff would sit by Rie for hours, just holding her hand. Jeff would tell jokes and keep us laughing while John remained serious. I took Sunny aside and asked, "Doesn't Doug ever come by to see her?"

"No. He's never been back since she gave his ring back."

"How sad. So, who's this John and Jeff?"

"John has loved Rie for years," Sunny said sadly. "Jeff has been Rie's close friend since the seventh grade. They come everyday after work leaving at midnight or until the nurses kick them out. Jeff, I'm not worried about, but I think John is getting in too deep." She spread her hands helplessly. "I don't know how to tell him not to get involved."

"You can't. Just the look on his face says he would rather be here than anywhere else."

When we walked back into the room, Rie held up her hand to show us John's graduation ring on her thin finger. It was so big it wobbled.

"Look what John gave me," she whispered proudly. Rie showed it to one of the nurses and she quickly wrapped adhesive tape around the huge ring to fit Rie's small finger. Rie waved it proudly into the air.

Tim, a respiratory therapist, walked in about that time and placed Rie on a breathing machine to clear her lungs. Turning toward John, he asked, "Are you Sunny Marie's boyfriend?" Rie's big eyes stared at John waiting for him to answer.

"I wish," John said in a clear deep voice. "I'm doing all I can to convince her I'm the right man." Sunny placed her hand on the young man's shoulder and explained, "Rie planned to marry a young man named Doug. They went together for four years."

"So why isn't Doug here?" Tim asked. "Rie gave Doug's ring back because she said she had too much work to do," Sunny hurriedly said.

Tim looked down at Rie. "So this Doug wasn't strong enough to stay up with you?" Rie shook her head, no. "Well, I've seen it happen before. You just outgrew Doug," Tim said with a big hearty laugh. Rie smiled back.

"Sunny Marie has known Jeff and John for a long time," Sunny said. "They're all good friends."

Tim looked long and hard at John and said, "Well, if you ask me, I think it's good riddance to Doug." He smiled down into Rie's eyes and winked. "I think you've got a winner in John."

Rie's eyes cut over to John. She smiled over the breathing apparatus and nodded her head in agreement. After that night, John's ring stayed on her finger night and day. Dale, Jeff, and John were all winners. These three young men were dear friends, always respecting Doug and Rie's relationship, but now that Doug was out of the picture it was their turn to love Rie. Rain or shine they were always there. It didn't matter to them that Rie was bald or that she was super thin. To them Rie was as pretty as ever. They were givers, not takers, giving Rie joy of laughter, companionship, soft soothing songs, but most of all they gave her their unconditional love. Everyone should be blessed with such friends.

Rie's girlfriends were another matter. They came nightly but their visits were short. Maybe it was the change in Rie's appearance that frightened them, bald, no make-up, unconcern with fashion, uninterested in gossip. Vanity was important to teenage girls. One girl remarked after she left Rie's room. "That could be me in there." Whatever it was, the girls would leave in tears. One mother and daughter came almost every night. They were the strong at heart. The mother told Sunny, "I can't imagine the pain you must be going through. I feel as if I need to be here. You never know when this can happen to my daughter and I would have to walk in your shoes."

Sunny's best friend and neighbor, Diane, came. This little woman was pregnant and her son, six-year-old Keith, was dying of leukemia. This mother found the time to give comfort. When she said, "Sunny, I know how you feel." It was true, because she was going through the same heartaches. Keith was constantly in and out of M.D. Anderson Hospital in Houston, Texas.

Thank God for John. He started bringing Sunny's boys to visit. He even bought the boys and himself matching black Windbreakers with the emblem of a Ford Mustang stitched on the back. John would take the boys out for Pizza or just drive them around in his National Mustang Pace-car. Philip and Derek loved the attention they were receiving. When Sunny complained to him about the money and time he was lavishing on the boys, John replied, "Philip and Derek are kind of lost right now without Sunny Marie and I really want to do it for them." Sunny tried to pay him for the jackets but he refused to take the money. He was constantly bringing Rie gifts of flowers, music boxes, and lovely cards.

One night, Sunny and I walked John down the hall. Sunny asked, "John, why do you come, day after day, night after night?"

Without hesitation, he answered, "I love Rie, Mrs. E." I watched Sunny search for the right words. In a voice full of anguish and pain, torn from the soul, she cried, "But John she's dying. There won't be anymore miracles now."

I'm thinking to myself, "No more miracles? Oh but that's wrong, Rie is our miracle. As long as one of us lives to tell the story of her courage and faith, her miracle will be never ending. There is no limit how long miracles last."

The young man took a deep breath and let it out slowly. "I know that. I've known that from the beginning, but I've been given this time. I'll take what I've been given."

My heart warmed to this young man. "God bless you, John."

"Yeah, Aunt Margie," he smiled back, "He has already."

Love, I thought. God surrounds us with His love. John was just another one of his messengers.

One day we had the windows opened wide enjoying the sunshine outside. We were sitting around Rie's bed talking softly when I noticed Rie wasn't listening to us but watching the corner of the room. In a soft voice, she said, "Go away."

Sunny stopped talking when she noticed I was watching Rie.

We both looked at the corner. "Go!" Rie whispered loudly.

Her eyes wide. "Go away."

Sunny stood up blocking Rie's vision. I said, "Rie who are you talking to?"

Rie shook her head. "I can't tell you." She glanced passed her mother. Sunny again moved into her line of vision and Rie said, "Get out!"

At first I thought the words were meant for her mother but then I realized she was looking around her mother. This had happened before. Chills danced up my spine. I searched my sister's face for a hint of the game they were playing. Sunny's face was blank. Whatever was there in that corner, my sister was standing between it and her daughter. "Tell me who you are talking to?" Sunny begged.

"Don't ask me," Rie said. She was visibly upset and we let the matter drop.

On the following day, I walked into the room and Sunny was standing on a chair hanging a large crucifix and pictures of Jesus on the wall with cellophane tape. I stopped in the doorway in amazement. "What is happening?"

Sunny looked over her shoulder at me. "Rie doesn't like this corner."

"Why not? What's in it?"

Sunny shrugged. "She doesn't want us to know." She continued to hang the objects. Then when everything was on the wall, she stepped down looking at her creation. Turning to Rie, she asked, "Now, does it look better?"

"Oh, yes." Rie gazed up at her mother. Her expression softened. "You've made my corner bright. It's my substitute sunshine."

Whatever she didn't like was gone for now, hopefully forgotten.

The next day everything hanging on the wall fell at one time. Rie was back talking to the corner again. I asked her, "Whom are you talking to in that corner?" She refused to answer. Sunny took her usual place at the end of the bed. "Are you talking to Jesus?" I questioned.

Rie shook her head vigorously and answered, "No!"

"Are you talking to Angels?" Again she shook her head. Sunny stood studying her daughter's face. I had the feeling she was waiting until I ran out of questions before she started with her own. "Please, baby, tell Aunt Margie who's in the corner. Maybe if we talk about it, it is will go away."

Rie looked over at me and slowly shook her head, no. Then her eyes encountered her mother's. For the first time, I saw fear in her pretty eyes. As a chill passed down my spine, I felt pure terror. Suddenly I knew. Rie wasn't afraid for herself but afraid for her mother. The corner held something ugly and she didn't want to put a name to it.

Sunny stood watching her daughter, reading the signs, knowing every expression on that lovely face. Sunny swore under her breath. "I know what's in that corner," she stated flatly.

Rie met her mother's eyes. "Don't say it, Sunny," I pleaded. "Please, don't give it a name."

"But don't you see, Margie, Rie is afraid for me."

"I know," I confessed.

"We have to face this thing together," Sunny cried out in anguish. She climbed into bed with Rie and took Rie's face between her hands. "Satan is in that corner, isn't he?" Rie's eyes were still watching the corner, she turned to her mother with a start and they stared at each other. "Yes," Rie finally admitted.

I hated the thought of that evil presence in the same room with our baby. I hated his name being spoken aloud. But with good comes evil. Sunny had referred before to the good, the bad and the ugly. Now we were faced with the ugly. I knew we had to face it in God's name.

"Is he telling you, you're sick because of God?" Sunny spoke defiantly. Rie answered with a nod, yes. "Do you believe his words?"

"No!" Rie whispered aloud.

"Are you afraid for yourself?"

"No!" again Rie cried.

Sunny was silent for a long moment. "You're afraid for your daddy and I…aren't you? He's telling you that if you die, we'll turn our backs on God." When Rie's eyes filled with tears, Sunny clutched her child to her chest rocking her in her arms. "He lies!" she shouted. "In God's goodness, He gave you to us to take care of. We would never repay God by turning against him. Please don't worry about Daddy and me. Whatever happens, we'll face what comes."

Rie brushed her mother's hair back from her face and kissed her. "Oh, Mom, I don't want anyone I love touched by evil. Don't ever blame God for my illness. I don't."

"No, baby, we won't. I promise."

Two days later, a new doctor came in along with one of the floor nurses. They stood by Rie's bed. Rie was sleeping. Sunny stood on the other side holding onto the sidebars. "Your daughter will have to go home to die, we need the room. Hospice can take care of her needs," the doctor said in a loud voice.

I jumped at the tone of his voice. The nurse grasped in shock. Rie's eyes flew open. The man had spoken the words without love or understanding of what this mother and child had been through. My sister slowly started to shake from head to foot in hard rigors. "My daughter knows she's going to die. Who the hell do you think you are to come here and tell us to leave? You're not one of her doctors and until I talk to someone I recognize I refuse to take my child home." Sunny grated each word through her clenched teeth.

The doctor looked from Sunny to his nurse. When the nurse nodded her head in agreement, he stammered, "I was under the impression she was comatose."

"Well, look at her," Sunny spat, "she's not! Now, I would appreciate it if you would leave us alone."

Rie, with great effort, in her weaken state, sat up in bed trying to reach her mother.

The doctor exited from the room as if the hounds were after him. The nurse got to Sunny before she hit the floor.

Sunny didn't faint. She just collapsed. It was like all the strength holding her together was suddenly jerked from under her. Her knees buckled and she slipped into the nurse's arms. "Mom!" Rie screamed in a loud whispered voice. "Mom! Oh dear God, help my Mom."

I held tightly to Rie. She was so concerned for her mother. Jerkingly, she cried, "Is my Mom all right?"

"She will be," I whispered back. "She's just mad at that doctor."

"Tell her it's all right, Aunt Margie," Rie said while patting my hand. "I don't want her to be angry."

"It's all right to be angry sometimes." I, too, felt angry with the doctor. How dare that man be allowed to be a doctor? All the other doctors had been gentle and kind…this one was neither.

"I'm so sorry, Mrs. Eppler" the nurse said, "That bastard is Dr. Milan's new associate but that doesn't account for his stupidity."

By this time, most of the nurses on the floor had gathered at the door. By the expression on their faces, all were deeply concerned and angry at the doctor's handling of the situation.

Dr. Milan hurried into the room. Evidently the other doctor had called him. No sooner than he came into the room, Sunny rounded on him and shouted, "Why did you send you associate when all you had to do was tell us it was time to go home. We know what has to be faced. We don't need someone who doesn't know us to waltz in here and tell us to get out."

The doctor's face was lined with concern. This large doctor humbly apologized for the incident and claimed it was all a misunderstanding. He said he had instructed the doctor to ask us if we wanted to go home so Rie could be around her family in her final days. Placing an arm around Sunny, he held Rie's hand. "Don't loose faith now. We doctors have never been able to predict what will happen to this child." He smiled down at Rie and she smiled back. "You, little lady, have surprised us at every turn."

Sunny wasn't as forgiving as Rie. She walked away from the doctor and stood glaring at him on the other side of the room with her arms crossed. She seemed to come to a decision. "We're ready to go home now," she informed the man. "It's time, our family needs to be together."

"You don't have to leave the hospital today, only when you're ready."

"Yes, we do," Sunny replied dryly. "Just as soon as you can release Sunny Marie."

"But…" he hesitated. One look at my sister's stern face changed whatever he was about to say. "I'll get the paperwork ready for you to sign," he stated. "I'm sorry things got so screwed up."

When the doctor left the room, Sunny lay down beside her daughter. Rie held her in her arms crooning softly. "Don't be afraid, Mom. God will take care of everything. Just rest for a while. I'll hold you."

The roles were reversed again; the child was giving comfort to the mother. Rie's words came back to me. The time before, when I left to go to the jungle I told Rie to take care of her mother and she responded by saying, "I always do."

THE LEFT SIDE OF BALANCE

They lie with little more than a Judas kiss of clarity. Set in reanimation from centuries past, they sow dissension among brothers and obliterate the Master's sanction.

They are unendowed with reason and lead others through their own self-deception.

Their mental poise is only the feeling of triumph at newly achieved strength.

They are found in solid mass, but they must exist for the balance.

They are not the stronger...the balance is even. The conception of good versus evil forever exist...on a balance.

It is inconceivable that they should ever overturn the scale.

CHAPTER 30

It was one of those perfect bright sunlight autumn days but it carried with it a stiff breeze from the north promising winter just around the corner. In the trees, one could glimpse a profusion of reds laced with gold. One more cold front and the remaining green would be gone. Normally the scene would delight us, but now our hearts were benumbed with a winter chill. We were making the trip home with our Rie, maybe for the last time. So on that beautiful day, in the middle of October, we left the hospital with a heavy heart.

All doctors except, Dr. Jimmy Jones, were dismissed. The Cancer Society furnished a hospital bed. We put it up in the living room so Rie could look outside from the large patio window Pawpaw and Phil had installed. The roses outside were in their splendor. Blooms that wouldn't be touched, but would be enjoyed by the girl inside. It was a hidden garden fit for our princess. As the days rolled by, we blessed each one. If Rie was in pain, she never showed it. Sunny took the day shift with her so their little family could be together. I took the night shift.

Rie was in the living room while Sunny worked throughout the house getting the boys ready for school or making meals. Sunny noticed that Rie's voice was getting fainter and she was afraid that if Rie needed her she wouldn't be able to hear her call out. Pawpaw, a retired telephone man, saved the day. He rigged Rie a buzzer on a board that stretched across her bed. When Rie needed her mother she would buzz. The loud buzzer could be heard all over the house and even into the back yard.

One day, while I was sleeping, I heard the buzzer going off. Oh God, I prayed, something must be wrong. I ran into the living room and heard Sunny and Rie talking. Sunny asked, "Rie what's wrong?"

Rie's eyes twinkled. "You said buzz if I needed you," she whispered.

Sunny laughed throwing her arms wide. "Well, here I am?"

Rie's eyes softened and her face became serious. "I need you, Mom. I really need you."

I heard Sunny catch her breath. She threw herself across her daughter and cried, "Oh, baby, I need you too. More than the sun, more than the rain, more than the rainbows, more than anything this life has to offer...I need you."

"That's the way I feel too, Mom," Rie whispered faintly. Rie held her mother while she cried.

Phil came through the patio door and sit beside his daughter. His face was somber. Rie saw her dad and reached around her mom to take his hand. "Daddy, I love you, too. I've always been proud to be your daughter. You and Mom have been the best parents any kid could have. Just remember how much I love you."

All Phil could do was mumble how much he loved her. The three just held each other crying. I stood there not wanting to intrude. I leaned my head against the wall and cried softly, "Please God, don't let this be their last good-bye." One of the family dogs, Madam Yen Chin, a cream-colored chow, wouldn't leave Rie's bed. We would literally have to force her to go outside. No sooner than she would use the bathroom she would return to her spot under the bed. There was no usual thumping of her tail or her usual begging for food from our plates. In fact, Sunny had to feed her by hand and place the water bowl under her nose to drink. It was as if she grieved with the rest of us.

Mother had the hardest time visiting Rie. She would come for short visits but always went home in hysterics. Daddy would sit for hours talking softly to the love of his life. Rie's face would beam as her Pawpaw told her stories of his youth, Daddy's voice never wavered, but the terrible pain he was feeling was visible in his eyes. We knew time was short. Watching Rie waste away before our very eyes, Sunny and I talked about having an early Christmas. When we told Rie, she became upset and told us in no uncertain terms that we were not to have Christmas early. Her words were, "I don't have time for Christmas." We gave up the idea. Rie began to sleep more during the day and staying awake nights.

On our nightly visits, Rie and I talked about many things. She wanted to talk about her mother and father and the boys. I told her stories of how much they loved her and the love Sunny and Phil had for each other. I told her how love could endure anything, warming and blessing everyone around it. I knelt beside her bed and told her how she was God's child and how bless we were because He chose us for her to live with. I told her how her name should have been Love, because she had done nothing but give love to everyone she came in contact with. She would listen quietly with a beautiful smile etched on her lovely little face.

We also talked about death. She wasn't afraid to talk about it. "I think I worry more about my mother and daddy and how my death will affect them," she said.

"I know," I cried. "It's hard for all of us to let you go. We're not as brave as you are."

Her honest eyes appraised me for a long time. "I'm not afraid, Aunt Margie," she whispered. "I know that God is there waiting for me just like he promised."

But I'm afraid I wanted to shout. We're all afraid. All the ones you're leaving behind are afraid to live life without you. We're afraid of the emptiness we're going to feel without our sunshine.

I told her stories of all the people she touched. One little tear slid down her face for each story. One night Philip, who frequently played in a rock band, came home late. He walked up to the bed and leaned over the side until his face almost touched his sister's face. The two little heads were so close but neither said a word. They only looked into each other's eyes, each other's heart. So much love and understanding passed between the two without a word being spoken. Then one little tear spilled from Rie's eye. Before it dropped onto the pillowcase, Philip drew it onto his finger. Then he dropped it into his opened palm. His fist closed tightly around it and he held it to his heart. "This is my tear, Sunny Marie," he tenderly whispered.

She reached out with a trembling hand and touched his face. In a soft whispered voice, she said, "I love you but you have to promise me, you'll be a good man when you grow up," Philip swallowed a large lump in his throat, then he replied simply, "I love you, too. I promise, I'll be a good man." He had given her his permission to turn loose.

They hugged and he kissed her cheek. They were saying their good-byes. I turned my head to conceal my tears. The pain had to be endured. Rie was showing us all what courage was about and none of us could fail her now. Much later I would thank God for these growing pains but for now it was too excruciating.

The next morning, Derek and Rie said their good-byes, Rie said, "Derek take care of Mom and Dad." With a catch in his voice Derek promised he would. "Always make them proud."

"I will, Rie," he cried, "you have my word." Rie smiled. "I know you will. I love you."

"Rie," Derek sobbed. "I love you, too."

We all wanted to say more at a time like this because we knew Rie was saying her last good-byes, but it gets too emotional, the heart nearly burst from a pain so great you think you're going to die from the sheer weight of it. All you can do is pray you have more time; pray these won't be the last words you utter.

Sunny decided to call Doug, thinking he might want to say a last good-bye to Rie. His roommate answered. The roommate asked who was calling and Sunny gave her name. He said he would get Doug. Long minutes later he came back, apologizing that Doug wasn't able to come to the phone. Sunny told the roommate why she was calling and that Rie didn't have long to live. The roommate cleared his throat. "Mrs. Eppler, I'm so sorry," he said, "but Doug refuses to speak to you." Sunny quietly hung up the phone.

One day Sunny and Phil were sitting in the living room beside Rie's bed and Rie informed us the devil was back. Sunny stood up and asked, "What does he look like?" It took an effort for Rie to answer but she managed to say, "Evil. He's smirking."

"Not in my house," Sunny stated, quickly hanging a crucifix over the door. "I rebuke him in the name of Jesus Christ. He'll not touch any of our family now or later."

It seemed to comfort Rie that her mother had the courage to confront Satan and stand strong. She gave her mother the thumbs-up sign.

All this time we had never seen pain registered in Rie's eyes but now she would catch her breath for just a second as if she couldn't breathe. She was being bombarded with intense pain but she still tried to hide it from us. The little house was being destroyed. It was time to let her run free. Our selfish love had held her back too long.

I asked her, "If the pain is unbearable, we can get you help. Is it your stomach or head that hurts?" When she did not respond, I said, "It's all right, little girl. You don't have to be brave anymore. Show me." After a long pause, she pointed with her finger to her head.

Sunny called the doctor. Dr. Jimmy ordered morphine at the pharmacy. I volunteered to run this dreaded errand. I waited in the drug store until the prescription was filled. Sobbing. Unable to stop myself, knowing that on my return Rie would become too drugged to respond.

When Sunny gave her the medication and Rie slipped quietly away into a pain free world of her own. It was the last time we were allowed to see her beautiful gray-green eyes. The nurse with hospice came to see if there was anything that we needed. She asked Sunny if she had told the boys that Rie was near death. Sunny calmly told the woman, "I'll talk to the boys later." Minutes later, the woman took it on herself to tell the boys that their sister was dying. The woman cornered Philip and Derek in the living room. "Cry and release some of the pain," she demanded.

It was the wrong thing to say. The boys went berserk. Philip cried out, "Get away from me. You don't know anything about my pain." Derek shouted to the woman, "Leave us alone, you old witch. We'll cry when it's over but not in front of you."

I felt sorry for the woman. When Doctor Jimmy came, she told him that he should make the boys face the fact that Rie was dying. The doctor sent the woman home.

Marilyn and Dave, Pastor Brock and his wife, Philip and Derek, Sunny, Phil, and myself sat around watching Rie's labored breathing. We prayed. This time our prayers were different. We prayed for Rie's release from her pain filled world and strength for ourselves. Sunny whispered, "Margie, I can't let my baby die here. How can I live with the sadness of knowing Rie's death was here? This house has always been filled with sunshine. I don't want it filled with the shadows of her death. Call an ambulance, we're going to the hospital."

As if Rie heard, a loud sound came from her. It sounded as if the soul was separating from the body. I have never heard a sound to compare with it. Sunny knelt beside her child and made sure she was still breathing. Rie's little heart was still beating strong.

The ambulance came and took Rie to the hospital. We all stayed by Rie's bed at the hospital the rest of the night. Her condition steadily worsened. John and his mother came to say their good-byes. I left to go after my mother and father. It was the morning of November 4th, one year to the day that Rie started the headaches.

Just as we got off the elevator I saw Steve, Phil's best friend, and his wife, Ella. Ella was sobbing against his shoulder. My knees turned to jelly and my heart jumped out of my chest. "Oh, God," I begged. "Please don't let us be too late."

Mother touched my arm and pulled me to a stop. "Marjorie, what's the matter?"

"Mother…Daddy, stay here. Let me go into the room," I pleaded.

Rie was propped up in bed looking as though she was resting. Two nurses stood at the foot of Rie's bed. Sunny was on one side of the bed holding Rie's hand, talking softly to her daughter. Phil was lying across Rie. When I touched him, he got up and moved away. His face wet with tears. The scene was calm, very quiet but Rie was gone.

One of the nurses was standing straight as a soldier. No emotion showing on her face. My first thought was this woman was cold, unfeeling. Then I saw the haunted look in her eyes. I said, "God bless you. This must be hard for you?" She made a soft noise and started to cry aloud. She said, "I know this isn't professional, but you're right. It's hard…very hard."

I walked around the bed and put my arms around her to comfort her. Sunny gently laid her baby's hand down and walked up to me. Tears were coursing down her cheeks but she was calm. "Rie's gone," she murmured softly. "I was holding her in my arms telling her she was my sunshine and rainbows. She took three little breaths before she left me." She searched helplessly around the room. "It's over," she stated simply.

At that moment, Mother and Daddy walked in. They stood there with their eyes wild with fear. Mother asked, "Our baby is dead?"

I hurried to Mother's side placing my arms around her. "Mother, Rie doesn't have to suffer any more." I was proud of Mother and Daddy that day. They didn't make a scene and they stayed strong for Sunny and Phil. We all took our turn kissing our angel good-bye. I stood by the bed and touched the still warm little cheek. She was warmer now than she had been the night before. I marveled at this perfect little girl, God's child. I rejoiced in the fact that God let us borrow her for eighteen years. I rejoiced in the knowledge that this brave child showed us not only the way to live but also the way to die. Her life, her many talents were not wasted. We needn't have any regrets or shame letting her go. Christians don't say goodbye, only see you later. Hopefully, when she sees us next, maybe she'll be just as proud of us as we have always been of her.

Sunny made us all leave the room. She said, "Rie, didn't want anyone to see her after death. She's not in this house anymore."

We waited outside in the hall until the funeral home came for our baby. Phil took Mother and Daddy home. Pastor Brock took Sunny and me to her house. We walked into the living room and were greeted by a loud buzzing sound. Sunny stood in the middle of the room searching around.

I asked, "What is it?" Sunny looked at me strangely. "I don't know?" She walked into the kitchen and called Pastor Brock and myself to come join her. She stood in front of her built-in oven. The timer was buzzing. "It hasn't worked since we bought the house thirteen years ago," Sunny declared.

She twisted it one way then the other. The sound continued. Then she giggled softly while tears rolled down her pale face. Pastor looked at me and I looked at him. "It's Rie," Sunny stated with a smile. "She's telling us she's still with us."

When the buzzer stopped without anyone touching it, I knew she was right. I felt the same way. That same day Doctor Jimmy came by to tell Sunny not to be surprised if odd things started to happen. She smiled and said, "Doctor Jimmy, things stated happening the minute we got home."

Dedo came immediately when she heard about Rie's death. She was only in the house a short while when Philip came up to her with a large box. He said, "I've been meaning to give you this for a long time."

Dedo looked at him questioningly while opening the package, inside lay Rie's fake fur coat. The same one no one could find just a few months ago.

"Dedo, in February, when Sunny Marie wasn't expected to live, Mother sent you here to take Rie's room apart," he said struggling with his emotions. "I tried at that time to tell you that I didn't want you to have Rie's coat, but I didn't know how to so I hid the coat at my friends house. The coat was special, Derek and I saved our money to buy it for her." He took a deep breath. "Now I feel differently. I would like you to have it."

It was a gift Dedo would always treasure. Sunny planned Rie's funeral. I asked her if she needed help. She smiled slowly. "You know, I've already taken care of most of it. God saw to that when she was in a coma. All I need to do now is plan her funeral the way she wanted it." She touched her head. "It's all here. I have to do it right."

"You will," I said. "Just the way she wanted you too." And it was. Everything that Rie told her mother was carried out to the last detail. The Evie tape, the one that Johnny bought in Indonesia, was played for all to hear. Woody was dressed in his blue police uniform and Dedo's husband, Hank, was dressed in his Louisiana's State Trooper uniform. They stood at attention on each side of the casket. It was Woody and Hank's way of pleasing Rie. I'm not sure most people understood why they stood there but Rie knew and that was the important thing.

So no one would see Rie after death, Sunny asked for the casket to stay closed. Pictures of Rie stood on easels around the room. A huge flower blanket of pink roses covered her casket. It represented the family hands she loved so much.

Dale sang a song that he wrote and the song "Sunny." Paul Gautier read Rie's poems. The service held by her friends was one Rie would have been proud of. It wasn't sad because Rie never liked sad things.

Flowers were everywhere in the large chapel. I'm not sure Rie would have approved of the flowers, but it was the people's way of showing how much they loved her. The chapel was too small for the people and flowers so they overflowed into the hallways and outside into the parking lot.

The area schools allowed students out of class to attend. The line seemed to go on forever. Rie had touched so many lives. Some of the young people drove a straight twelve to fourteen hours to come from colleges in Texas, Louisiana and Oklahoma.

One boy came up to us and said, "Mrs. Eppler?" Sunny turned. The young man was tall and slim. He appeared nervous as he twisted a tissue in his hands. "Mrs. Eppler, would you mind if I stay for the funeral."

"Of course not," Sunny affirmed. "Were you a friend of Sunny Marie?"

"No, not a friend." The young man shuffled his feet. "I'm not sure she even knew my name, but I knew her." He had a pained expression in his eyes. "I used to be a dope head. Popular girls like Sunny Marie didn't have anything to do with me. Every morning when your daughter came to school, she would pass me and wave as if I was someone special." His eyes soften. "It was as if she smiled just for me. It made me ashamed that I was smoking pot. I wanted her to be proud of me, so I stopped. I cleaned myself up but I didn't dream she would notice." He smiled sadly. "One day…" his voice cracked and he stopped talking. Then his voice became shrill as he replied. "One morning she came up to me and told me how proud she was of me." He drew a breath trying to cover the tears. "She noticed…she really noticed. Could I please stay…?"

Sunny put her arms around the sobbing youth. "It's all right, son, stay. Sunny Marie would want you to."

A woman walked up to me, and said, "There's something wonderful in this room. It's something," she patted the middle of her chest, "if you don't have it when you come in, you want to take it with you when you leave." I agreed. Where God is, love is. That's what filled that room—our hearts—our lives.

Pastor Brock gave the most beautiful eulogy. At the very
end he said, "Now, Sunny Marie runs free with the Angels." It was this exact message I telexed Johnny. "Our Sunny Marie is now running free with the Angels."

DON'T CALL ME BACK
A silver thread can not hold my soul to this earth.
I will never be bound.
My companions now are angels with gold halos
Their thoughts and words profound

I am a child of heaven totally without skin.
I can be a star, the wind, or just a grain of sand.

I witness wonders unseen by living men.
I can hold this universe in my outstretched hand.

Do not blame my God because I died.
Do not burden your heart or fill it with hate.
Because I walk along with God, take pride.
It's time to rejoice, give thanks and celebrate.

I now am a part of this universe bright,
Only a small heartbeat away.
I live and breathe in our Savior's light,
Happy forever, with Him and His angels I'll stay.

CHAPTER 31

Death? Yes. Gone? Never. Rie's spirit will be with us always. She's passed over to a wonderful place where the rest of us earthbound humans can't go…not yet. But when we do, she'll be there waiting for us with that beautiful smile of welcome.

Rie will be remembered as the girl who sang her songs for Jesus. She was a girl who sang His praises as long as she had a breath. Her voice will echo in our hearts and souls as long as we live. That's how miracles work.

What do we do now? For a full year from November 4, 1979 to November 4, 1980, our thoughts, prayers, energies were directed toward Rie and her illness. Every morning our days were occupied with keeping each other's spirits up and all the ups and downs that go with serious illness.

Years ago, I saw a play at a school UIL contest, where a woman had a husband and three sons who were fishermen. She never slept a full night because she was always keeping watch over the sea until her family returned.

One by one, she lost her loved ones to the sea until she had one son left. When she lost her last son to death, she said, "Tonight, I will sleep for the first time because I do not have to wait, worry, and watch anymore. It's over." Over? Oh, if that were only so. The pain of knowing we won't see her today, to touch her or to hold her. The pain suffocates us. We are in agreement, that we will see Sunny Marie again in heaven. We get less earthbound and begin to look forward to that wonderful reunion. We know now that it's not if we lose our loved ones, but when.

We keep reminding ourselves to love each other and be tolerant of others. We have to prepare our souls and forget about the silly unimportant things that clutter our lives.

The wonderful thing is that through all the tears and pain, we are comforted knowing Rie is in God's care.

Sunny Marie knew her God. She was strong and unafraid through that year. Her time was used more to get us to the point where our faith grew strong enough to let her go.

Sunny and Phil received letters by the hundreds. People letting them know how special Sunny Marie was to them. From teachers to Sunny Marie's peers. Her friend, Paul Gautier, the young man who offered to fix soup for Rie, wrote one such letter. It read:

Dear Mr. and Mrs. Eppler & Family,

May God bless you with peace, understanding, and growth in His love. Through Sunny Marie's strength, courage, and faith I have grown closer to God and closer to myself in my relationship to God. She will always be there for me. I know that. Giving me the strength to "go on." She will always be alive, giving that inspiration that I so often need.

Had I one-tenth the nib of her pen I could more eloquently describe my feelings. But I am simple. I wrote a simple poem to say how I feel. I love you all dearly, God Bless you, Paul Gautier

The wind is blowing, it's Sunny.
The sky is dark, it's night.
And I can see her smile in the stars
While I think about days gone by.
And I hear her voice
Soft as a butterfly
She talks to me.
She walks with me.

She lives in me
She lives…
The rain is falling, it's Sunny.
The sky is dark, it's night.
I can feel her touch just as much
As the raindrops when they fall.
My ears aren't alone, they hear the tone
Of her strong, sweet, loving all.
She prays with me.
She stays with me.
She lives in me.
She lives…
The dawn is breaking, it's Sunny.
The sky is bright, it's day.
I watch her sigh as she says Good-Bye
But it's only for just a while.
For she's going home and it won't be long
'Til I am there by her side.
She talks with me.
She walks with me.
She lives in me.
She lives…she lives.

In another letter, the Superintendent of the Orange County school system wrote about the time when he came to work for the county. He said that one of his first duties was to tour the area schools. On his day to tour the high school he was assigned, he thought, a faculty member to assist him. He explained how he was walking around the school with this beautiful intelligent person talking shop. He said it wasn't until later that day, when he was commenting to his staff that if all his staff was on the ball as Ms. Eppler was then he was really going to have a great year. They informed him that Miss Eppler was a senior in high school. He concluded his letter by saying, "I had hoped that your daughter, Sunny Marie, would be a teacher. She was one of those special people that would have made a difference in students' lives. We have lost a wonderful person. She'll be missed."

Much later after Rie's death, Stephanie, Rie's best friend, wrote:

Dear Mr. and Mrs. Eppler:

I don't know that I ever told you how Rie affected my life...after she died I was so devastated, I never really got a chance to talk with you again. I don't know if you remember or not but the kindest thing you did was invite me to sit with you all, in the family section, at Rie's funeral. That meant a lot to me then and now. I wanted to say so much then but I completely retreated into myself (even throughout her illness).

I had lost my one and only best friend and when she died. I felt alone-so very alone. Truthfully, when it came time for me to choose a college to attend, I had entertained thoughts of going off to school but I chose Lamar University because Rie had planned on going there and we talked about being roommates. And so, I gave it no other thought. I thought Rie might recover and eventually come on to school and join me because I believed in miracles too. That year did not go well-I couldn't get over my anger and shock.

Rie and I had an exceptional friendship-my childhood was rewritten because of our years together. I remember the day we actually met at Salk Elementary like it was yesterday. It was the first day of school and all the kids were pouring in the classroom to find their seats-there was a flurry of children everywhere. I was already seated and so was Rie (about 3 desks away from each other) when our eyes met and we smiled/laughed we moved next to each other. It was instant friendship! We really always did laugh together (I never remember sad times between us, we just thought so many things were funny.) We truly were always "in trouble"-all the way through high school. She really was my sunshine. After her death, it took along time for me to become friends with anyone else but I think it began preparing me for some of the things I was going to encounter in my life. Rie was but the first of my family and close friends to die of cancer.

I still miss Rie and I am still so very sorry for your loss but God bless you.

Sincerely and with much love, Stephanie

*   *   *

It would take at least another book to tell all the strange and wonderful things that happened after Rie said good-bye, but I will pass on a few of these wonderful events.

I stayed for a couple of weeks longer. The day Sunny and Phil took me to the airport in Houston, I asked them to stop at a religious bookstore. We picked a mall at random and went inside a large cluttered shop.

Just as I pushed opened the door, a song was playing. It was one of the songs from Johnny's Indonesian tape. The sweet clear voice of Evie was singing, "Jesus, I believe what You said to me."

We all froze. We looked at each other and started smiling. Big broad smiles. Tears filled our eyes. Sunny said, "Can't you feel it? Rie wants us to know she's happy."

There was an older woman working in the shop. I asked her if she had any more recordings of the song that just played.

She looked at me strangely and laughed. "I don't think so. I've never heard that song before."

I told her why we were interested in that particular recording. I shared Rie with her, showing her all the photographs I carried. She replied, "Oh, don't you know the Angels in heaven are rejoicing to have her with them."

What a wonderful thing to say, another messenger of God. We didn't consider the incident of the song a coincidence. It wasn't a song you heard everyday. Out of all the songs that could have been on the tape it was one that meant something to us. It was a message from our Rie.

When it was time for my plane to leave, I put my arms around my sister and said, "Are you going to be okay?

She looked at me with tears shimmering in her eyes and replied "No, but I'll work on it. I'm still angry with God for taking her," she shrugged, "but I know He won't mind." Then like the sister I knew so well, she grinned. "God knows I love Him."

"Please don't be mad," I begged. "Rie wouldn't approve of that."

Sunny looked off into the distance for a long moment, then back at me. "Don't worry, I'll work it out." She swallowed a lump in her throat. "After all, I can't disappoint Rie." Oh, God, who could? Rie set us an impossible task. My sister would keep the faith just like her daughter asked her too. I went back to Indonesia. Back to the blue and green jungle that was my home, back to my Johnny.

The first day I was back home, I walked around my house feeling lost. There was really nothing for me to do except unpack my suitcases. The house was empty and quiet, too empty and way too quiet. When the telephone rang, I jumped. It was Johnny calling from the plant to make sure I was doing okay. I was standing in the dining area, in front of two large windows, assuring him I was all right. Suddenly, I found myself face-to-face with a tiny bird peeping in the window. It wasn't just a bird…it was a redheaded bird perched on a huge green leaf.

I laughed out loud and said, "Johnny, you won't believe what's sitting outside my window looking at me." When I told him, we both laughed. I went back to unpacking feeling as if I had just received another love message.

When Johnny came home from work at five in the afternoon, we heard a loud whistle. Johnny started for the door and said, "I wonder who that could be."

I followed him and looked out the window expecting to see a friend, but there sat my little bird. When it saw me, the tiny bird whistled again.

It was more like a man's whistle, shrill and loud. The little bird cocked its head to the side and whistled again until I came closer. I pressed my face to the window. It turned its tiny head from side to side, watching.

Every morning after that, it came at six in the morning, at noontime, and at five in the afternoon. It would always whistle to let us know it was there. Sometimes, it would fly in and out of Johnny's parked jeep and gaze at itself in the mirror. It let Johnny take pictures of it with a flash and it wasn't afraid. It seemed to pose.

I shared it with my friends and neighbors. Rie had said to look for her in the birds, flowers, butterflies and rainbows. A happy little messenger. Probably the little redheaded bird had always lived in Indonesia, but as God as my witness, I had never seen it before, nor had my neighbors. I know that God in his love used the little bird to comfort me as he promised. Jesus said, "Blessed are they that mourn: for they shall be comforted." He had kept his promise.

One morning, I received a call from one of my friends who informed me that three of the men in camp had been rushed to the hospital with high fever, vomiting, and were extremely ill.

We had a well-equipped hospital in our camp and they were able to take test to determine what was wrong. Having just been through the terrible illness with our Rie, I said prayers for the men asking God not to let it be serious. A few days later, two had showed improvement. The other, Craig was getting worse. He was hooked up to IVs unable to keep anything down. I didn't know this young man personally, but he continued to stay on my mind. I knew he was getting the best of care and that his wife, Bonnie, was at his side. For some strange reason every time I tried to say prayers for Craig, I thought about potato soup. I know that sounds crazy, it did to me too. It was strange. It doesn't take much skill to fix but it's not on the top of my list to make for just anybody. I never made potato soup for anyone outside my family. And then it was always made in the winter months to eat, not for illness.

Here we were a few miles from the equator, where it's summer all the time and I'm thinking potato soup. Just the thought made me want to turn the air conditioner up a notch. I tried to fight the thoughts but my mind kept saying, "POTATO SOUP." I stood in my kitchen arguing with myself, feeling like I had finally gone over the edge.

"POTATO SOUP my brain kept repeating. No," I cried, "I don't even know this man." I walked around with my hands over my ears hoping to somehow close out the potato soup obsession. It was a losing battle. I finally made the potato soup telling myself I was making it for Johnny. That didn't work. As soon as Johnny stepped through the door, my mouth took on a life of its own. "Honey, I know you'll think I've lost my mind but would you go see Craig and take him some potato soup?"

With everything that I had been through with Rie, I could tell by Johnny's expression that he had reason to believe I was not quite myself, to put it mildly.

When he didn't answer, I said, "Craig has to have it now."

"Who told you that?"

"I don't know. But someone has been telling me all day, Craig has to have potato soup."

Finally, he said gently, "I don't know Craig very well except to speak to him." He cleared his throat. "Honey, he's very ill. I don't think he could eat it even if I took it to him."

"Johnny, I'm sorry but you must take it to him," I stressed. By this time, I was wringing my hands. "All day I have felt this urgent need to get him potato soup."

Johnny loves me and tries his best to please me. He agreed. "Okay, if you feel that strongly about it, I'll do it." I put the potato soup in a Thermos and also sent a tape recorder with the New Testament Bible tapes. I kissed Johnny good-bye and thanked him for taking care of it for me. I waited with apprehension for his return.

When Johnny walked slowly into the house, I stood up expectantly. A bewildered expression creased his face but there was a gleam in his eyes.

He shook his head slightly and said almost in a thoughtful tone, "I can't believe it."

"What happened?" I asked.

"Honey, I walked into Craig's room and asked him how he was feeling. He told me, 'not so good.'" Johnny sat down in the nearest chair and stared out into space.

"And?"

He swallowed a lump. "I told him you sent him some potato soup but if he didn't like it or was too sick to eat it, we would understand." Johnny's eyes filled with tears. "Honey, Craig started to cry."

"Oh, Johnny, why?"

Johnny cleared his throat of the tears. "Craig wanted to know how you could have known that every time he was sick at home his mother would make him potato soup. She died a year ago. I watched Craig eat part of the soup and he told me he would save the rest until later. He turned on the Bible tapes and was listening to them when I left."

I clapped my hands together and said, "Dear God, I'm not sure how you worked this but thank you. You're so good." I felt better that I wasn't losing my mind after all. It had been a message sent by the Holy Spirit.

The next morning when Johnny checked on Craig, he was sitting up in bed. He had just finished eating the rest of the leftover soup for breakfast. Now that he had begun eating again, the IVs were removed.

That night, his wife Bonnie came by to see us. When I asked how Craig was doing, she said, "He's so much better, but I have to know something. I've been married to him a year and I knew nothing about his mother making potato soup. How did you know to make him potato soup?" Her voice began to tremble with emotion, "That was the first food he was able to keep down."

"Bonnie, all I can say, is it must have come from the Holy Spirit. God's ways are mysterious, I'm still trying to understand all this myself." She stared at me as if she didn't believe me. I laughed. I knew the feeling. "It's true." I chuckled. "You have no idea how I felt when all I could think of was getting potato soup to Craig."

I told her about how things had been with Sunny Marie. Bonnie ended up staying until well after midnight.

I told her that I felt as if my soul had become a sponge, soaking up everything I can about God. What I didn't tell her was how overwhelming it was at times. Since Rie's death, my life had new meaning and I seemed to be on the very verge of knowing what God wanted from me.

After the soup incident, God seemed to be bombarding me with knowledge and answers to questions that had gone unanswered for years. Many times I threw my hands up into the air and said, "Wait a minute, just wait a minute, God. You're going too fast. I need time to digest all these wonderful things." I was so elated and at the same time totally overwhelmed.

Craig soon got out of the hospital. The doctors never could give a reason for his illness.

A few days later, while Johnny was at work, I was on my knees talking to God…something that had become so natural that calluses had actually formed on my knees. Tears were streaming down my face. I prayed to God, "Guide me. Give me a sense of purpose. Use me for Your glory, but please more slowly."

I said, "God, if I have wronged anyone, please forgive me. If there is anyone I have failed to love as I should, please help me to make it right."

At that very moment the telephone rang. When I said, "Hello," a voice softly asked, "Do you need me?" Recognizing the voice immediately, I nearly dropped the receiver from my hand. It was the only person in camp I didn't feel close to. To put it bluntly, we just didn't like each other. I never actually felt dislike…exactly. It was just nothing at all. For all the years we have been in camp I can honestly say that I loved the people here, except this one lady. There was no tangible reason to feel this way toward her but she acted the same toward me, so I knew that it was mutual. There was just a wall between us.

My heart overflowed with wonder. As the tears continued to flowed down my cheeks, without hesitation, I answered, "Oh, yes, Betty. I need you."

She explained, "Marjorie, all of a sudden I felt an overpowering sensation that you needed me."

"I do need you," I said, "Please come down. I would like to talk with you."

When she arrived, we talked for hours. The wall between us came tumbling down by Gods hands. Again I was so overwhelmed, that I could love this woman so much in a few seconds when I had felt nothing for her before. To God, I give the glory.

Johnny and I had friends in for Thanksgiving dinner. One of them strolled out on our pouch. He made a comment about my orchid plant. "Has this thing ever bloomed?"

"No," Johnny replied. "Margie bought it from one of the yard boys when we first came here." After inspecting the plant carefully, our friend was an expert on orchids but all he could tell Johnny was that it appeared one of the healthiest plants he had seen.

Several mornings later, Johnny was having coffee on the porch and called to me. I walked out and he pointed to my orchid plant. A long stem protruded from the plant. It was four feet long. It kept growing daily until hundreds of blooms appeared.

Then we knew what kind of orchid plant we had. It was a very rare and protected tiger orchid. As the last orchids died on that shoot another shoot would take its place with another hundred flowers on it. Our orchid expert had never seen one bloom so profusely before and it was the center of attention for all those that came to visit. The huge orchid plant bloomed continuously for an entire year. I was again reminded of the time Rie said, "Look for me in the flowers, butterflies, birds and rainbows." Not only did we have a Rie Bird, but now we had a Rie Orchid."

During that year, a new couple with two little boys moved into the house next door. I went over to welcome them and offered to help in any way I could to get them settled in.

Anyone moving to the jungle for the first time has a cultural shock. You come with clothing and the company supplies everything else. In the jungle, we have to share with each other.

A few days later Jerri, my new neighbor, came over to visit. She had never been in my home before and she took her time looking at my framed family photographs scattered around the room. Then she came to the one of Sunny Marie. She became silent, pursing her lips in concentration. Finally, she said, "I've seen this girl."

With a deliberate attempt at lightness, I assured her it wasn't so. I smiled tightly. "Jerri, that's my niece. She passed away a few months ago."

The tone in my voice made her hesitate. She shook her head and picked up the 8 x 10 photograph to get a better look. She held it up to the light coming through the window, turning the picture first one way then another. "Marjorie, I've seen this girl before." This time her voice was more determined.

The room became quiet. Still clutching the framed picture in her hands, she looked at me and said excitedly, "Wait a minute…wait a minute. Was she in Lake Charles at St. Patrick's hospital?" All I could do was nod my head in agreement. "I can't believe this," she intoned. "My next door neighbor's mother worked as a nurse at St. Patrick. She was visiting my next-door neighbor and showed us this very picture, but it was smaller. She told us of the miracle of Sunny Marie coming out of the coma and how excited the entire hospital was. She said that Sunny Marie's mother gave her the picture." Her face became sad. "I'm so sorry, I didn't know Sunny Marie had passed away."

Jerri wanted to hear more about Sunny Marie and I shared everything with her. Finally after I finished about Rie, Jerri sat looking off into space. "Are you angry with God?" she asked.

"Oh, no," I replied, "We love Him more than ever."

"Well, I'm angry with Him!" she suddenly declared. I was shocked at her statement. Jerri's lips twisted and in a troubled voice she said, "My mother loved God but he took both my parents away at a young age. Mother would always sing songs about Jesus. Her favorite was 'One Day At A Time.'" Then, she murmured, "I don't think I can forgive Him for taking them."

I walked over to the young woman and sat down beside her. "Don't waste your energy on anger. Don't you see that you were truly blessed by God? You know where they are. You had Christian parents, Jerri. You can now rest knowing they're in God's care. Death for Christians is not a punishment but a reward. I truly believe that Rie was our blessing and that her illness made us stronger Christians. In the past year, I made three trips to the states to be with Rie and my sister, Sunny, and I grew from each trip."

Jerri said, "I wish I could feel that way but I don't want anything to do with Him."

"Give it time, Jerri. God's always there. It will come. You have two beautiful sons that will need a good foundation on which to grow."

"We'll see." She started to leave but seemed rooted to the spot. "Oh, my God! Marjorie, were you on a plane from Beaumont to Houston around July."

"Yes."

She covered her mouth with her hand and looked pale. In disbelief she asked, "Did you sit next to a lady about my size and she looked a little like me?"

"Yes," I replied. "Just a minute. I think I still have her address." I retrieved it from my purse and handed it to her.

She took the paper and looked at the name printed on it. "Oh, my God! I can't believe this," she cried. She sat back down hurriedly. "This is my very best friend. We've been friends for years and when she found out my husband and I were going to Indonesia, she told me she had met a nice woman who lived there, somewhere. She told me if by some miracle I could live by that woman, she wouldn't worry about me." Jerri's eyes filled with tears and she nervously giggled. "She'll be so happy to know I did just that very thing. She couldn't remember your name or which part of Indonesia you were from, but this piece of paper is proof that you were the one. This is unbelievable! She'll never believe this. I don't believe this."

After all I had been through with Sunny Marie I could believe it. How could I tell this young woman that God never wastes a moment or meeting? I hugged her tightly, still in awe of our meeting. It was going to take time to gather everything that had happened in such a short time.

"You're doing it to me again, God," I whispered. As if God whispered back, a sudden understanding came over me. No, this wasn't for me. This was for Jerri because of her anger.

A few weeks later Jerri, a picture of health, started having severe kidney trouble. Both her kidneys stopped working and she had to move back to the states. From the letters I received I found out that Jerri's sister donated her a kidney and it was compatible. Later I received a letter from Jerri thanking me for sharing Rie and her faith in God. Jerri claimed she couldn't have made it through the operations and recovery without that knowledge. She could now give God all the glory.

During this time Sunny worked as a volunteer for The American Cancer Society. God managed to put her in a place to help others through the same ordeal she had just been through. What better person to reassure grieving families. When she would say, "I know how you feel at a time like this." They knew it was true.

There is no way anyone can tell me that God doesn't put us where we're needed.

GONE WITH THE WIND

I don't try to stop the feeling any longer. I see things the way they were, now, but the feeling still comes, and surrending, I remember.

The pain is dulled. I've started laughing again. The tears are sweetly diluted; besides, they always fell for the wrong reasons.

I'm beginning to know myself again and looking at life through clear lenses. The rose colored glasses were thrown away long ago-you took them off for me. I guess I put off letting them go for sentimental reasons. Now I can't recall any of those reasons, probably because they had no substantial backing…dreams are made of clouds, and clouds disperse with the wind.

The Red-headed bird

Tiger Orchid

CHAPTER 32

Four months later, Johnny and I went into Singapore to locate and commission an artist to paint Rie's portrait for Sunny and Phil. Time and again we were met with disappointment. None satisfied us with samples of their work that could do justice to a portrait of Rie.

Unfruitful days passed and our stay in Singapore was drawing to an end. We had just about given up any hope of finding someone on this trip.

On the last day of our vacation, I went to the hotel's beauty shop to have my hair washed and nails done. I started talking to the girls that worked there about how we had spent the week searching for an artist. The manager of the shop said, "Oh, I have a friend who works at the TV station as a set designer but his first love is portrait painting. I can talk to him and see if he would be interested."

I told her we would be leaving early the next morning to go back to our camp in Indonesia and tonight would be the only time we'd be able to meet with him.

That night about 9 p.m., we received a call from the front desk saying there was a man downstairs wishing to speak with us about painting a portrait. We told him to send the man to our room.

When the knock came at the door, Johnny and I were excited. The visitor introduced himself as Lee See Sin. He was a small built man appearing much younger than his 40 years. He apologized for calling on us so late, but he had just gotten off work. He also apologized for bringing just two samples of his work. The larger painting was of Beethoven and the smaller one was of the First Lady of Singapore. Both were beautifully done. Very life like and the soft hues of color begged to be touched. I could picture Rie in the pastels and knew this man was the one.

We explained to him what we wanted to do. We showed him a picture of Rie and he sat for several moments gazing at it. We told him about the past year during her illness. He listened patiently. After along time, he said, "I never copy a photograph if I can help it. I like to get the feel of a person mentally and than paint them." He sat forward on his chair and smiled.

"I need to have Sunny Marie's mother send me many photos of her over the last few years with as much information about Sunny Marie's likes and dislikes. I must get to know her personally."

"I can do that," I said, but I was wondering if Sunny would part with her photographs that were one of a kind.

We explained it would be at least four months before we would be back in Singapore to pick up the portrait and he said he would do the best he could.

We called Sunny that night while Mr. Lee was in the room and gave her his name and address. At first when I told her about having the portrait painted, Sunny's reply was expressionless.

"Margie, I don't think that would be a good idea. I don't have many photos of Rie and what I do have I would like to keep." Her voice broke on a sob. "There can never be any more, you know."

"I know, but honey, that's what Johnny and I are giving you. It's going to be a sixteen-inch by twenty-inch oil painting of Rie. Something that you can put up in the house and see everyday." I was met with silence.

"Margie, as an artist myself, I know that it's hard to get the perfect likeness of someone. I don't want an abstract or an Oriental Rie."

I knew my sister's concern. During the Korean War, our brother had her portrait painted by a Korean artist. He made her eyes slant at the corners.

"Believe me, Sunny, it just feels right."

"What makes you think he's qualified?" I gazed over at Mr. Lee with a secure feeling knowing as far as I was concerned it was a done deal but I had to convince my sister. "Faith," I answered simply, "Blind faith."

Again, I was met with silence across the thousands of miles that separated us. I couldn't tell her that her precious photographs of her daughter would not get lost in the mail. Something that precious couldn't be insured.

I knew if Sunny sent them immediately, she wouldn't have time to make copies. I couldn't tell her that this man wasn't a con artist or irresponsible, but I could tell her that I had a gut feeling that God was with us, leading us through every step. "Trust me," I whispered.

Finally, she answered with a laugh, "Am I obligated to hang the painting if it doesn't look like Rie?" I laughed out loud and replied, "If the painting isn't the exact image of Sunny Marie, you'll never see it. This, I promise you."

"Oh, all right," she conceded. "I'll send everything tomorrow but please tell Mr. Lee to take care of Rie's photographs and poems. They're more precious than gold." After that we said our good-byes. Johnny gave Mr. Lee three hundred dollars to buy materials that he needed to do the oil painting, knowing we wouldn't have any contact with this man for four months. We told him how he could contact us if he needed us through the company office in Singapore.

Next morning, bright and early, we left for Indonesia feeling as though we had made the right choice. Actually that God had made the choice for us.

Several days later we talked to Sunny and she had confirmed that the photographs and written materials were on the way. As it turned out, it was five months before we were able to get back to Singapore. All that time we had no contact with Mr. Lee and our friends chided us about being taken for three hundred dollars from someone we would never see again. We never faltered in our trust of him.

Johnny's job in Indonesia ended. Now we were leaving this part of the world, being sent home to the United States. I flew into Singapore three days ahead of Johnny to get some last minute shopping in before returning to the States. When I arrived at the Hotel, I called the TV station and asked for Mr. Lee. I was told he wasn't there at the moment but they would have him call when he returned.

Later that afternoon, Mr. Lee called confirming he had completed the portrait and promised to bring it to the hotel after work.

When he arrived he placed the covered painting on the table. I stood quietly, waiting. I held my breath in anticipation as he removed the cloth. The instant my eyes beheld the painting, I placed both hands over my mouth and said, "Oh God! Oh God!" completely overwhelmed at the beauty that radiated back at me. Rie's large eyes were alive. I was expecting her to take a breath before laughing that musical way I remembered. I started to cry. All I could say was, "It's so beautiful, so— so very beautiful."

I touched the pastels shades of softness. It was Rie, full of sunshine, just as I remembered her on the day in the rose garden. Her face was caught in a gentle grin showing her many dimples. Her hair danced around her shoulders in springy natural curls. The way Mr. Lee had painted her; she could have been a girl from centuries past or a girl of the future. Utterly feminine, suspended in time.

"Mr. Lee," I said trying to control the trembling in my voice, "how did you get her so lifelike. Her eyes, dimples, hair and even the amusement in her grin are exactly the way I remember her."

He sat down in the nearest chair and murmured softly, "Her eyes were the first thing I put on canvas."

Of course, I thought silently, mirrors of the soul. How often had I heard that saying before, but I knew in Rie's case it was true.

He continued, "My wife got very nervous. She wanted me to hurry and get the painting out of the house." He shrugged. "She felt it was alive." He nodded his head in agreement. "It was the truth. To me Sunny

Marie was alive." I smiled at the man that couldn't take his eyes off his own painting. I understood.

He stood up and paced the room. Finally he took a deep breath. "I had to take two weeks leave from my job. Once I started to paint Sunny Marie, I could not stop." He gazed up at me almost apologetically. "It became an obsession, but I had to finish her."

He lovingly touched his painting. His action showed just how emotionally affected he was by the girl he managed to capture on canvas.

"I read all her poems her mother sent me. I studied all the photographs. Sunny Marie interrupts my sleep…my life," he whispered softly. He turned toward me. "She's a beautiful person. Please tell me more about her?"

My heart ached for this man. He was affected just as much as anyone else that had come in contact with her. Once again, like it was the first time, I began telling him everything about Rie. For a while, he was content to sit quietly soaking it in. Then later, he began asking questions about Rie and her family. Hours later, by the time we finished talking, Mr. Lee knew everything about Rie.

When he finally decided it was time to leave, I handed him the remaining payment we had agreed upon. Because I was so happy with the portrait, I tried to give him a bonus but he refused to take more. I said, "I would be glad to recommend you to our friends that still live in Singapore and Indonesia. I know they would love to commission you for paintings." He raised his hands and shook his head. "No, please don't do that."

When I stared at him in confusion, he smiled apologetically. "I don't want to paint for a while." He shrugged. "Maybe one day, but not now." His face became sad and tears formed in his eyes. "No one has ever affected me the way Sunny Marie has. I sent the photographs back to your sister."

"I know Sunny will be happy about that. But Mr. Lee," I said, "You have a God given talent, don't stop painting. Sunny Marie would be the first to tell you that you need to continue as soon as possible."

He gazed over at the painting, then back at me. He sighed loudly. "Someday," he murmured. "Maybe someday but not now." We hugged good-bye. I knew by taking the portrait away from him that we were also taking a part of his heart. I walked across the room and Rie's eyes followed me. I stopped, drinking in the loveliness of the painting. Yes, she was real.

Johnny arrived the following morning and when he walked into the hotel room he came to an abrupt halt just inside the door. I realized the painting was facing him and he was seeing it for the first time. The sun spilled golden rays across Rie's hair capturing each brilliant highlight. So many times we had seen her playing in the sunlight with just that same mystical appearance.

Johnny slumped down in the nearest chair facing the portrait and cried. Later when he could talk, we discussed how we would take it to Sunny and Phil. It would be carried by hand aboard the airplane. We couldn't trust it in the baggage compartment.

One of our dreams for Rie was that after graduation she could visit with us in Indonesia. As we stayed several days in Bangkok we unwrapped her portrait and placed it on a table. She was now traveling with us. Every morning we would both say, "Good morning, Rie." And every night we blew her a kiss.

It was at this time that Johnny decided he really didn't want to turn loose of "HIS" painting. I laughed and said, "Get real. It's not 'YOUR' painting. It's never been 'YOUR' painting. It goes to Sunny and Phil. Period!" He laughed. "Okay, but if they don't want it, I keep it." When we arrived at my parent's home in Orange we called Sunny and Phil to come over as soon as possible. We placed the covered painting on a footstool in Mother's living room. We wanted to be able to greet Sunny and Phil in the entrance hall before leading them into the living room. We wanted everyone to see it at the same time.

When we greeted Sunny and Phil as they came in, Sunny didn't mention the painting. Hardly unable to contain my excitement, I said, "Okay everyone, it's now time for the unveiling."

Johnny and I led everyone into the living room. Mother and Daddy were seated while Sunny and Phil stood. Proudly, I uncovered the painting. Mother and Daddy grasped loudly, I heard Mother say, "My God!" Daddy sat very still, his eyes glued to the portrait. His hands hung loosely between his knees and he started to cry. Phil stood as if mesmerized. But before making a comment nay or yea, he turned his eyes toward his wife. She was the one we waited for. She was the one that needed to approve the painting. At that moment we all held our breaths waiting in silence, hardly able to tear our eyes from her face.

Silently, my sister stood. Her face and eyes wore a noncommittal expression. Finally, almost cautiously she knelt in front of the painting touching the brush strokes gently. Like a blind person reading Braille, her fingers traveled over the dimpled cheek, the gentle grin, finally following the red curls down to the shoulders. I wasn't sure what was going through her mind and I wondered what she thought of the painting. In anticipation all of us waited for Sunny to say something. When the seconds ticked by without her uttering a word, I knelt beside her, touching her shoulder, willing her to face me.

Turning slowly, she looked at me, her eyes registering my presence but by the expression on her face, I was still uncertain of her response to the painting. Gently, I said, "Honey, if you don't like it, you don't have to accept it."

"Like it?" she said vaguely, almost in a whisper, "I love it." She smiled her approval. "It's my baby. Thank you," she cried. "It's my Rie."

We collapsed in each other arms. I sighed in relief while silently blessing Mr. Lee in his role in another beautiful miracle.

The painting affects everyone that sees it. It hangs in Sunny's and Phil's living room, blessing them everyday when they walk in and see those gorgeous eyes gazing back at them and that grinning face just one step away from laughter.

One day, Philip and Derek were talking. Derek said, "If the house should catch on fire, the first thing that needs rescuing is Rie's portrait."

"Yeah," Philip agreed. "I don't want anything to happen to it. Since I'm the oldest now that painting will someday belong to me." "Says, who?" Derek wailed while physically pushing his brother backward. A mild argument occurred. I had the impression this was going to be an ongoing battle between the two of them for some time.

Later, when I told Sunny the story about Mr. Lee bringing two pieces of his work for us to view. She asked what they were.

"One was of the First Lady of Singapore and the other one was of Beethoven," I said.

Sunny smiled slowly and replied, "No wonder Mr. Lee was the right artist to paint Rie's portrait." I looked at her questioningly. She laughed. "Oh, Margie, Beethoven, was Rie's favorite composer."

I never knew that. Now as I look back, it wasn't odd at all that Mr. Lee brought a painting of Beethoven to our hotel room. It was very fitting. God had already picked him to do Rie's portrait.

THE ARTIST

I reached for my paint and brushes,
Not knowing what was to come.
I knew I was an artist,
Not great but better than some.

I stroked the canvas before me,
In pigments of softest hues.
My hands took on a life of their own,
As over the canvas they flew.

The eyes were the first thing I painted,
Your soul for the whole world to see.
They mirrored the love and compassion,
You had for others and me.

Oh, too soon, the portrait was finished.
I stood back with wonder and awe.
The portrait was that of Jesus.
Whose love was all that I saw.

EPILOGUE

By rights some would expect me to end this book now, but it can't be done. As long as there is one left here on earth that can repeat Sunny Marie's story or that has been touched by it in some special way, her story will go on forever.

In the years after her death, we have endured more heartaches and growing pains, but because of Sunny Marie we have faced them with courage and faith.

I wish I could say the pain gets easier to bear but it's just as acute as it was in the beginning, only now we have learned to live with it. Now we can talk about the sunshine and shadows of that time and celebrate Sunny Marie's life, not mourn her death.

It was extremely hard for Philip to accept his sister's death. He missed her terribly. During college, Doug was Philip's big brother in his college fraternity. During this time, Philip confided to his mom and dad how much he missed his sister. It was then that Sunny suggested that maybe it would help if he could write a letter to her. He did, pouring out his heart and all the pain he felt. It was the beginning of his healing.

After serving four years in the Navy, Philip decided to make California his home. He's a Sales Representative for a biomedical equipment company. He is married to Lei. They reside in the San Francisco area and have a beautiful little girl. They named her, Riana Skye, but they call her Rie.

Derek met his wife Victoria while he was in the Air Force during Desert Storm. Together they have three lovely children, Britney, Christopher and Alexandra. To Sunny's and Phil's delight, Derek and his family now live close to them. Derek is a Program Developer/Information Technologist at a chemical company.

Philip and Derek kept their promise to Sunny Marie. They turned out to be very good men, fathers and husbands making their parents very proud.

When Derek was stationed at Ellsworth Air Force Base in South Dakota, Sunny flew up for Britney's two-year-old birthday. During her stay, Britney and Sunny shared a bed together. Every night after prayers, Britney would demand, "Ganny, say good night to my Nangel."

Sunny pretended to carry on a conversation with Britney's Angel. This went on for days. Sunny asked Derek about Britney's angel and he informed her that he was indeed aware of an imaginary playmate, but every time he questioned Britney about her friend's appearance, Britney responded by telling him that he knew what her angel looked like.

Sunny finally asked Britney, "Please just for me, tell Granny about your angel."

In her baby voice, Britney replied, "Her is beautiful and her tells me her loves me bery bery much…and Ganny, her says she loves you too."

"That's nice, Britney, but what does your angel look like?" Sunny questioned.

"Sunshiny bright," replied Britney.

"Sunshiny bright?" Sunny questioned.

"Yeah," Britney nodded, "her has long orange hair."

Sunny said that cold chills ran up her spine. She asked Derek if he had ever showed Britney any photos of Rie. Derek assured his mom he had not, simply because when he was transferred with the Air Force he was afraid they would be lost in the many moves.

Sunny took a photo from her wallet and showed Britney. Britney giggled and said to the waiting adults, "That's my Nangel. Ganny, do you know my Nangel?"

"Oh, yes," Sunny replied. "I've known your angel for a long time. In fact, she's my angel too."

During the same visit, Britney asked to see more pictures of "her Nangel." Sunny took all she had from her wallet and gave them to her. Britney kept placing one away from the others while she inspected the others closely. Sunny asked, "Don't you like this picture?'"

"No," Britney replied, "My Nangel don't like it. I don't like it too."

Sunny said it was the same school picture that Rie hated and had asked her not to buy. Rie had refused to give it to anyone. It was comforting to Sunny to know that Rie was there for Britney.

Our beloved parents, Rie's Mawmaw and Pawpaw, have gone to be with God. They died within a year of each other. Phil's dad, Rie's Pepaw, died also. How happy they all must be to be reunited with Sunny Marie.

Sunny and Phil keep busy loving each other. Their marriage is very solid. They weathered the storm and came through it. So many marriages in today's world would have collapsed.

Johnny and I are still gypsies and loving it. We no longer live in Indonesia, now it's West Africa, on a small island called Bioko off the Cameroon coast. One thing about living all over the world, I share Sunny Marie's story with everyone and no matter what race or creed hears about Sunny Marie they are affected by her great courage, faith, and love.

In a letter, I mentioned to Sunny, that I wished Johnny and I could buy a home in the Orange area before we retired. The very same week we came to visit, Sunny was walking down the street and a house had just come up for sale. She called me at Dedo's house and told me that God had a house for me. I agreed it would be nice to have a home but we weren't ready for retirement. That next day, out of curiosity and never dreaming it could be possible to buy, Johnny and I looked at it. It was a lovely house.

I got down on my knees and prayed, "Okay, God, I'm putting all this in your hands. Only You can tell us if this is the right time to live by my sister and finish Sunny Marie's book." Evidently God thought it was. The same day we made an offer on the house, the owner accepted it and we signed the papers, that very same day. In two weeks time, Johnny went back to Africa leaving me to get settled in. A month later, Sunny and I were busy writing Rie's book. God took care of everything. It was all too perfectly timed.

One of my eight grandchildren, Keith (Benny's son), also felt Sunny Marie's closeness. At an early age, he wouldn't go to sleep without Rie's little stuffed lamp in his hands. Many a time I would watch him scribble a note to tie at the end of his helium filled balloon and send it toward heaven to Rie. It didn't matter that he couldn't really write; he knew that Rie knew what it said. Today he's serving in the Army. He has Sunny Marie's name tattooed over his heart.

By the time my great-grandson, Taylor (Dedo's grandson), was two years old, we hadn't been around him very much because of living in Africa. On one of my visits home, I was showing him a picture book of angels. He pointed at the drawings and cried, "No! Not Angels, Mawmaw!" When I assured him that they were indeed Angels, he refused to listen to reason. He walked out of the room and came back later with a small picture of Rie that I kept on my dresser. To my knowledge, no one had ever called his attention to it. H e pointed to the photo and said, "Angel." I agreed. I knew this angel well.

Over the years, several of Sunny Marie's close friends have called Sunny telling her of dreams they have had about Rie and because of the dreams they have made important changes in their lives. Quite often when Sunny goes out to the cemetery, she finds beautiful arrangements placed besides Rie's headstone. No cards, no names. The arrangements are always made with roses. Sunny has inquired at the local florists if they made the arrangements. So far the area florists have denied doing so. To this day, the donor still remains a mystery.

One day Sunny, Phil, Johnny, and I were visiting at Phil's mother's house. Sunny and I had been busy writing on the book for weeks. Sunny and I were drained from reliving all the emotions again. It had rained all week and I noticed that while we were talking the sun was shining through the windows. It was a strange glow, not bright but a dark gold in color. Phil and Johnny walked outside to check it out.

I said, "You know, Sunny, what we need is a rainbow to cheer us up." She agreed. About that same time, Johnny knocked on the window and shouted, "Come see."

Phil's mother, Sunny, and I walked outside and saw a sky alive with rainbows. Phil and Johnny were standing in awe looking up at the gorgeous sky. How God managed the miracle will always remain His secret, but it was the most amazing thing Sunny and I had ever witnessed. Rainbows seemed to bounce off the clouds making each cloud a different color. There were blue and purple clouds, pink and orange clouds and some were even yellow and green. In my heart I could hear Sunny Marie's voice saying, "Behold, the Master's hand." It gave us inspiration to continue. We gave thanks to God.

Rie is still keeping her promise to me. The island I live on in Africa is alive with butterflies and rainbows. Every time I get a little depressed a rainbow appears over the bay. How I envied the day when Rie reached her finger out to the butterfly and he actually perched upon the end. Now when I walk outside in my new blue and green jungle, thousands of butterflies actually swarm around me in every shape, size, and color, but ever so often a special one will actually brush my lips with a kiss. That's the one I call my Rie butterfly. I guess now, when I die, I'll keep my promise to her and come back as a fat little Ghost and scare the hell out of everyone.

So you see, Sunny Marie is still watching over all of us. Some dream about her. Some still bring her flowers. Even the babies in the family are visited by her. Some of us see flaming sunsets, witness a rainbow, caress a flower that blooms out of season, or get visited by a little redheaded bird. These are all love messages from our Sunny Marie. She's still very much with us and only a heartbeat away.

NEVER THE END

AFTERWORD

The cause of primary brain tumors is unknown. Environmental agents, familial tendencies, viral causes, and other possibilities are under investigation. Brain tumors are NOT contagious but they are on the rise. Doctors are still trying to find a cure.

According to the publication, <u>Brain Tumor Facts</u>, in 1995, a study predicted that more than 100,000 people in the United States would be diagnosed with brain tumors. Brain tumors are the second leading cause of death in children and young adults.

With cancer rates soaring everyday and in every nation, there are more volunteer groups forming, trying to give grieving parents support when they lose a child.

ABOUT THE AUTHORS

The co-authors of SUN-SHINE AND SHADOWS are sisters who both live in Orange, Texas. Although this is their first book written together in 1994, SUNSHINE AND SHADOWS won a nonfiction award at the Golden Triangle Writers' Convention in Beaumont, Texas.

Sunny C. Eppler is a self-employed art teacher. She has also worked as a social writer for the local newspaper and has served as a volunteer in just about every organization in her hometown. Married for 40 years to the same man, she is the mother of two married sons and grandmother of four.

Marjorie M. Woodcock is the mother of four children, grandmother of seven, and great-grandmother of two. She has been married for 50 years to her high school sweetheart. Margie doesn't like to think of herself as a missionary, but finds herself spreading God's word wherever she goes. She said, "Everywhere I go, I feel as if the Lord places me there for a reason. God puts the words in my mouth and I simply deliver them."